OUT OF THE ROUGH

JACK NEWTON scored more than twenty tournament victories in Europe, the USA, Africa, New Zealand and Australia. In July 1983 he was involved in a near-fatal aeroplane accident that ended his professional golfing career. With the same determination that had made him a successful golfer, Jack fought back and became a respected television and radio commentator and part-time journalist. He is prominent in promoting junior golf, served as chairman of the PGA Tour of Australia, has designed golf courses and a range of golf accessories and apparel, and is in constant demand for corporate days and speaking engagements. He lives in Cardiff, near Newcastle, New South Wales.

PETER STONE is the president of the Australian Golf Writers Association and has been writing about golf for more than thirty years, first with the *Age* and then with the Melbourne *Herald*, where he was Sports Editor in the mid-1980s. Since 1992 he has been golf correspondent for the *Sydney Morning Herald* and the *Sun-Herald* and has covered golf around the world. In 2000 he was awarded the Australian Sports Medal for services to golf. Peter lives in Sydney.

To everyone who has touched my life,
especially my immediate family –
father Jack senior, mother Meg, wife Jackie,
children Kristie and Clint and sister Jan

OUT OF THE ROUGH

THE JACK NEWTON STORY

Jack Newton with Peter Stone

VIKING

Most of the photographs in this book were supplied by the author and every effort has been made to contact the copyright holders for permissions. The author and publisher welcome any further information regarding ownership where relevant.

Viking
Penguin Books Australia Ltd
487 Maroondah Highway, PO Box 257
Ringwood, Victoria 3134, Australia
Penguin Books Ltd
Harmondsworth, Middlesex, England
Penguin Putnam Inc.
375 Hudson Street, New York, New York 10014, USA
Penguin Books Canada Limited
10 Alcorn Avenue, Toronto, Ontario, Canada M4V 3B2
Penguin Books (N.Z.) Ltd
Cnr Rosedale and Airborne Roads, Albany, Auckland, New Zealand
Penguin Books (South Africa) (Pty) Ltd
5 Watkins Street, Denver Ext 4, 2094, South Africa
Penguin Books India (P) Ltd
11, Community Centre, Panchsheel Park, New Delhi 110 017, India

First published by Penguin Books Australia Ltd 2001

10 9 8 7 6 5 4 3 2 1

Designed by Melissa Fraser, Penguin Design Studio
Cover photographs supplied by the author
Typeset in 11.5/16pt Esprit Book by Midland Typesetters, Maryborough, Victoria
Made and printed in Australia by Australian Print Group, Maryborough, Victoria

National Library of Australia
Cataloguing-in-Publication data:

Newton, Jack.
 Out of the rough: the Jack Newton story.

 Includes index.
 ISBN 0 670 83829 2.

 1. Newton, Jack. 2. Golfers – Australia – Biography. I. Stone, Peter.
 II. Title.

796.352092

www.penguin.com.au

Contents

Acknowledgements vi

Prologue 1
Golf in the backyard 3
A kid from down-under 19
Enter Jackie 33
Have clubs, will travel 51
One stroke from glory 67
A golf course made in heaven 87
Sweet victory at Metropolitan 115
The battle in the USA 133
The accident – and a fight for life 165
Getting down to business 193
Playing golf again – with a handicap 215
Of Tiger Woods, appearance money and other concerns 229
Epilogue 245

Career record 248
Index 253

Acknowledgements

The idea of writing a book about my life was never something I used to contemplate seriously. Although it is fashionable these days for just about anyone to put pen to paper, I was always against 'has-beens tipping the bucket on their contemporaries' in print, at times with sensationalist accusations and quite often with far-reaching effects.

Following my accident, I had a number of approaches about a book – an assignment I had originally reserved for my twilight years, if ever – along the lines of 'Yours is a story that should be told, given the twists and turns of your life'. Finally, in 1990, I decided to do it, with the aid of an experienced writer, for fear of someone else getting in first and possibly misrepresenting my thoughts.

With much of the book already written, court proceedings over my compensation claim (which I am legally not at liberty to discuss) dragged on for almost seventeen years before settlement was finally reached at the end of 1999. The delay created a nightmare for my co-writer, Peter Stone, and publisher, Penguin Books, and I am grateful for the patience they have shown. I thank Peter particularly for taking my heavy use of colloquialisms and murder of the English language and turning it into some semblance of good prose. At Penguin, publisher Robert Sessions and editor Katie Purvis have been extremely helpful and instrumental in getting the book published at last.

It would be remiss of me not to pay tribute to the many thousands of golfers around the world and others who supported my family at the time of my accident by way of a massive fundraising exercise. In addition, I was afforded incredible moral support by many wonderful people. The videotapes sent by my peers were extraordinarily motivational at a time when circumstances were at their most desperate.

The Newton clan, while quite small in numbers, has always been close-knit. I have no doubt that the love, affection and attention I received from my family – particularly my amazing wife, Jackie – after the accident, and the inspiration provided by our two children, were the main factors in enabling me not only to 'dig deep' in order to survive, but also to be strong enough to face the challenges that lay ahead. I am extremely proud of Kristie and Clint's achievements, especially given the additional pressures they have been subjected to as 'Newton kids'. Thank you.

Prologue

Tom Watson and I stood on the 18th tee at Carnoustie. It was pouring with rain, we were both drenched and it was becoming difficult to maintain any grip on the golf club. Everything was soaked.

We were square at one under par, the day after we had tied for the 1975 British Open Championship. Today hadn't been an easy day for scoring, but both Watson and I were playing fairly decent golf in the conditions. Here we were, after 89 holes, still tied.

Watson hit a fine drive up the right-hand side of the fairway. Mine was a fraction to the left and I was satisfied with it even though it meant I had a shot over the burn and a greenside trap to the pin. On his next shot, Watson cleared the burn by a couple of yards and his ball galloped up the front portion of the green, but still a fair distance from the pin. The breeze was coming into me from the left and I had the corner of the bunker to contend with plus the wind blowing the ball away from where I wanted it to go. I hit a fade and the ball appeared to be going straight for the flag, but it caught the lip of the bunker and rolled back down. Just 6 more inches would have done it.

Because of the rain, the sand in the bunker was compacted. My sand iron skidded a little, but the ball came out hot. It had a lot of spin on it and landed about 12 feet past the pin. Watson hit his putt stone-dead. I was convinced that the line on my putt was left lip, but I hadn't taken into account the water on the green.

Even today, if I looked at that shot again, I couldn't see it as a straight putt. I hit it left lip and that's exactly where it stayed. The championship had been won – and lost.

Golf in the backyard

Life as a kid in Wollombi Road, West Cessnock, in the early 1950s was as it should be: uncomplicated. Each day my father, Jack, rode his pushbike at first light to the coalmines, where he worked underground with his father, Bill, or 'Da' as I called my grandfather. I waited, sitting on the letterbox, for his return each afternoon, chatting with anyone who came past.

Inside, my mother, Meg, always had the kettle on the coal-and-wood stove and the smell of freshly baked scones and biscuits usually filled the air. The men would stop off at the pub for half a dozen pints after work and then be home by 3.30 in time for tea. They would head back to the hotel or the local football ground before we had supper around 8 p.m. After that we played cards, dominoes and all the other games people played before their lives became dominated by television. We listened to *Dad and Dave* on the wireless, Smoky Dawson or the fights from the old Sydney Stadium.

They were good times, carefree times, I thought, and I would sit listening, fascinated, to the stories my father and grandfather told of their work in the mines. A pick and shovel, plus a canary in a cage, were the only equipment they had as they crawled into the underground pits to extract the coal for a wage of four shillings and sixpence a ton. On good days my father and his workmate would shovel 30 tons, always keeping a watchful eye on the canary that was their lifeline. If the bird suddenly turned up its toes, it was time to get out, and quickly, as the level of gases in the mine could potentially be fatal.

The harder they worked the more they were paid, and when the working day was over they played hard, too. It was a rich heritage, a working-class background in which, though we were poor, we never missed out. We ate well, with my mother and my grandmother, Isobel, who was simply 'Gam' to me, able to whip up delicious meals from offal like tripe and tongue. They were hardly the best cuts, but they were all we could afford.

The real hardship of that day and age in Cessnock was rarely discussed, and for a time I remained oblivious to the continuing uncertainty of working the mines. In 1949, the year before I was born, both my father and grandfather were involved in the nationwide coalminers' strike, which sought a 35-hour week and certain long-service leave provisions. It lasted from late June until mid-August and was only broken when the Chifley Labor government sent in troops to work the mines.

The strike may have been broken but the instability

remained, with short strikes and lockouts occurring regularly. This of course meant even less money in our household. They were tough times and I think it was that early background which gave me much of my determination. I've never been scared of getting my fingernails dirty, because that was the road on which I started life.

In January 1956, just before my sixth birthday, my father, who was in his mid-twenties, was cabled out – retrenched – from the mines. Cessnock now thrives on the wine industry, but then everything revolved around the coalmines. There was no alternative work in the district for the old man. A friend of the family, the local inspector of police, Charlie Kennedy, suggested the police force as a career, which meant Dad would have to take the huge step of moving to Sydney, away from the small community in which he'd lived all his life.

He took that step and moved to Sydney with my mother and my sister, Janet, eighteen months younger than me. I was just starting school at West Cessnock Primary and it was decided I should stay with my grandparents while the family settled in Sydney. I had always been particularly close to both Da and Gam and became even more so during the short time I lived with them.

Da had a big influence on my life. He hadn't travelled widely but his knowledge was worldly. He read a lot, mainly newspapers, and had a tremendous experience of life, albeit not an international one. Objective in his opinions, his philosophy was one of good sense, hard work and honesty. He never raised his voice, never became flustered and, in short, was the epitome of all things good.

He would say to me, 'If you're not going to give

something your best shot, don't do it in the first place.' It was an attitude he'd instilled in my father as well. Whether it was cricket, football, golf, anything, Da would say, 'Don't be like I was: good at most things, master of nothing.' I have tried to carry that advice through life.

My mother was a nursing sister, as was her mother before her, and Janet would follow the same career path. On arrival in Sydney, my parents found a house in Surrey Street, Epping, owned by an old lady, a Mrs Raison. Her son hired Mum as a live-in housekeeper-cum-nursing-aide to take care of Mrs Raison, and Mum's wages paid much of the rent of our share of the large house. After they had settled I came down from Cessnock and was enrolled at Epping Primary School, which seemed very big after West Cessnock.

Mrs Raison was something of a tyrant and gave my mother a hard time, but Mum at least got the old girl out of bed and walking again during the three years we lived there. We moved to another large house just around the corner in York Street, Epping, where we again shared, this time with an old bloke who lived in one room of the house. His name was Frank Sullivan and he was a former expert in wireless telegraphy, now a hopeless alcoholic. He was a grubby old guy with bottles of beer at the ready in the house or garden wherever his path took him – in his room, on the back lawn, in the gas meter – just in case his fancy was a drink, and it always was. The beer was never cold, which I'm told is the way of alcoholics, and whatever food he ate came from cans. Very occasionally he would ask my mother to cook him a meal.

Frank was an incredibly generous man and a sports fanatic. I was into every conceivable sport. Soccer, rugby, cricket, a bit of golf, tennis – you name it, I was playing it, and the old bloke would always turn up to watch me play.

The backyard was quite a long block of land and when I was about ten I started playing my own version of golf on a course I'd mapped out. It started in the yard and went down the driveway and across the road to the front lawn of the house opposite, where the owner allowed me to include his land in the improvised course. Part of it also included chipping the ball over a sweet-pea vine in our backyard.

I played with a perforated plastic ball that didn't go too far but didn't break too many windows either, and I played to jam tins dug into the grass, using bits of kindling as flagsticks. Each morning before school I'd be out playing my course and the old bloke would be there watching.

'A zac for a two, a zac for a two,' he would say, nominating which hole he wanted me to get down in two shots for the lure of sixpence. It was my first experience of playing anything for money and brought out my competitive streak.

It was the same with cricket. We had a pitch of about 15 or 16 metres in the backyard and the old guy devised another way to add to my pocket money. He would put a shilling on the stumps and take the bat while I had the six-stitcher in my hand. He'd have no pads on and be half drunk, but it wasn't easy to get the ball past him to knock the shilling from the stumps and thus claim it. I rattled him around the shins and various other parts of his body, but he didn't care. All he wanted was to give me another challenge.

Frank Sullivan also got me my first job, delivering telegrams from the Epping Post Office where he used to work. I worked school holidays and weekends to supplement my 'winnings'.

I guess it took a couple of years or so to rid myself of the feeling that I was a stranger at Epping Primary. All the other kids had grown up together in the local area and I was the boy from the bush. Sport broke down the barriers, as it always does.

I went to Sunday School at the Congregational Church, which had a big soccer club through all grades known as the Epping Congs. I threw myself into it. I played soccer with the Congs, rugby league and cricket at school, golf in the backyard, gymnastics on Friday night in the church hall and cricket at weekends for Epping RSL in Sydney's Northern Districts league. In my last two years at primary school I made the State schoolboys' team in rugby league. Scholastically, though, I guess you'd have to say I was a battler.

Dad settled well into the police force, though it was a huge change from working in the mines. One of the big snags was the shiftwork and there were times he'd be sleeping when I came home from school. I sometimes saw him for only an hour or so a day. He was settling into the sporting scene himself, playing midweek rugby league for the police.

Later, Dad was one of the first to join the new Muirfield Golf Club in Sydney. He had been a member at Cessnock for a couple of years before moving to Sydney, but didn't play for about four years until joining Muirfield with a handicap of 12. He was down to single figures within a year and then became a scratch marker, a handicap he held for years.

She was a rough old golf course in the early days when I caddied for my father. There were huge rocks everywhere and it wasn't uncommon to see your ball ricochet off a rock and into the bush. Eventually they gelignited the rocks out and it's now a very good course and a very successful club.

Apart from backyard golf, I hadn't played the game until I started caddying for my father, who played pennants for Muirfield in 1961. I was eleven. After his match Dad would go for a beer with the others while I went to the practice fairway to hit balls. He always said to me, 'Get your swing sorted out and then worry about playing the golf course.'

I progressed from the practice fairway to playing a few holes on my own until the old man finished his schooners or it became dark, whichever came first.

I joined Muirfield GC immediately after my twelfth birthday. My first handicap was 22 and a couple of years later I got that down to four. In those early days, breaking 90 became an obsession. Try as I might I couldn't, until one day I blew the barrier away shooting 84. Then it was on to the next challenge of breaking 80. Same thing. Just as Roger Bannister and John Landy had hammered at the four-minute mile I, in my small way, smashed through the 80 score, firing a 74. I hadn't even celebrated my fourteenth birthday. It just sort of happened. Like a war of attrition. You're out there trying your best and it all goes right.

Soccer and rugby had come naturally enough, but a whole new world opened in golf. There were a few tricks to master and a lot more to it than met the eye. I liked what I'd found.

My first major competition was the State schoolboys', when I was thirteen. I won the under-14 trophy at Northbridge with a round of 80 and then proceeded to the schoolboys' title itself at Long Reef, where in fairly windy conditions I shot rounds of 89–84 that left me pretty well up the list. I had borrowed my mother's clubs rather than use my own, which were a hotchpotch collected along the way. Her clubs were a full matching set of hickory-shafted clubs from East Bros, forerunner of the PGF company.

One of the first times I broke 70 was around the Gosford course in an annual tournament conducted there. I was only fourteen and fired a two-under 68 followed by a 72 to beat guys like Phil Billings and Kevin Donohoe, whose reputations in amateur golf were something akin to star status.

My grandfather caddied for me, as he often did in those days. He had never played golf in his life and could never understand how anyone could miss a 3-foot putt. If you missed one he would fly off the handle, crying out, 'Je-e-e-sus bloody Christ! I could have knocked that in with my forehead.'

Though he knew little about club selection, Da was a very steadying influence. He would give me a serve if I did anything stupid and emphasised the importance of taking my time, thinking about the shot I was about to play. I was never much of a club-thrower in my youth, but I did get uptight inside, probably because I was so much of a per- fectionist. Like most kids, I didn't think I could hit bad shots. You learn later that everyone hits bad shots from time to time and you come to accept it. But youth has no fear.

My old man was notorious for missing short putts, and at Muirfield one day we were both playing in a Wednesday comp when Da was down in Sydney. He trailed us around and on the 16th, Dad missed a very short putt. Da dragged out his line about knocking it in with his forehead and on the next tee the old man swung on him, saying, 'All right, smart alec. Let's see how good you are.'

'Okay,' he replied and took a 4-wood from my bag. He obviously knew that if you're going to swing a golf club for the first time you don't take the driver. He calmly teed up the ball and to our amazement knocked it about 170 yards straight down the middle of the fairway. 'Fluke,' we said as he marched resolutely towards his ball.

We let him tee up his second shot and again he used the wood, knocking the ball to about 50 yards short of the green on the 330-yard par 4. He then took out a 9-iron and pitched it onto the green about 20 feet from the pin. By this stage, my father and I were just looking at each other in disbelief.

And he wasn't finished. He took my putter and calmly stroked the ball into the hole for his par 4. He turned to us and said, 'There y'are. I told you there was nothing to this game. Now get on with it.'

It was the one and only time he ever played a hole of golf, and he made par. We tried to persuade him to take up the game, but I reckon he was too smart. He had made his par and wasn't about to undo all his good work.

A year after my win at Gosford, I gained selection in the NSW junior team to play the interstate series in Brisbane. There was a frightful hullabaloo as there were some in high places who reckoned I was too young at the age of fifteen to be in the team. It didn't worry me, but later in life I guess I didn't take so kindly to the foolishness of officialdom.

I copped a bit of flak when I first started at Epping Boys' High, which, like most schools in Sydney, was rugby union oriented. I had never played the game and when the list came round for students to indicate which sports they wished to play I chose soccer.

The sportsmaster at the school was a chap called Brian Moffatt, who played Union for NSW and was at that time the coach of the Gordon Rugby Union Club, one of Sydney's most successful clubs. I hardly gave my decision to play soccer a second thought until at general assembly I heard my name called. 'Newton, fall out and report to the sportsmaster's office.'

Waiting for me were Moffatt – a short guy who played half-back – and his assistants Alfie Mitchell, who was the Australian javelin champion, and Dave Prince, the Australian hurdles champion, later to be president of Athletics Australia.

'Newton, I see here you played State schoolboys' rugby league. Why aren't you playing rugby here?' Moffatt said.

'I don't want to. I'd rather play soccer,' was my reply.

'That's not the rule of Epping Boys' High. This is a rugby school. That's what you'll play,' Moffatt fired back.

The sudden declaration of what I would or wouldn't do left me a little taken aback, but I continued to argue. 'Well, my father doesn't want me to play rugby. He wants me to stick with soccer,' I said, and the stand-off continued.

Moffatt then threatened that things wouldn't go too well for me if I didn't play rugby, but my stubborn streak surfaced. 'I'm not playing. I've never played rugby union in my life and I'm not about to start now. I'll get my father to come and see you,' I said.

Moffatt replied, 'Well, it won't take us long to convert you. Don't worry about that.'

I maintained the stand and didn't play rugby that year. The following year I was voted in as junior house captain and in that position had to pick the team for an intra-school touch rugby tournament. Naturally enough I selected all the guys who played rugby and then threw my own name in as well. Prince called me aside, saying, 'How come you're playing rugby in the touch side?'

I attempted to explain that it was for the house and that we wanted to win the tournament. Prince replied sarcastically, 'You're a soccer player, son. You don't play rugby at this school.'

'Well, that doesn't mean I can't play touch,' I answered back. I did play and we won the tournament, but I continued to have a stormy relationship with Moffatt.

I had also started playing competitive tennis. Dad was a pretty good player and there was a woman down the road who let me and a few mates use her court. I started playing in the school team, which played on Wednesday afternoons. One evening my father asked me if I had anything scheduled for a particular Wednesday afternoon. After checking, I discovered the tennis team had a bye. 'Good,' he said. 'We'll play with Tommy Moore [club pro at Muirfield from the mid-'50s to the mid-'70s and a big help to me in my formative years] in the I.K. Harrison Shield that day.'

The I.K. Harrison Shield was a fairly prestigious event played at the toffy Elanora Golf Club each year, with one professional and two amateurs making up each team. Boys from the western suburbs didn't get too many chances to play at Elanora and I jumped at the opportunity.

On the day, school classes finished at noon and the old man was waiting outside in his car to drive us to Elanora. I didn't have permission to leave, but didn't give it a second thought. As it happened, we won the event and it was duly reported in the newspapers the following morning.

'Newton, fall out and report to the sportsmaster's office,' came the order at general assembly. Moffatt was waiting for me. 'Where were you yesterday, son?' he demanded.

'I went home,' I said boldly, trying to tough out the impending trouble.

'No, you didn't. You played golf. It's here in the paper,' he said. I attempted to explain that there had been a bye in the tennis and, rather than go to Room 19, where all the wimps who didn't play sport spent their Wednesday afternoons, I thought it would be okay to play golf.

'Did you have permission to leave the school?' Moffatt said.

'No, but I'll bring a note from my father tomorrow,' I replied.

'That won't make any difference. You left the school without permission,' he said, and then accompanied me to the headmaster, who tore strips off me.

That night I told the old man about the events of the day and he wrote a note saying he had given me permission to leave the school grounds on the Wednesday. I showed this to Moffatt the following day, but he was singularly unimpressed.

'I'm afraid you didn't produce this note before you left and it's too late now. I'm going to cane you. You'll get six, but not at this time. I'll call you out when I'm good and ready,' he said. Moffatt was only a little guy, but he had a reputation as the best caner in the school. I thought, 'This is bloody nice. What do I do now?'

I made no mention of it to Dad. A couple of months later I was walking past the sports room when Moffatt emerged. 'I haven't caned you yet, have I?' he said.

'No, sir.'

'Right, in here,' he ordered and proceeded to give me three on each hand. The damage to my left hand was the greater: a blood blister formed across the forefinger knuckle where the cane had bitten into the bone. I gritted my teeth and went on my way to the next class.

That day after school, the old man suggested we go for a hit of golf and I declined, saying, 'I don't think I can grip the club properly. I've got a bit of a sore hand.'

'What from?' he said.

'He what!' he thundered on hearing my reply. 'I'll go down there and pull his nose.' He never did, but he and Moffatt had a friendly chat about it next time their paths crossed.

I called a truce with Moffatt after that. It was all getting too hard. I agreed to play rugby union in the next school season and as it happened, Epping Boys' won the Waratah Shield for State interschool rugby two years in a row. I was the fullback and captain on both occasions.

My chance to get square with Moffatt came in an unlikely way. He was a pretty good golfer, playing pennants for Roseville in Group 2, and I was playing for Muirfield, which had risen from Group 3 to Group 2. It was during 1965, probably about nine months after I received that caning, that the two teams met. Roseville had a very good player called Norm Maish playing at No. 1, while Moffatt usually played No. 2 or No. 3. I was playing No. 1, having beaten the old man in the club championship, but that day I asked to be dropped down the order.

'Whatever happens, I want to play Moffatt,' I said. As luck would have it, we worked it out correctly and Moffatt and I met on the first tee. I played some great golf that day and smacked his arse, beating him 6–5. As we shook hands at the end, I remarked that it was nice to even the ledger in such a manner.

Whatever our differences, Moffatt was a damn good sportsmaster and a great motivator. The school was the worst in the zone for swimming when he arrived there, so he decided to do something about it and ordered the entire school to swimming training three mornings a week at the Epping pool. It was a massive exercise but had the desired result. We won our zone.

I was only an average swimmer, unlike my sister Jan, who got to the State trials. She trained every morning at 5 o'clock and then again after school. On one occasion, she was giving me a bit of lip about how good she was at swimming. A challenge eventuated over 50 metres. I beat her and said, 'Now, get on with your training and don't bother me.' In fairness to her, she was predominantly a breaststroker and our race had been freestyle.

In my last year at school, rugby league was introduced. I was the only one who'd ever played the game, but we won a State knock-out comp with $500 going to the winning school. I guess there was a certain irony in that, given the poor start to school sport I'd had with Moffatt.

Some years later, during the Australian Open, I was signing my card when a chap approached and said, 'Would you mind coming over here to say hello to an old friend of yours?' I went with him and there was Brian Moffatt in a wheelchair, the victim of a mystery virus that had paralysed him. He could only talk from the corner of his mouth and it was a sad sight to see.

In the late '80s I was invited to a surprise party for Moffatt on his retirement from Hurlstone Agricultural College, where he went after Epping Boys' High, and it was great to chat about old times again. He had completely recovered from the illness and was as fit as a Mallee bull. His only legacy was that he still spoke slightly from the corner of his mouth.

Cricket also took a fair bit of my sporting time in my early teenage years, playing with Epping RSL. In my first year with the twelves and under I averaged 90 and then the following season I averaged 139 batting at first drop.

But it got to the stage where golf simply overran cricket, and I've got to say I didn't enjoy the fielding side of it, standing out there on a Saturday afternoon when it was 54 degrees in the water bag and chasing leather balls. I didn't mind smashing the ball around, but chasing? Forget it! Golf was becoming a consuming passion.

A kid from down-under

The tragedy of Norman von Nida's playing career was that he never won the British Open championship. He had a chance at Hoylake in 1947 when he shared the lead with Fred Daly, Arthur Lees and Henry Cotton with just 18 holes to play. But those were the days when they played 36 holes on the final day.

As Daly, the eventual winner, completed his final round of 72, von Nida and Cotton were about to tee off. When they walked up the first fairway, a fearsome wind blew up to wreck the chances of the late players. The Von, who never did relish playing in the wind, fired a 76 to finish in a tie for sixth, four shots behind Daly. The following year he finished third to Cotton at Muirfield, but to this day he regards 1947 as his best chance.

The presence of wind was the reason I joined the New South Wales Golf Club, that magnificent course on a rugged stretch of coastline at La Perouse, in 1969, my last year as an amateur. I was a member of Muirfield and also Ryde-Parramatta, but they were both inland courses. Partly on the Von's advice, I went to the New South Wales to simulate the conditions of the links courses in Scotland and England and learn to play in the wind.

The Von played a key role in my formative years in golf. He was mentor in all things golf to the managing director of Slazenger, Noel Morris, from the identification of young talent to the development and promotion of the game, to personal tutelage of the Morris swing. The likes of Peter Thomson, Bruce Crampton, Bruce Devlin and the young Gary Player, who won his first professional tournament outside South Africa at Yarra Yarra in Melbourne in 1956, were all taken under the Slazenger–Morris wing. So, too, were Bob Shearer and I. Slazenger saw us as an investment in the company's future.

It was a similar situation with the young tennis players. Neale Fraser, John Newcombe, Tony Roche, John Alexander, Phil Dent, Evonne Goolagong and Margaret Court were among those employed by Slazenger. With the tennis players it was a way of feeding them in the days when their sport was still amateur.

Slazenger looked after me from the age of fifteen, when their great old clubmaker, Scottish-born Sandy Faichney, hand-forged my first set of clubs. I also received a dozen balls per month. After I completed my Higher School Certificate in 1968, the company offered me a job in what was euphemistically described as 'public relations'. What this meant was that I did a few promotional tours, clinics and film nights with John Sullivan, a golf pro who was retained by Slazenger at the time. It also meant that I had most afternoons off to practise and play golf. Rules of amateur status were pretty strict in those days, and while I could work for Slazenger, it couldn't be advertised or used in promotional material that I played with Slazenger equipment.

I also had the opportunity to play practice rounds with people like Player, Arnold Palmer, Devlin and Crampton whenever they came to Australia. As they were contracted to Slazenger, the Von would organise for me to have a game. Though I was a bit awestruck at the time, it was a great advantage later because I knew them and realised they only had two arms and two legs like me.

So a career as a golf professional more or less fell into place. In my last couple of years at school I'd had aspirations to become a physical education teacher, but because of the influence of von Nida and Slazenger I was pointed in a different direction.

It was the Von who suggested I play in the 1969 British amateur championship at Hoylake. Slazenger provided the air ticket – which, had it been known, would have buckled my amateur status – and the members of the Muirfield GC in Sydney raised some cash for me. The Von also looked after me financially and was my 'chaperone' while I was in England.

He picked me up at London's Heathrow airport in a very large Jaguar and told me we were going to Sunningdale, where he based himself whenever he was on that side of the world. The club professional at Sunningdale, York-shireman Arthur Lees, was legendary. He had only won a handful of tournaments in Britain and Europe but was regarded as the best player for money on the continent. I'd heard stories of the Von and Lees playing Gary Player and Harold Henning when the South Africans were in their heyday. The old-timers murdered them, particularly on the day when Lees fired a 62.

As we drove towards Sunningdale, the narrow road became increasingly snarled with traffic. There was a big race meeting on at Ascot, which is just down from Sunningdale, and we virtually came to a standstill. The Von, an impatient man at the best of times, swung into the oncoming lane.

The cars, bumper to bumper on the left, became a blur as the Von drove merrily on for about 5 kilometres. Suddenly a car appeared from the opposite direction and the Von moved back into half a gap between two cars. The driver of the approaching car had to take evasive action, scraping the side of his car along the hedge as he went past.

The next moment, a bloke got out of his truck about three vehicles back and walked up to the Jag and began hammering on the window. The Von bristled as he wound it down. 'What's the matter with you?' he snapped.

The truck driver, all 190 cm of him, demanded menacingly, 'What do you think you're up to?'

It should be remembered that the Von is not frightened of anyone, no matter their size. In the US, he once refused to sign the scorecard of American golfer Henry Ransom because of certain irregularities with the Rules of Golf along the way. The disagreement became physical, with the Von trying to throttle the big man, who resisted to the point that both Norman's feet were off the ground while he maintained his hold on Ransom's neck. The late Harry Hopman, writing for a Melbourne newspaper, called it a disgraceful incident and called for the withdrawal of von Nida's passport. But the US PGA saw it a different way, suspending Ransom and praising von Nida for his courage.

'Get back in your truck, you Pommie bastard!' the Von yelled on the road to Sunningdale. The truck driver started to turn a different colour in the face and returned the abuse only to be halted in mid-sentence by the Von, who said, 'If you don't get back in your truck, I'm going to punch you in the nose.'

I started removing my coat. There I was, after a 34-hour flight from Australia, about to be involved in a stink within an hour of arriving in London. But I'd seen the Von in action before and now, just as on every other occasion, the truck driver suddenly backed off to return to his vehicle and leave us to continue to Sunningdale.

The Von had prearranged a match with Lees and David Wickens, owner of British Car Auctions and a multimillionaire. Wickens had got into the car business quite by accident after he bought an old MG and restored it with the intention of selling it. He advertised in the newspapers but couldn't get a buyer, so decided to auction the car, doorknocking homes in his local area to tell people of the sale. He ended up getting far more for the MG than he expected, and presto, he had a business for life.

'What's the pairings?' I asked the Von.

'You've got it all wrong. We are playing the new course; you go to the old course over there. Just play nine holes and get the flight out of your system,' he replied. I did his bidding and was just about to hit off when a chap in his early forties staggered up to the first tee with a woman. He looked as though he'd had polio as a kid and could barely walk. He asked if I minded if they joined me. Of course I didn't.

'Do you play for a few shillings?' he enquired, and naturally I answered in the affirmative. Long flight or not, I reasoned it would be easy pickings. 'We'll play for £10 the front nine and then we'll negotiate,' he said, and once again I agreed. It seemed fair enough, as he hadn't seen me play and I guess I didn't think too much about how he could play.

'My wife will have the same,' he added. I began to smile to myself. There was this bloke, incapacitated in both legs, and his wife. 'Oh, by the way, I play off one and my wife's off ten,' he said as we tossed for the honour. I still reasoned it would be easy pickings, but the jet lag caught up with me a bit and I shot one over par for the nine. The chap and his wife beat me to death and I handed over the twenty quid.

'Well, how did you strike the ball?' the Von asked after he'd completed his round.

'I lost twenty quid to this fellow and his wife,' I replied.

'Who was it?' he asked, and when I told him it was a guy with crippled legs, he fell about laughing. 'You didn't tumble for him, did you?'

It was probably the first time I'd been hustled in my life. The guy's name was Patrick Tallis and he was a good player, a wealthy guy who was notorious at Sunningdale. He and his wife would play for any amount of cash, but she was the one you really had to watch; she played some quite brilliant shots when necessary.

———————

The Von is passionate about horseracing and, as it was Royal Ascot week, had arranged for us to go to the races with Wickens the following day. Wickens was a very large, stately-looking man who was also a tough, tough cookie. He had a large limousine with a female chauffeur and the Von and I, along with half a dozen others, settled into the car for the journey to the course.

Once again we were confronted by a traffic jam. Wickens, I discovered, was an even more impatient man than the Von. 'Out and around the traffic,' he instructed his driver, who replied, 'David, I can't do that.'

'Do as you're f— told,' he ordered, and she did. We arrived at the main gate of Ascot just after the Queen's horse-driven carriage had arrived. 'Drive on,' Wickens commanded and again his driver protested.

'I'm telling you to drive in the front gate,' he said, and she did as she was instructed, with the result that a horde of security guards descended in our direction. Wickens told them to go forth and multiply in language I'm certain is not taught at the best English schools and, amazingly, we drove in the front gate, parked the car and proceeded to his private box.

Smoked salmon and champagne awaited us. 'Have a few bubbles,' he invited and I watched and listened wide-eyed as he talked with his guests – several of whom were knights and ladies of the realm – in language that would not be unfamiliar to those in shearing sheds in the Aussie outback. At that stage I'd never heard a guy swear so much – and in public.

After the experiences of Sunningdale and Ascot I travelled to Hoylake, or, more precisely, the Royal Liverpool Golf

Club, which was the first venue of the British amateur championship back in 1885 and has hosted the British Open ten times.

All went well until the round before the quarterfinals, where I met the universities champion, Peter Moody, who beat me 2–1. The winner of our match was to play Michael Bonallack, who'd won the title in 1961, 1965 and 1968. I confess to thinking too far ahead instead of concentrating on my match with Moody. I felt I could beat Bonallack, who had an unbelievable reputation, and go on and win the championship. The Von believed this was the world title in amateur golf and felt the contracts when I turned pro would be more substantial if I won it. I watched Bonallack that week and really fancied myself, as he had the funkiest swing you've ever seen. But in the end, he went on to win his fourth title. The following year, Bonallack, now secretary of the Royal and Ancient Golf Club, won the championship for a fifth time.

It was at the British amateur that I met South African Dale Hayes. We'd both planned similar trips. We played in the French Open at St Nom La Breteche, where I fired rounds of 75, 68, 74 and 75 to finish tied for seventeenth behind Frenchman Jean Garaialde, who beat Roberto de Vicenzo on the third hole of a sudden-death play-off. Then Dale and I proceeded to Frankfurt for the German Open and German amateur titles, both played on the same course – Frankfurt Main-Neiderrad – in successive weeks.

We were both babes in the wood. Dale celebrated his seventeenth birthday in Germany and I was only nineteen. We roomed together in a little pub. For the first week we ate nothing but tomato soup and Wiener schnitzel, as that's all we could understand from the menu – but it didn't seem to affect our golf. Hayes beat me in the amateur final.

During that week I met a local girl called Becky van Gulpen, who was playing in the German amateur ladies' championship that was being held in conjunction with the men's title. She spoke perfect English and after a week of tomato soup and schnitzel, Dale and I were able to change our diet. Again it did no harm, though Dale had a far better tournament than I did. He opened with a 65 and closed with a 63 to finish in third spot behind Garaialde and South Africa's Cobie Legrange. My rounds were 75, 68, 69 and then a dreadful closing 81 to finish tied for twenty-first.

I can't say I would have been overwhelmed by the cheque had I been a professional. Those pros on the same scoreline as me collected the equivalent of just $25.20. Dale would have picked up $1263, but instead that went to the fourth place-getter, Britain's Bernard Hunt.

I wasn't to know it at the time, but Becky was to re-enter my life at a later date under strange circumstances. I met up with her again in 1971 and 1972 and then, a year or so later, received a telegram at home in Sydney from her mother. I'd met the family in Germany and her father, I remember, was one of those angry Germans who basically sat in a dark room thinking of the war. When he did emerge he more often than not belted his daughter with his walking stick.

We learned from the telegram that Becky had been hit by a car on a pedestrian crossing and was in a semi-coma. She kept repeating my name as she lay dangerously ill. Her mother asked me to write to Becky, which I did. I wrote that I hoped she would be better soon and signed the letter, 'Love, Jack'.

Someone apparently read the letter to her and she came out of the coma. The next thing I knew was another telegram arriving, this time from Becky herself, saying that I'd saved her life and she was coming to Australia to marry me. By the time I got the message she was already on the boat with just a suitcase of clothes and her golf clubs.

It was all very confusing. She arrived and spent quite a bit of time staying at our house. There's no doubting she wanted to get married, but there was no way I did – I was just embarking on my professional golf career. I helped her get a job and she joined a golf club in Sydney. After that I saw her only once, a few years later, during one of the Kerry Packer Australian Opens at the Australian Golf Club.

On my return from Europe in 1969, I decided the course of action I wanted to take in my life. I would turn professional after the Australian amateur championship at Royal Adelaide in August that year.

I went through the interstate teams series unbeaten for New South Wales and then Barry Burgess and I shot rounds of 68–70 to win the national foursomes title by seven shots. The Australian title, I thought, would cap an amateur career that had included winning the New South Wales amateur title at the age of eighteen.

In Adelaide a 76 in the first of two qualifying rounds for matchplay was less than ordinary, and that's the way I felt. I'd picked up food poisoning and was as crook as a dog on the way round, very nearly quitting after thirteen holes. The following day I felt much better and went out to fire a four-under 69 that, at the time, was a course record for both amateurs and professionals. I was safely through to the matchplay.

My first opponent was former national amateur champion Kevin Donohoe, and after going to four up after seven holes I was never in trouble, winning 4–3.

New Zealander Bruce Rafferty attempted to throw a spanner in the works in the quarterfinals, taking the match to the 22nd hole before I won, and then I met my good mate, Victorian Bob Shearer, in the semifinals. We both worked for Slazenger and I had played with him many times, and against him in interstate junior golf, but he had never beaten me. It looked as though the pattern would continue after I went to an early two-up lead. It didn't. Shears fought back to beat me one up and then went on to beat New Zealander Ross Murray in the final to thumb his nose at the Victorian selectors, who had left him out of their team for the interstate teams matches.

There was a last bit of cleaning-up to do that week when I represented Australia in winning the Sloan Morpeth Trophy against the New Zealanders in a teams match. And that was the end of my amateur career.

Only three top amateurs had turned professional since 1962: Vic Bennetts, Graham Marsh and South Australian Bob Mesnil. I guess Bob is the odd name out, as most golf enthusiasts have heard of Marsh and Bennetts. Mesnil was another young golfer in whom the Von took a kindly interest, but he tended to be just a touch wayward in what he did, both on and off the golf course. He loved the punt and could have $2000 in his pocket one day and nothing the next.

In those days you had to become a tournament trainee professional, which basically meant you could play in

Australian tournaments by invitation only and for twelve months you could not accept prize money. It was a system you had to accept, and for the next 11 months and 29 days I did, though the cheques I might have won would by no means have put a dent in my expenses.

I had to quit my work with Slazenger when I turned pro, but Barry Burgess arranged for me to work with him at the Haymarket, which was then the central fruit and vegetable market in Sydney. The job started at 3 a.m. and I had to load and unload semi-trailers until around nine or ten in the morning. The pay was good – $20 a day – and it left me with the remainder of the day to play and practise golf.

Mind you, the hours had their hazards. I'd just started driving a car and not too long after that I was taking a few girls out. Throw in a few beers each day and at times it was pretty tough trying to get up to make it to Haymarket for the 3 a.m. start. One morning I was driving to work along Parramatta Road and suddenly woke as I heard my car horn go. I'd gone to sleep, my head nodding onto the steering wheel, and had been woken abruptly as the front wheels were mounting the median strip. It gave me a helluva fright and I swore instantly off booze, women and late nights. You can imagine how long that resolution lasted.

I learned a lot at the markets. It was the first time I'd been in the fair-dinkum workforce and I met a marvellous array of characters. Con the Greek was one of them. He was the strongest bloke at the markets and could unload a semi in seventeen minutes flat; Barry wasn't too far behind him. Others around the market had surely been at the back of trucks when goods fell off and there were always cheap watches and clothing and so on being offered. You heard talk of the presence of the Mafia, but I had no first-hand experience of that.

What I did experience was the joy of a couple of beers at the ten o'clock opener before heading home for a couple of hours' sleep and then practice.

The first day of the 1970 New South Wales PGA title at Castle Hill in Sydney was exactly twelve months after I had turned professional and I reasoned I could start picking up the cheques that week. Not so. The Australian PGA ruled that as my probationary period ended on the day the tournament started, I was not entitled to any prize money until the following week. I finished second to Billy Dunk but had to sit and watch as Queenslander Randall Vines picked up second-place money of $400. I'd been patient for twelve months, but that day I was impatient.

Nothing spectacular happened for the remainder of the 1970–71 circuit. I picked up a few minor cheques here and there, but was already planning my full-frontal assault on Europe for 1971. I had a return airfare plus $500 in my kick – and my set of golf clubs. The Von suggested I telephone David Wickens, who could perhaps set me up with lodgings from which to base myself, and a car.

'Is there any chance you know somewhere I could sleep nights? And is there a possibility of a car?' I hesitantly asked Wickens.

'When you get here, just ring me. I'll have something organised,' he replied.

I made the phone call from Heathrow and Wickens

gave me an address to go to in the Sunningdale–Ascot area. 'I'll meet you there in an hour,' he said.

It was a small cottage and I arrived before Wickens. When I knocked on the door, two Australian girls answered. I introduced myself. 'Oh yes, we know you're coming to base yourself here. Playing golf, they say,' one girl said. I was thinking my luck was about to change when Wickens pulled up followed by one of his henchmen driving a small Hillman Imp, which was to be my car.

'Well, I see you've settled in all right. You've met the girls. They'll look after you, give you anything you want,' he said, bursting into guffaws of laughter. It didn't quite work out that way, but the girls were terrific. They were both from Melbourne and the cottage became quite a home away from home. It was brilliant.

My feeling was that Europe was only a stepping stone to the US and I wanted to go it alone. I felt if I could play well enough I could get enough bread to go to the States without the noose of a sponsor around my neck. (At that time David Graham was going through the Bucky Woy experience and in the end it cost him around $250 000. Woy was a Yank who gave David an American Express card, but when David started winning, the 60–40 split, or whatever it was, became a very expensive proposition. Lee Trevino went through the same experience with the same man.)

I didn't think the European circuit was that tough a nut to crack. There was a core of good players: Neil Coles, Peter Oosterhuis, Brian Barnes and, of course, Tony Jacklin. But basically I felt there were only about ten who could really play, with the remainder being average stock who could throw together the odd good round. I was ready to play.

Enter Jackie

After my first trip to England and Europe in 1969 I had returned home via the US, where I met a woman through Bruce Devlin. We met at a cocktail party at her home, which was on the 4th fairway at Winged Foot in New York, and it soon became obvious she had big money. Her name was Susan Hayes and she was a good-looking woman in her early thirties who was the daughter of a guy who'd made a fortune investing in run-down pharmaceutical companies and then resurrecting them. One such company had developed the contraceptive pill, worth millions.

Bruce was playing in the Westchester Classic and fired a first-round 67 to be just one stroke off the pace. He was off late the next day and I arranged to have a game at Winged Foot with Susan before heading to the Westchester Country Club to watch Bruce play his second round. Susan was obviously impressed with the way I hit the ball and started questioning me about whether I had intentions of turning professional. She was sponsoring American Mike Reasor on the Tour, but he wasn't exactly fulfilling his potential.

Susan made me an offer of $500 a week expenses and a 60–40 split my way of any prize money I made. When I got home, I talked it over with my father and we decided it was best to remain independent. Also, when I did take the step into professional golf, we thought I should start somewhere other than the toughest circuit in the world.

Two years down the track, in my first earning year as a pro, I could certainly see why other players accepted sponsorship deals. I picked up small cheques for around $1500 in eight tournaments in Europe and Britain, but expenses were high. I was playing in places like Crans-sur-Sierre, a millionaires' playground in the Swiss Alps where it cost an arm and a leg for food and accommodation. My money was fast running out, but the experience was invaluable.

I qualified for the 1971 British Open at Royal Birkdale and played a practice round with the Von and Gary Player. The Open itself was larger than life, awe-inspiring, and I was pretty proud of myself to play all four rounds and shoot 73, 72, 76, 77, even if the cheque for £129 didn't quite cover my expenses.

A couple of weeks later I arrived at the Dutch Open at the Kennemer club in Zandvoort with just $200 in my pocket and my return airfare home. It was my last tournament before heading back to Australia, and even though Holland was nowhere near as expensive as Crans-sur-Sierre had been a week earlier, I didn't think $200 was going to be enough to get me through.

There were no more worries about money when I won that Dutch pro-am. In those days, American Express sponsored all the pro-am tournaments in Europe, with each of them worth $5000, including $1000 to the winner. The Dutch Open itself was only worth $22 000, so by winning the pro-am I'd virtually finished in fourth place in the Open. In reality, I tied for twenty-third place and pocketed another $190.

Back home I picked up a few cheques without really threatening the victory dais. In New Zealand I tied fifth in both the New Zealand Open and the Otago Classic in back-to-back tournaments, won respectively by Peter Thomson and Bob Charles. It all went towards a bank for my second sortie to Europe and Britain in 1972, a schedule which took me to Asia before I headed to the Northern Hemisphere.

Through Dale Hayes, with whom I had teamed up on my first trip to Britain and Europe as an amateur in 1969, I met Simon Hobday, Tertius Claassens and Vinny Baker, who all had Southern African origins. Tertius was an Afrikaner, a crazy blond bastard who was hell-bent on having a good time wherever he went. Vinny was an English South African and a very staunch patriot, while Simon was from Northern Rhodesia (now Zambia).

We decided to team up and travel together in 1972, and it's fair to say we enjoyed a pretty wild lifestyle while remaining reasonably successful on the golf course. Golf writer Jack Wood took me to task in an article in *Golf World* that same year after I suggested I needed to work on my short game and putting. Wood wrote, 'I suggested that it was difficult to do this when so much of his time was spent in the clubhouse nursing a pint or the prettiest girl available. Mr Newton is adept at both.'

My reply was, 'Look, I like a drink. Maybe there are times when I take a little too much. I like females and fortunately some of them like me. I have been brought up in a tough sort of school where people do these sorts of things. Some blokes relax by going to the cinema or taking a book to bed. I'm not all that keen on reading.'

But Wood wasn't done. He continued: 'I observed that I had heard it said that he left a tournament or two behind in the bar and between the sheets. Newton considered the suggestion for a moment or two and replied with a wide grin, "I like a good night's sleep." As a playboy, he is off plus two. As a golfer, he certainly has the talent to make his mark on the world golf scene.' So it was that I was rightly or wrongly tagged 'The Wild One' by some sections of the British press.

If I was off plus two, my travelling companions were off plus one and Tertius in particular was always looking to slice yet another shot off his handicap. He never wore a watch and was forever asking me the time, to the point where I suggested I buy him one. 'No, man. I don't want no watch. If I'm at a nightclub at four in the morning and I'm off the tee at eight, I don't want to spoil the good time I'm having,' he said.

In Europe, we more or less had the language barrier covered. Tertius, being an Afrikaner, spoke Dutch and German, while I had studied French for eight years at school at my mother's insistence. It was due to the inability of some people to understand Tertius's heavily accented English that a great lady, Jackie Butterworth, came into my life.

We were playing the Piccadilly Medal tournament in April at Hillside. Rothmans, the sponsor, always employed a number of stunning girls to add a touch of glamour to the hospitality area and Tertius took a fancy to one of them, Salli Raymond, a tall, lovely girl whom he affectionately named Big Bad Sal-Sal.

Both Vinny and I won our first-round matches, but Tertius exited after shooting an 80 to Scot Bobby Walker's 76. Naturally enough, he was hot to trot that evening. Vinny and I went back to the hotel where we were staying and an hour or so later Tertius burst in and said, 'I've been talking with Big Bad Sal-Sal. I've got a date with her tonight and I need you to come as she might not under-stand my English.'

'Nah, I'm not going,' I protested, but he would hear none of it. Tertius's date was for 7 p.m. and he was to meet Salli in the foyer of a hotel where she and the other Piccadilly girls were attending a function for the press.

Eventually she emerged with two other girls. As they approached, Vinny said, 'I fancy the blonde bird.'

'So do I,' I said. The only gentlemanly thing to do was toss a coin. I lost, leaving Vinny to focus his full attention on Patsy Bass-Walker while I paired off with Jackie. The six of us went off to dinner, the casino and then a disco.

It was the first lucky break in my life, though I didn't quite see it that way at the time. Jackie and I sat talking until four in the morning and she resisted every effort I made to share her bed.

I was beaten 74 to 79 by English player Mike Ingham in the second round of the Piccadilly Medal and Vinny fared no better, shooting a 79 against Tony Jacklin's 78, but we both received £98 as second-round losers.

I didn't see myself as a loser. Jackie was different from all the other women I'd met. She had genuine qualities and class. She'd done a bit of film work, been a model and was very mature. Her mother and father were separated and her mother was deaf and very ill, so Jackie had the responsibility of looking after her and Christopher, the younger of her two brothers. As the person responsible for hiring the Piccadilly girls, she was like a mother duck to them too, the one whose shoulder they cried on, the one who stayed calm in difficult situations. And that is still one of her greatest qualities.

She and I went out again the next night and then Tertius and I headed back to London and the Traveller's Rest private hotel in Earls Court (or 'Kangaroo Valley' as it was known in the late '60s and early '70s), which we'd made our headquarters because the owners were prepared to store our excess junk. Earls Court was also one of the few areas in London, before England became Fosterised, where you could buy Australian beer.

We rang Jackie and Big Bad Sal-Sal a few days later to ask when they would be in London so we could get together again. Dinner was arranged on a boat on the Thames that had been converted to a restaurant called the Sloop John B. Fair dinkum, I reckon the girls must have thought we were a pair of hot-shots ready to be taken for a ride. In the end, the bill was £200. Tertius fumbled, coming up with only a fiver, and when we left I was fresh out of travellers' cheques.

A complicating factor to any lasting relationship with Jackie was that she had just ended one long affair to begin another, with Romanian tennis player Ion Tiriac, who played the straight man to Ilie Nastase in doubles but also had a cute party trick of chewing glass. A former ice-hockey player for Romania, Tiriac turned to tennis and later became manager of German champion Boris Becker and, more recently, president of the Romanian Olympic Committee.

I next saw Jackie in May, when she was working at the British hardcourt tennis championships in the same week as the Penfold tournament at Queens Park Golf Club in Bournemouth. Tertius and I played a practice round early one day and then went, unheralded, to the tennis. I knew Jackie would be there and after watching a bit of tennis we went to the bar to find her sitting with Tiriac. He and I both suggested we would knock each other out and I could see Jackie was distinctly uncomfortable about the situation. She was going out with Tiriac, and suddenly I'd appeared on the scene to complicate the whole affair.

The Bournemouth tournament was the start of a great run for me on the circuit. I finished one shot out of the play-off in which Peter Oosterhuis defeated Christy O'Connor Jr on the first hole of sudden death, and followed that up with a tied fifth in the John Player Trophy, a second to Brian Barnes in the Martini International, a tied eighth in the Carrolls International and another tied eighth in the Scottish Open, to give me five top-10 finishes in just five events. I earned a new tag from the press: 'Mr Consistency'.

All the time I was ringing Jackie and writing to her. In one letter I suggested she accompany me to the Dutch Open in early August, but she knocked me back. She missed a hell of a good party when I won. An opening 64, nine under par on the Haagsche Golf and Country Club layout near The Hague, was followed by 75, 69, 69 with a birdie birdie finish in the final round to give me a one-shot victory over Oosterhuis and Englishman Malcolm Gregson. It was my first tournament win on the European circuit.

The following week it was the Benson & Hedges tournament at Fulford Golf Club in York, where Vinny, Tertius, Simon and I stayed at a bed-and-breakfast joint run by three little old ladies. They looked after us as though we were their grandsons, and showed a remarkably tolerant attitude to our youthful excesses. I made it back-to-back victories with rounds of 73, 70, 67 and 71 to score by a shot from Harry Bannerman. Across the Atlantic, Bruce Devlin made it a great week for Australia by winning the USI Classic in New York. Jackie missed another party, which included a spot of rough-and-tumble wrestling in the carpark on the way from the Benson & Hedges marquee to the club-house bar as the night wore on. We continued the drinking session at the bar only to be interrupted by a gentleman who approached and said, 'Jack, I think this belongs to you.'

It was my winner's cheque for nearly £3000 and had obviously fallen out of my pocket while we were wrestling.

I saw Jackie again the following week in London when we were playing the PGA championship at Wentworth, but any hope of making it three wins in a row went out the window with an opening 77. I was starting to grow very fond of the tall, elegant girl who was a couple of years older than me. I liked her sense of humour and her sincerity. I was putting on all the parties and every freeloader who needed a quid was borrowing money from me, but Jackie wasn't there for the good times. She had substance and I guess I was starting to feel I was ready for the stabilising influence she seemed to have on me.

It wasn't your normal boy–girl courtship. It wasn't as if I lived down the road from Jackie and could call and say, 'Let's go out tonight.' Rather, I'd ring and say, 'Come and spend a week with me.' She came to the John Player Classic at Turnberry in Scotland in late September and travelling up on the plane I asked her if she would come to Australia with me for Christmas. Just as Jackie was involved with Tiriac when we first met, I had been in a fairly heavy relationship with a girl I had left behind in Sydney. I was fairly keen on her, but the greatest test of any relationship is to be travelling away from someone for six or seven months and I had come to the conclusion it wasn't right.

Nor did I want to get married at that stage. Not to Jackie, not to anyone. I was only twenty-two, far too young. But I had got to the stage where I had a great respect for Jackie, a growing love for her, and if we were ever to get married, there was no way I was going to live in England. I thought the best test for us both was for her to come to Australia to see if she liked it. Anything else down the track could take care of itself.

She agreed to make the journey and we met up in Auckland, the site of the last event of four in New Zealand late in the year. The tournament was the City of Auckland Classic and the big import was 1969 US Masters champion George Archer, with 1963 British Open winner Bob Charles playing his home circuit. Archer led into the last round and Jackie walked the course following Charles, Archer and me. For once, she didn't miss the party. I shot a final-round 64 to Archer's 66 to beat him by a shot and reach an important turning point in my career. To beat a recent Masters champion in such a fashion added a pretty big scalp to the belt.

Traditionally my family spent Christmas with my grandparents, who had moved from Cessnock to Arcadia Vale on the shores of Lake Macquarie. As I've said, they were a strong influence in my life and I would always take any serious girlfriend to see them. Mind you, I'd only taken a couple, and each one had been met with these words from my grandmother: 'So you're the one trying to steal my grandson!' She wouldn't have met them for five seconds before she uttered those lines, but she only had my best interests at heart. She was tough and matriarchal, but a wonderful lady.

Jackie and I stayed with my grandparents and on Christmas Day went across to Caves Beach for lunch with my uncle and aunt, Basil and Audrey. All the relatives were there. Given that Jackie only has a handful of kin, she must have thought there were hundreds there that day. Later, we went swimming and Jackie didn't have to say a word; I knew it had been a difficult experience for her.

We stayed at Arcadia Vale for several days, spending most of our time fishing. Before you can go out in the boat, you've got to get the worms, and my family had a very simple way of collecting worms by wading into the lake and digging. The blue mud would be deposited on a covered floating tyre and the worms would emerge. Jackie learned to shovel for worms and we still joke that I gave her a hard time if she split one in two. 'So this is our love life. Digging worms and going fishing,' she said at the time.

Jackie spent two months down-under before returning to London. I stayed home to play the February tournaments of the Australian circuit. When she left I knew I still wasn't ready to get married, but she was certainly the most important person in my life outside my immediate family. Maybe I'd found Jackie too early. I still wanted to go to parties and raise a little hell. I was still learning the ropes as a professional golfer and didn't want to be saddled with a wife and possibly kids as well. Yet when she left to return to London, there was a certain emptiness. I didn't want her to go.

I missed Jackie a lot in the ten weeks we were apart. She met me at Heathrow at the end of March, and after spending a couple of days in London, we flew to Spain for the Madrid Open, the opening tournament on the 1973 European/British circuit.

On-course was nothing spectacular but one day there was quite a scene during a few drinks around the hotel swimming pool. Stewart Ginn and his wife, Sam, were with us and all hell broke loose when a waiter made a remark about Sam. Ginny was going to punch the waiter – and any-one else who moved – in one of his rare moments of rage. He doesn't fly off the handle often, but when he does it is spectacular.

He was going to 'kill' Ian Stanley one night in a pub in London and punched him through the toilet door. He probably didn't hit him hard enough – maybe it might have knocked some sense into him. Stan was always acting the goat, never more so than at the pro-am we played that was sponsored by the Durex condom company. Each player was given a box and Stan created havoc by blowing them up and letting them loose on the first tee.

The Australian contingent in Europe and Britain was growing. Ginny, Shearer, Stanley, Tasmanian David Good and I formed the nucleus, with the likes of Thomson, Kel Nagle and Marsh joining in around British Open time.

Shears' best tournament placing for the year, a tie for eighth, came at the Penfold event at Bournemouth, where Jackie and the other Piccadilly girls were once again working at the hardcourt tennis titles. Shears met his lovely wife, Kathie, that same week. It was Jackie's birthday on 8 May, two days before the golf tournament started, and we decided to have a party with forty or fifty people from the golf and tennis assembling in one of the larger hotels to drink and dance the night away. Shears drank more than his fair share and was virtually knee-walking as the evening wore on. I knew he fancied one of the other Piccadilly girls, Kathie Melvin, but they hadn't met. When I saw her dancing with Scottish golfer Harry Bannerman, I thought it time she and Shears were introduced.

I had no time for Bannerman whatsoever. We'd been involved in a slight altercation at the Dutch Open the previous year over remarks he made about Gary Baleson, one of the South African guys. Bannerman came into the clubhouse and started shooting his mouth off about Baleson, suggesting he may have cheated. I went to bat for Gary, saying that if Bannerman thought someone was wrong, he should have said it out on the course rather than coming into the clubhouse to bad-mouth him.

Bannerman then turned his verbal attack on me and I said, 'Right. We'll go outside and settle this.' But he wouldn't budge, his feet firmly planted to the spot. I reached out and grabbed the front of his Pringle cashmere sweater and started walking, but he did not. The result was that his sweater stretched five paces as he continued to resist.

So when I saw Bannerman dancing with Kathie, I intervened. 'Never mind about this Scottish prick. Get over here and look after my mate Shearer.' Shears was not in great shape, but it was at that moment that he and Kathie began their life together.

Dad took his long-service leave from the NSW police force in 1973 and he and Mum came to Europe for three months. Dad caddied for me and also played in the British amateur championship at Royal Porthcawl in Wales, reaching the third round. The first tournament in which he caddied for me was the Martini, in Scotland in early June, and I was glad to have him around as a backstop considering that Christy O'Connor Sr would be playing.

Christy Sr and I have been great mates through the journey, but 'Himself', as he is known to every Irishman, did used to have one very annoying habit when he was drunk. He would throw punches at you, pulling them at the last moment. We had been in the bar during the French Open a couple of weeks before the Martini when Christy appeared and got up to his old party trick.

'Knock that shit off. It's driving me mad,' I said.

'What's the matter, Skippy?' he taunted, and threw another punch that caught me flush on the chin.

'Christy, if you do that again, look out,' I warned. He advanced towards me and I could tell he wanted to fight.

I didn't want to hit him, so instead thrust my arms around his armpits and started squeezing. His feet lifted off the ground and I knew if I let him go it would be on for young and old, so I continued to squeeze until he began to turn red in the face. Simon Hobday, who was with us, said, 'You'd better let him down,' and I released my hold. Christy crumpled onto the floor and I thought it time to take my leave. Next day, he withdrew from the tournament after he was diagnosed with three broken ribs.

There is one thing about Christy – he never holds a grudge. We remain firm friends, but I was thankful to have Dad around just in case there were any repercussions so soon after this incident.

My relationship with Jackie was getting stronger and she travelled with me whenever her work would permit. She had the week off during the Coca-Cola young professionals' championship for players under 25 at Bristol in June, and joined Mum, Dad and me. We didn't book ahead and while I practised Jackie and my mother went in search of accommodation. Mum, being the very protective lady she is, was asking for two single rooms and a double at each hotel they went to, but there was no joy. Finally, at the fifth hotel, the manager said he only had two double rooms and Jackie, without looking my mother in the eye, said, 'That will be fine, thank you.'

We stayed in contact, mostly by mail, through the summer of 1973–74, but decided it would be a period of time where we could both decide how we felt about each other. I went out with other women and I'm darn sure Jackie went out with other blokes.

I arrived back in London on 14 February, St Valentine's Day, and convinced Jackie to come to Africa with me. We had been through a few ups and downs over the previous few months, but I believed now that all our troubles were over. They weren't!

In late April after we had returned to England, almost as a passing thought Jackie said, 'Oh, by the way, I'm flying to New York in a couple of days to join the *QE II* on the voyage back to England.' It was another job as a hostess, for a big backgammon tournament on the ship. I felt that every shyster under the sun would be on board and I was unimpressed. Jackie went anyway.

On her return, her next job was at Wimbledon. There was no golf tournament that week and I was staying at her house in Dulwich. A couple of my African mates, Gordon Wadey and Bobby Bolton, were in London for a social rugby match and on the night of the first Friday of Wimbledon we were at Jackie's playing snooker for money on her three-quarter-size table. Naturally enough, there was a bit of grog being consumed. Jackie retired to bed fairly early.

It was about 5 a.m. when we quit playing snooker and by that time I had made a decision. My Dutch courage was up and I was going to propose to Jackie. 'How about we get married?' I said as I sidled into the cot. She said yes and I was asleep within moments. Next morning when I awoke, she had already left.

At Wimbledon, Jackie was apparently in a bit of a tizz. She wanted to say something, but with all the newspaper guys around she had to keep quiet. She told one of her friends, Sandy, about what I'd said at 5 a.m. and they decided to telephone me. It was Sandy on the line and she said, 'Do you remember what you said last night?'

'No. What did I say?' I replied. Next thing Jackie was on the phone, saying, 'Do you remember asking me to marry you last night?' My head was a bit fuzzy, I wasn't quite with it and I answered, 'No.' Of course I remembered, but there I was facing twenty questions rather than Sandy offering her congratulations or whatever.

We announced our engagement at Royal Lytham and St Annes during the British Open a couple of weeks later and were married at the Dulwich College Chapel on 1 September. Shears was my best man. Ian Stanley, Stewart Ginn and a lot of the blokes were there, too, but Peter Thomson declined an invitation. 'No, I won't come to this one. I'll come to the next one,' Thommo said. Jackie has never forgiven him.

The reception was at Jackie's house and we saw through the bay windows my caddie, Charlie Mackie, approaching. Charlie was one of the best caddies I ever had. He hadn't been at the ceremony but was there for the drinks, which wasn't at all surprising. I knew he'd been drinking before he arrived. 'I told you not to get married, you f— wanker!' he called.

With that, Jackie's mother, bless her, took hold of him and said, 'Now come on, Charlie. I'll look after you.' He had put on his best suit for the occasion and proceeded to top up very nicely.

Without Jackie even changing from her wedding dress, she and I went from the reception to Gatwick Airport to spend the night before going to the Canary Islands for a one-week honeymoon.

The following week I won the British matchplay title at Dundee, beating Mexican Cesar Sanudo 2–1 in the final – but earlier that day I played some of my finest golf and was 10 under par after thirteen holes in beating Neil Coles 6–5. I had a further £3500 in the bank to begin married life.

Sadly, Big Bad Sal-Sal is no longer with us. Nor is Vinny Baker. Salli married George Hammond, who started the Piccadilly world matchplay championship at Wentworth. She died of cancer in 1990. Vinny died in tragic circumstances the same year. Fishing was his love and one day he took his four-wheel-drive vehicle to a river in South Africa and went out in a small boat for a day's fishing. On his return he disturbed three men who apparently were attempting to steal his wagon. He fought for possession and lay dead on the ground for his trouble.

Both Salli and Vinny were very dear friends, and I miss them.

Have clubs, will travel

It wasn't fashionable for Australian golfers to play the full British and European circuit in the early '70s. Sure, the Von, Thomson and Nagle had carried the flag through the years, but others, like Alan Murray, Col McGregor and Teddy Ball, focused their overseas travels on the Asian circuit.

My first encounter with Asia in early 1972 wasn't love at first sight. In fact, it was the total opposite. I hated the place and its golf. Firstly, there was the stinking-hot, humid weather which attempts to suffocate you. It wasn't unusual to go through three or four gloves in a round.

Secondly, there was the manner in which the tournaments were conducted. I won't say it was shonky, but it certainly left a lot to be desired. Although I'd felt that Europe wasn't terribly well organised in 1971 in my first year over there, at least the rules were set down as to how many players were in the field, and there were tournament officials on the golf course who made rulings.

Not so in Asia. If a given set of circumstances didn't suit the locals, particularly in Singapore, they changed the rules. My first encounter with such indifference was in the prequalifying for the Singapore Open. The field for the tournament proper was to be 144. After qualifying, the officials felt there were not enough locals in the field so they simply increased the size of the draw to include another two local players.

I also soon discovered there was a lot of cheating going on. If you reported it, you invariably came off second-best. It was almost a case of anything goes, with guys out there who couldn't count and didn't know the rules. It wasn't uncommon for players to change their scorecards after you'd actually signed them. I recall signing one bloke's card for a 73 and on arrival at the course the next day there he was with a 72 beside his name on the board.

To me, all this was totally unacceptable. I'd been brought up to play everything down the line and I couldn't take this insane situation in which you basically had to turn a blind eye. While things have improved since, I feel those circumstances had much to do with the demise of the Asian circuit and the rise to power of the Japanese circuit, where even though there are tight rules regarding foreigners playing, everything is strictly according to Hoyle.

After Singapore, the next tournament was the Cathay Pacific in Hong Kong, worth $150 000, which was pretty big brass in those days. I shot 70 in the opening round before rain halted play with less than a quarter of the field still to complete the round. Under normal circumstances, with so few to finish, those still on the course would mark their balls and return the following day to finish the round. Not in Hong Kong.

Graham Marsh had turned professional in 1969, a year before I did, and in 1971 had made some impact on golf, winning the New Zealand Spalding Masters and the Indian Open on the Asian circuit. He negotiated a good contract with Cathay Pacific and was very much a favourite son of the Hong Kong-based international airline. The trouble was, that day in Hong Kong he fired an opening round of 78. Even Greg Norman knows, from bitter experience at Augusta, that such a score is an invitation to miss the cut.

So what did the tournament organisers do? They scrubbed all scores, abandoned the first day's play and ordered a re-start the following day, when Hughie again did his best to drown Hong Kong, rendering play impossible once more. There we were, two days into the tournament, and there wasn't a score on the board. It was decided to make the event a 36-hole affair with a one-round cut, which I missed after firing a 74.

I sat thinking about that for a while. I'd shot 70–74, which would have been pretty close to leading any normal tournament in those days – and despite this I'd missed the cut. I was out, gone.

'Leave me out of this,' I muttered to anyone who cared to listen and caught the first British Airways flight to London, turning my back on the Asian circuit forever and a day.

After the 1972–73 Australian season there was a vacuum in my tournament golf before travelling to Europe, so I decided that in 1974 I'd play the African circuit. They had a few small tournaments over there and the British PGA had decided to annex them to give the British players somewhere to play in preparation for the mainstream European circuit.

The tournaments were in Nigeria, Kenya and Zambia, with just a couple of thousand pounds to the winner each week. But from an economic point of view, it made good sense to me. There were virtually no overheads, and I had a contract with British Caledonian Airways so I could travel there for nothing. Because of the lack of European-style hotels, players were billeted in the homes of British expat-riates and the like, who, through the years, welcomed the annual invasion of golfers.

First stop in 1974 was Nigeria, and it was quite a shock to find that the tournament was to be played on sand greens. I wasn't entirely unfamiliar with sand greens because I'd been sent as an amateur kid to various places in country New South Wales by the NSW Golf Association, to play in local events. But it wasn't until I had a 9-iron to one of the greens of the Ikoyi Golf Club that I remembered some of the tricks of the trade. It looked a fairly straightforward 9-iron, but as soon as the ball hit the green it bounced as high as the trees beside the green and carried to about 15 yards behind it. From then on it was pitch and run.

I guess you'd have to say there was a fair bit of interest in my appearance in the Nigerian Open that year. I'd started to make a bit of a name for myself in Europe, winning the 1972 Dutch Open and Benson & Hedges tournaments, and I was also the first Australian to play in Nigeria. As well, I was feeling quite at home. The heat was drier than that of

Asia – good beer-drinking weather – and the local manager of Barclay's Bank, with whom I was staying, kept his fridge well stocked.

With rounds of 74, 65, 69, five under par, I was three shots behind Nigerian Amadu Baba, who'd started in golf as a caddie and despite his anonymity elsewhere was something of a local hero. I was drawn to play with him in the final round and on arrival at the course was stunned to see what seemed to be thousands of black kids running around wearing identical T-shirts with 'Baba d'Winna' printed on them. Some enterprising businessman must have done a rush job overnight and flogged them cheaply to the kids.

I was in a strange country and suddenly thought, 'What happens if I beat him?' Then I thought, 'To hell with it. I'll give him "Baba" out on the golf course.'

The poor kid played well early but then suffered a huge attack of nerves as the round progressed. I shot 67 to beat Irishmen Christy O'Connor Sr and Eamonn Darcy and Scotland's Ronnie Shade by four shots, while Baba fired a 75 to disappear back into the obscurity whence he came.

The courses in Kenya were mostly built by the old British colonials and are a very fine test of golf. Nairobi is around 1500 metres above sea level and the first thing I noticed was that the ball would go forever. We were using the old Slazenger B51s in those days, which went like rockets under normal circumstances, but in Nairobi even the wimps became long-hitters. I was hitting 9-iron into 550-yard par fives, which took some getting used to.

My ability to crank the ball out a fair distance got me into real strife in Zambia, which used to be Northern Rhodesia before the country was split in two with black rule in the north. A lot of white people stayed on in Zambia because of the copper mining, but there was a fair amount of tension.

I played the African circuit for three years, from 1974 to 1976, and in the first year met a local Zambian player called Bob Katontoga, whom we called 'The Cat'. This guy was beautifully built, around the 190 cm mark with broad shoulders and a body that tapered to a slim waist. He was very definitely Mr Universe material and ebony black. He was also a member of the famous Ecoye tribe, one of the elite of Zambia.

That first year, and in the following years, the Cat couldn't understand how I continually hit the ball farther than he did. Each time we met he challenged me to an armwrestle to prove he was stronger than I was and I'd fob him off, saying the reason I could drive the ball farther than he could had nothing to do with power but rather timing, and so on. But it became an obsession with him and each time he confronted me he was more aggressive.

In 1976 we played three tournaments in Zambia and I won the first two, the Mufulira Open and the Cock o' the North title at Ndola. I was attempting the hat-trick in the Zambia Open at Lusaka Golf Club the following week.

Along with Bobby Bolton, the local manager for Rothmans, and Gordon Wadey, a well-known footballer and big guy, I backed myself to win the three tournaments. After two rounds, I led the field by a shot. On the Saturday evening, as always, a Calcutta – a sweep where the contestants are auctioned off to the highest bidder – was held on the final day's play. Bolton, Wadey and I decided we should buy J. Newton. The way I was playing I thought it would be a formality.

We were standing in Castle Corner in the bar – so named because of the Castle Lager that was consumed there by the expats and visiting golfers – as the Calcutta dragged on. The mission to buy me was accomplished and the first money in the Calcutta was the equivalent of about £3000. Everything looked rosy until the Cat arrived on the scene.

'I want to armwrestle you – now!' he demanded.

He'd been drinking and I thought the best way to placate him was to agree. 'Okay, tomorrow night. After the tournament's over. We'll do whatever you like, but not until then. I want to win the tournament,' I said. He seemed satisfied and left. But blow me down, he was back inside thirty minutes, even drunker. 'Armwrestle – now!' he again demanded.

'Listen, f— off. You're driving me crazy. I'm going home,' I said. Before I'd finished the sentence, he'd taken a swing at me. I saw it coming and ducked, while at the same time giving him my Sunday-best left hook. I knocked him out, and as swiftly as the punch had been delivered, silence engulfed the bar.

'Jesus, you're in trouble now,' said Wadey, as the black bartender came from behind the bar to throw a jug of water over the Cat's head to revive him. 'Just stand at the bar and do nothing. We'll finish our drinks and get out of here.'

We turned our backs on the Cat and tried to appear as though nothing had happened. The next thing I knew I was flat on my back on the floor. An enraged Cat had kicked me in the back and then proceeded to put the boot in as

I lay there helpless. Not one person, black or white, was coming to my aid.

Finally a guy called Jimmy Walker, a tobacco farmer who had earlier given me a present of a lion skin, threw his body on top of mine to prevent the Cat from kicking me further. 'That's enough. No more!' he cried out and mercifully the kicking stopped. My friends dragged me out of the bar and I surveyed the damage through half-closed eyes. I was red raw, missing skin from all over my face, and my body felt as if it had suffered similarly.

The guys got me back to Bolton's house. Jackie had left the bar before the trouble started and her face fell as they carried me in. She helped me undress to reveal a bloody mess and I spent most of the night in the bath, attempting to rid myself of the pain and stiffness.

I could barely walk from the car to the clubhouse the following day and was immediately called to the PGA office to give my version of the events of the previous evening. The Cat had already been interviewed and had admitted throwing the first punch. No action was taken against me, but the Cat received a suspension and I've not heard of him from that day to this.

I was so stiff and sore I didn't think I could play. It was as though someone had taken one of those dolly hammers used for tenderising steak and hit me all over. The net result was that I fired a final-round 75 to lose by a shot to Englishman Peter Cowen. I guess all up, with the prize money and my share of the Calcutta, it cost me about £4000, which made it a pretty expensive left hook.

That same year, just a couple of weeks earlier in the Cock o' the North tournament in Ndola, I had had cause to get my gear off rather quickly because of another painful experience. Both the Ndola course and Mufulira have the fairly distinctive feature of being dotted with anthills. Not anthills as most Australians know them, but huge mounds, some of them 20 or 25 metres high and around 9 to 12 metres at the base. It's not uncommon for them to have trees growing out of the top. They're the home of Matabele ants, which, folklore has it, were once about 8 cm long and used by the indigenous people to torture their enemies. These days they are only about the size of a big Australian bull ant, but they do make their presence felt.

The anthills are actually hazards on the golf courses and if you hit your ball behind them, the only shot you've got is to chip out sideways. There is also a local rule that if the ball gets in a Matabele trail, which can be up to 1.5 cm wide trailing around the fairways, or among some of the ants, you get a free drop. I'd seen people attacked by these ants before; they jump onto the body and bite with enough ferocity to draw blood. You can literally be covered by hundreds of them in a matter of seconds, and then the only way to get rid of them is either to have a shower or to strip off and pluck the wretched things off your body.

I was playing with Englishman Brian Barnes in the third round with a gallery of about three thousand – and playing pretty well. At the 17th, a par 5, I hit my second shot just short of the green. My caddie, a black guy who stood about 200 cm but weighed no more than 60 kilos, threw the bag to the ground and bolted, yelling as he went, 'Ants, bwana! Ants!'

I looked down at the ground and couldn't see any ants, but within seconds I felt the first bite. I started slapping at each sharp pain, just as I'd seen others do when they'd been attacked, but it seemed only to increase the creatures' fury.

It was a vital stage of the tournament and, as there was no shower immediately available beside the 17th green, there was nothing for it but to get my gear off – and quick. Jackie and a few friends formed a circle around me and then helped pluck the ants from various parts of my anatomy. It's pretty embarrassing to get your gear off in front of three thousand or so people, but there was no lasting damage and I went on to win the tournament.

My golf in Africa was not confined to tournament play. On my first visit to Zambia, the Foreign Affairs minister, Aaron Milner, telephoned and asked if I'd be prepared to go over to the palace to play golf with President Kenneth Kaunda. Now that's the sort of invitation you don't knock back. Inside the 6-metre-high wall of the palace was this lovely little six-hole course that had obviously been there for yonks. After meeting the president, he and I played the course three times to tally up 18 holes.

I then lunched with Kaunda, who even at that first meeting struck me as an all-right guy. Everything was very formal, as though we were at Buckingham Palace, and Kaunda himself poured the tea. He seemed to be either Oxford- or Cambridge-educated, but in truth was the product of a mission school. His influence in Africa was enormous, yet as we sat sipping tea he was nothing more, nothing less than a bloody good bloke. On each visit to Zambia I gave him a lesson and then played a round of golf with him. He was far from a useless player, shooting in the low nineties. Quite a few years later I heard that he had beaten former Australian prime minister Bob Hawke in a round of golf in the West Indies and I rang Bob, saying, 'I guess one of my oldest pupils is too good for you.'

The friendship with Kaunda and his staff had its advantages, as I guess is the case in any situation where you know people in high places. Before going to Zambia in 1976 I needed advice and sought it from David Phiri, Kaunda's right-hand man. My sin, if you can call it that, was to play two tournaments in South Africa – the South African Open and the Dunlop Masters – as a prelude to going on to Nigeria and Zambia. I had top-10 finishes in both events, but then heard rumblings that I might not be allowed to enter Zambia because I had been to South Africa. This took place at about the time when the black list was started on those who had sporting contact with South Africa.

I went with Simon Hobday to his home in Southern Rhodesia to kill a little time before the Zambian tournaments started and telephoned Phiri to test the waters and ask for advice. He said not to enter Zambia from Rhodesia, a trip which would have been no more than 160 kilometres from Simon's house, but rather to go to Nairobi and enter from Kenya, which was considered a neutral country.

I was told to deny going to South Africa, and did just that when a newspaper guy confronted me. He produced a cutting from the *Sunday Tribune* of South Africa, which listed 'J. Newton (Australia)' as playing in the South African Open. 'How do you explain this?' he demanded.

'No, that's not me. That's my brother,' I replied, and

incredibly he bought the story and the headlines the following day declared: 'Newton denies playing in SA'.

I'd told a white lie for the sake of convenience and I guess I was lucky it was a fairly naive Zambian sportswriter asking the question rather than one of the Fleet Street beasties, who relentlessly pursue mud even if it hasn't rained.

The other occasion I had to seek help from the palace was in 1975, when Jackie's mother fell gravely ill. I was being sponsored by Zambian Airways that year and we managed to book Jackie a flight to London on the evening that we received the news of her mother's ill health. It was a 10.30 p.m. flight and we left in good time for the airport. After the usual delays with ticketing and checking the luggage through, I farewelled Jackie and she headed to passport control.

A couple of hours later a cab pulled up outside the house and a hysterical Jackie emerged. Tears flowed down her cheeks as she told of her ordeal at the airport. What had happened was that the officers in charge of passport control had been sitting around smoking cigarettes and refused to stamp her passport. 'Too late,' they said. 'The person has gone off duty.'

Jackie then went out to the plane, which was preparing for take-off, but the crew wouldn't let her board because her passport wasn't stamped. She went back to the passport guys, who were still sitting around smoking and chatting among themselves. Again they refused to stamp her passport and once more she returned to the aircraft. She pleaded with the crew to let her board. 'Look, my mother is dying. I've got to get back to London.' But they wouldn't budge, and as she walked down the steps the doors of the plane were closed. Her luggage, mind you, was on board.

I was as mad as all get out and picked up the telephone and called David Phiri at the palace. 'You bastards keep telling me black is beautiful and yet you've got a guy at the airport who wouldn't stamp Jackie's passport so she can get on a plane to go and see her mother who is dying. It's crap!' I said, forgetting any sort of protocol.

All hell apparently broke loose that night. Phiri phoned back to say there was a free ticket for Jackie to travel British Airways to London the following morning. Her mother died just a few hours after Jackie arrived home in London, and the world had lost a great lady. Jackie telephoned that night to tell me the sad news.

I fired an 11-under-par 62, one of my finest rounds ever, in the pro-am of the Mufulira Open that day, which I guess was somewhat ironic. Perhaps I sent Jackie's mum out in the right way.

Despite what had happened at the airport that evening, David Phiri was right. Black *is* beautiful, and Zambia and the other African countries I visited are stunning. I am occasionally guilty of using the expression 'He's where elephants go to die' on television to refer to deep trouble confronting a player, and I guess this has its origins in my African experience. Another favourite TV expression of mine is 'bundu', a Swahili word that roughly translates as the stuff in which Werribee ducks or Bondi swimmers occasionally find themselves. I reckon 'bundu' sounds a whole lot better than the English word, or the more refined comment that the ball is 'dead'.

They were good times in Africa, but sad times as well. The death of Jackie's mother was paramount, but I also lost another good friend while there. As I've said, when a golf tournament came to an African city, it was the big event of the year. The expatriates looked forward to the week because they were starved of the companionship of outsiders and of top sport as well. It was party week, like the Melbourne Cup, and they threw their homes open to us.

During the Mufulira Open of 1976 I was leading after the third round. As was the custom, there was a social function in the clubhouse after the end of play and among those present were a couple of young British players, David Moore and Gary Smith. They were staying with the captain of a copper mine and his wife. The mine captain was quite famous as some years before he had shown bravery beyond the call of duty when he risked his life to save about 100 workers after a mine disaster. He was basically a non-drinker, but that day he broke out with a bee in his bonnet in the form of a suspicion that one of the English golfers was having it off with his wife.

The mine captain went to the golf club at 10 a.m. and then sat in the bar drinking until around 8 p.m. He was drunk and showing it. He danced with some of the black women, which, while blacks and whites fraternised freely and went out to dinner together, was a social 'no-no'. But everyone kept smiling because the guy was something of a local hero.

Around 9.30 p.m. Smith, who was just three shots off the lead, decided it was time for bed. Moore, who had missed the cut, said, 'I'll go, too.' The wife drove them home and the two golfers went their separate ways to bed. Some time later the husband arrived home and an argument broke out between him and his wife that the two young English lads could hear from their bedrooms. The mine captain left no doubt that he felt his wife had been paying too much attention to one of them. Next moment, the mine captain burst into Moore's room and a gunshot rang out, leaving Moore dying on the floor. With that, the husband headed to Smith's room. Having heard the shot, Smith locked himself in the toilet and stood terrified as the mine captain shouted, 'Open the door! You're next. I'm going to shoot you, too!' Suddenly the mine captain snapped out of it and went to the aid of Moore. He was barely alive. The husband and Smith drove Moore to the hospital, but it was too late. He was dead. The mine captain then turned the gun on himself.

It was a sad, sad day for golf in Africa. Dai Rees, who was on the Tour board, made the decision the following day that the tournament should go ahead as he believed it was what Moore would have wanted. But it was a very hollow day, even in my victory. Golf is supposed to be a pretty safe sport, but one of our number had died, murdered by a jealous man. David Moore had been just twenty-three, with everything to live for.

One stroke from glory

Bobby Locke stood out like a sore thumb among the hardened musclemen of golf in their trendy clothes. He looked like a portly politician as he ambled around the course dressed in a white business shirt, a Welsh golf club tie and old-fashioned black trousers that showed his green socks.

He was called 'Old Muffin Face' or 'Droopy Jowls' even before he was thirty and nothing seemed to have changed from the old photographs I'd seen of him, apart from maybe a few centimetres around the girth.

I first met him when he was in his mid-fifties, and jumped at the invitation to play a practice round before the Martini tournament in 1975.

He was a legend. Someone said he had been involved in a level-crossing accident and it was suggested this left him with a memory loss, but the day I met Locke I realised just how wrong rumours can be. The thing the storytellers did get right was that he was a gentleman among professional golfers and a master player in his prime.

I'd also heard the stories of his right-to-left movement of the ball, even on his putts, and as we played the early holes I found the truth in this, too. That is, until we came to a hole with a very sharp dogleg to the right, where there were trees down the right that would prevent him starting his ball down his legendary line to allow for the hook.

I asked, 'Mr Locke, how are you going to get on here where you've got to hit a fade?'

'Excuse me?' he replied.

Remembering the story that he might have been a little affected by the accident, I repeated, 'Mr Locke, how are you going to play this hole with a fade?'

'Excuse me?' he said again, and suddenly it dawned on me that he was taking the mickey. 'Master,' he said, 'that word is not in my vocabulary.' (It was always like that with Locke. Everyone was 'Master'.) With that, he stood on the tee and hit the most perfectly straight shot you've ever seen in your life, with the ball never deviating one yard from right to left, to position it in the middle of the dogleg and give him a straightforward shot to the green.

'That's how I play a dogleg to the right,' he remarked before ambling on up the fairway.

Later, in the clubhouse, I sat enthralled as we shared a few noggins while his fellow South Africans got him going. He told of the Tam o' Shanter tournament in the States, at the time the biggest-money tournament in the world, when he needed three at the last to beat Lloyd Mangrum, who was in the clubhouse, or a par 4 to tie.

It was a very long par 4 and Locke was never a long

hitter. 'You know, I knew I had to hit my very best shot from the tee and then my very, very best to get anywhere near the green. But as luck would have it, I hit a perfect drive down the right-hand side of the fairway with a little draw, and I hit a perfect 3-wood which just trickled onto the front of the green. You know, Master, it must have been 60 feet from the hole,' Locke said. 'You know something? I almost missed it,' he added.

Locke went to the US on the advice of Sam Snead, who, at the end of 1946, had gone to South Africa for a series of head-to-head matches with Locke. Snead won only twice, halved four and lost the other twelve, and it's said that this may have been the beginning of his yips.

'Do you think, if I went to America, I could make a bean?' Locke asked Snead, who replied, 'With that putter, you could get rich.'

And so it was that Locke did go to the States, where he won not only the Tam o' Shanter but also twelve other tournaments, finishing second in a further ten. It got to the point where the Americans began to set up their courses with the pins on the far right of the greens so that he had to aim outside the green to get anywhere near the flag. This didn't stop him and he continued to hit shots with a predominant right hand and accept cheques with his left. I left the clubhouse that evening with the feeling that I had met someone quite special in golf.

The next time I saw Locke was at Carnoustie, a few days before the start of the 1975 British Open. Carnoustie was back on the Open rota for the first time since 1957, when

Ben Hogan had won, but the accommodation problem that had caused officials to abandon it as an Open course still hadn't been solved. Jackie and I decided to stay in the very fine Russucks Hotel in St Andrews and take the short hovercraft trip across the Firth of Tay each day. We could be away from the madding crowd yet still in close travelling distance of the course, where the hovercraft docked right next to the practice fairway.

It was a fairly laid-back preparation as there were no other major tournaments scheduled in the week before the Open, but rather a series of pro-ams, one of which was run by the comedian Jimmy Tarbuck at Dalmahoy in Scotland. My partner was 007 himself, Sean Connery, who is among the more enthusiastic celebrity golfers.

One of the first blokes I ran into on the Monday of Open week was Locke, and I seized the opportunity to ask him if we could play a practice round. 'Master, that would be my pleasure,' he replied. At the Martini, after my practice round with the legendary South African, I had lost by a shot to Brian Barnes after taking a nine on the 12th in the third round. I'd been striking the ball very well, but wasn't entirely happy with my putting and Locke was a genius putter. Maybe, I thought, I could pick up a few tips from him. The other thing, of course, was that he'd won four British Opens.

Locke's touch around the greens was incredible. He did the same with his putts as he did with his long shots, setting himself up to the right to almost pull the ball into the hole. He believed a hole had four sides and was a great advocate of the theory that if a ball was hit too firmly to catch any side of the hole, it would spin out. So his method was to let none of his putts go more than 3 or 4 inches away from the hole. With the spin he had on the ball, it didn't seem to matter which part of the hole it caught. It always went in.

Along the way around he gave me a couple of putting tips, saying I had my hands too close to my body. As we came to the 18th hole, Bobby turned to me and said, 'You know, Master, I think you can win this tournament, but there's one thing you must remember: the most important club in the bag is the fifteenth club.'

I've heard the expression many times since then, but at that stage, I'd never heard it. I looked at him and thought, 'Well, this old bugger *is* senile – there's only fourteen clubs in the bag.'

'The fifteenth club, Bobby?' I asked.

'Yes,' he replied. 'The one between your ears.'

Of course, he was right. And, as well, he had given me a fair dose of confidence when he said he thought I was playing well enough to win. Everything he said on the way around made sense.

That day I also ran into Tom Weiskopf, who had won the Open in 1973. He reminded me, as he did on every occasion we met, that he wanted the chance to get his money back from the time in '73 at Melbourne's Yarra Yarra when Tony Jacklin and I had ripped off about $400 from him and David Graham.

'Well, now's your chance,' I said. My Irish mate John O'Leary and I had won the Sumrie Better Ball title at Bournemouth earlier that year, and I reckoned we would make a pretty good combination against Weiskopf and anyone he could convince to come along.

The time of high noon the following day was set. After

John and I had practised, we arrived on the tee, where Weiskopf was waiting. 'Well, come on then, where's your partner?' I said, and the next moment Jack Nicklaus strode onto the tee. It was the first time I had met him.

Bets were agreed. It would be £50, £50, £50, with automatic one-down presses. This meant that every time you went one down you were allowed to press for a further £50. Now that sort of action can add up to a sizeable amount of money.

I birdied two of the first four holes and we had already got them for two presses, with the result that I was feeling pretty cocky about the state of affairs. 'You'd better send back and get another partner,' I somewhat facetiously yelled to Weiskopf across the 5th fairway. Immediately he and Nicklaus went into a huddle. Weiskopf told me later that the Bear had growled, 'We'd better teach this young pup a lesson.'

From that point on, they played golf as I've never seen it played before or since. Weiskopf had a hole in one on the 8th and ended up shooting 64, while Nicklaus had a 65. I shot around 67, but we were absolutely annihilated, losing six or seven presses plus the front nine, the back nine and the match.

I started to wonder how on earth I was going to settle, and I guess John was thinking the same thing. But I wasn't about to give Weiskopf the pleasure of taking my money and said, 'I'll pay Jack.'

'No,' Nicklaus replied. 'I don't want your money. I'll settle for a beer and a sandwich in the clubhouse.'

It was as though I'd won the lottery – in more ways than one. It had been a tremendous experience to witness the marvellous golf they played that day, and I had also watched them putting with Bobby Locke's tips still in my mind. I noticed that Nicklaus and Weiskopf both had their hands higher than I was carrying mine, and after I paid for afternoon tea I rushed back to the practice green and worked on my technique until darkness fell.

In the first round of the tournament I holed a couple of good putts early, but as I progressed I really peppered the flag and got it to five under after fourteen holes before dropping the 15th and 16th. I shot 69, but conditions had been ideal, with none of the notorious foul weather of Carnoustie. Sure, 69 in the first round of the Open is acceptable, but I felt I really hadn't taken advantage of the situation in which I had put myself.

The second day was a repeat, with a lot of run on the ball and very gentle sea breezes, even in the afternoon when I played. The scoring was sensational and players were beginning to refer to Carnoustie as the Sleeping Giant. I got it to three under after nine holes and felt I was cruising, but then had a lapse in concentration with a three-putt green and a couple of very poor shots. The result was a 71, which left me four shots off the pace set by a little-known Scot, David Huish, who fired rounds of 69–67. The big round of the day was from South African Bobby Cole, who shot a course-record 66 after his opening 72.

Staying at Russucks meant I spent very little extra time at the golf course. I practised on a park between the Old and New courses at St Andrews, with Jackie picking up the balls, and then took the hovercraft across to Carnoustie, leaving myself just enough time to hit fifteen or so pitch shots and a few putts before teeing off. Dinner in the evening was pleasant, too. There were no other golfers staying at the hotel and we were away from the hubbub of the Open.

The third day dawned with perfect weather again, and we had a real tournament on our hands. Apart from Huish, they were all big names on the leaderboard – Johnny Miller, Tom Watson, Nicklaus and Graham Marsh. Bobby Shearer and I were there, too.

The third round of any tournament is the most vital, the make or break, and I was drawn to play with Nicklaus. It was fortunate that I had played with him on the Tuesday as there could have been a few butterflies if it had been my first time with the great man. I was not overawed or intimidated by his presence, but rather by his record in golf.

I holed a 20-footer for a birdie on the first hole, looked across at Nicklaus and remarked, 'I'm a quick learner, aren't I?', referring to our Tuesday practice round. He gave a wry smile and any pressure I might have felt was gone. I picked up another birdie on the 3rd and felt I was really on a roll. After going out in 33, I came home in 32 to shoot a course record of 65, holing every makeable putt and knocking the flagstick out all day.

Nicklaus fired a 68 and it was a touch ironic that I'd done to him in that third round what he'd done to me in the Tuesday practice round. As he handed me my scorecard, he said, 'You know, I felt I was taking 78 playing alongside you out there today. That was one helluva score.' I felt an inner glow of pride after such praise from the Golden Bear himself. I trailed Cole, who'd had a second successive 66, by just one shot, with Miller a shot behind me and Watson a further shot behind him.

That evening Jackie and I had dinner with Weiskopf and his wife, Jean, at the Craw's Nest restaurant in nearby Crail, which has one of the oldest courses in Scotland and is where the Crail Golfing Society was formed in 1786. Tom basically held court all night. There was a fair bit of chiacking going on until we got down to the serious business of what lay ahead the next day.

Tom talked of concentration and rhythm and told the story of going to his locker at Troon before the final round of the Open in 1973 and finding a note from Nicklaus pinned to the door. There were just three words: 'Concentration and rhythm'.

The next morning we checked out of the hotel, packed all the gear in the car and drove across from St Andrews. In retrospect, and I don't mean it to be a slight on Bobby Cole, I think the end result might have been different had I been drawn with either Miller or Watson in the final round rather than Cole. Sure, he had shot back-to-back 66s, but it was a whole new ball game in the final round of the Open championship. Like me, Cole was erratic at times, and after a pretty good start his world started to fall apart. I don't think that helped me, particularly on the back nine.

I held a two-shot lead on the field standing on the 15th tee, where I hit a good drive and had a 6-iron to the green. You've got to remember it was a typical Scottish course, with knolls and mounds to contend with, and my intention was to land my 6-iron about five or six paces short to let it bounce onto the green.

As fate would have it, my ball caught one of those knolls on the downslope at the front of the green and skipped onto the green and just trickled through the back. I had a fairly straightforward chip, but the green sloped quite sharply from left to right as you played the hole. Obviously my chip shot had the opposite contour and I aimed it right, expecting the slope to work the ball down to the hole.

The trouble was that the wind – the first wind for the week – was blowing over my left shoulder and had the effect of holding my ball up on the right side of the hole. It was a 10-footer, which I missed. A bogey 5 went on the card and I was pretty disappointed, as I felt my second shot shouldn't have been penalised to such a degree.

It's a fair walk from the 15th green to the 16th tee, and as we walked over the top of the hill we saw two groups waiting on the tee. Miller, Nicklaus, Watson, and a South African guy called Andries Oosthuisen who'd had rounds of 69, 69 and 70. So, after the disappointment of a bogey, I now had to wait for the two groups ahead to play the 248-yard par 3. The long, narrow green creates a demanding tee shot at the best of times, and with the wind blowing it was going to be a driver. I was forced to sit there watching the problems encountered by those ahead of me. My mind started to scramble a bit. They were obviously given heart because they had seen from the carryboard that I'd just come off a bogey.

By the time I got round to playing my shot, I was cold and there were all manner of thoughts tumbling around in my brain. I let my tee shot go to the right a bit, maybe 10 or

15 yards, and my ball was in thick rough. Given that there was no green to work with, my recovery shot to about 9 feet short of the hole wasn't too bad in the circumstances. I hit a good putt that hit the right corner, but stayed out. I wish Locke had putted that one for me.

I didn't panic, but things were certainly becoming a little unstuck. I was still one ahead of Miller and Watson and two clear of Cole. The 17th, a par 4 of 454 yards, is an unusual hole with two burns running across the fairway. Generally it is a 2-iron shot from the tee to carry the first burn and lay up short of the second, leaving a 4- or 5-iron shot home.

My caddie, Charlie Mackie, had no time for yardages. If you wanted them, you did them yourself. He was a freak. No matter how strong the wind, he could pick the right club. On the 17th tee we discussed the shot and settled for the 2-iron, which I hit as well as I could. But we'd both made a mistake failing to recognise that the wind was coming from a slightly different quarter, and my ball was lucky to clear the first burn. In fact, I had one foot on the upslope as I addressed the ball.

I had no chance of making the green and it would have to be an extremely fine shot even to keep the ball in play. I had to aim at the 18th tee, to the right, which has an out-of-bounds behind it, an aim that was probably 80 or 90 yards further right than I would have liked. The idea was to hit a roundhouse hook and at the same time make sure I cleared the second burn. I also needed a fair loft on the club to get it up from the slope. I took 7-iron and all went according to plan, with the ball finishing over the second burn and running up to about 120 yards from the green.

My next shot was a 9-iron and it was slightly blind

because of the undulation of the green. I played it and was happy with its flight, but when I got to the green I was dismayed to see the ball had run 20 feet past the hole. My putt grazed the left edge to give me three bogeys on the trot.

As I tapped in, I heard an enormous roar from up ahead. Watson had holed a huge putt for birdie and I subsequently discovered that Miller had blown his chances by taking two to get out of a fairway trap at the 18th. Watson's birdie meant I had to birdie the last to win the championship.

I was calm as I hit a good drive and then a 9-iron to about 20 feet. It was an uphill putt to start with and then ran away from you at the hole. If you knocked it too hard it could very easily run 4 or 5 feet past, which was certainly the last thing I wanted to happen.

Thoughts began flashing through my mind. As a kid, I'd always imagined myself playing against Nicklaus and having a putt to win the British Open championship. But here I was at Carnoustie in 1975 and it was for real. The only difference was that it was Watson I had to beat.

I took a couple of deep breaths and tried to keep the tension out of my hands. I didn't want to choke the club to death. 'Just keep the tension out, put a good stroke on it,' I said to myself.

'Damn it, I haven't given it enough,' I muttered as the ball pulled up 1 foot short and that putt then looked like a 10-footer. I was bitterly disappointed as I checked the line. I hadn't won the Open – but then I suddenly thought, 'Well, I haven't lost it either.' As I lined it up, the hole looked about as big as a mouse's ear, but relief came as my ball rattled the bottom of the cup.

Jackie came to console me, congratulate me, whatever.

I could see Watson and his wife, Linda, behind the green and then, within minutes, there was a mock ceremony with both of us with our hands on the auld claret jug to give the photographers their morning picture. All I wanted to do was seek the sanctuary of the locker room.

I had a couple of beers as I sat alone. People were coming past saying 'Well done' and 'Bad luck', but it was all a blur. I looked straight through them as my thoughts and emotions ran riot. There was disappointment, and yet the knowledge that I still hadn't lost my chance to win the Open. I'd built myself up for a grand finale that day, and now I had to turn around and do it all again.

And then there was a feeling of emptiness. There had been no resolution. A tie is like kissing your sister.

A tournament official came past to take me to the media interview tent. You've got to do it, but it was the last thing I wanted. All that was on my mind was how I took five at the 15th and then pulled the wrong club on the 17th. My mind screamed out to me. I wanted to be alone.

———————————

Jackie and I drove back to Russucks, where we were given the same room as before, and decided to wander up the road to a little restaurant for dinner. We talked of what might have been and what might still be and came to a consensus that 'whatever would be would be'.

We got back to the hotel around 10.30 p.m. and found Jackie's brothers, John and Christopher, waiting. They had been watching the golf on television in London and had jumped on the first available plane to Scotland to watch the play-off the following day.

As we hadn't had coffee after dinner at the restaurant, we ordered four cups, and following a tradition we had established in London, decided to have brandy with it. I went to the bar to purchase four brandies and noticed American sports writer Dan Jenkins there. It would have been a surprise if he hadn't been. He watched as I carried the drinks out and later wrote that the number of brandies I'd consumed that night was roughly equivalent to the number of strokes I had taken in shooting my course record in the third round.

It still hacks me off when I'm told with great authority by fools that I was drunk that night. These sorts of statements about drinking have followed me through my golfing career and beyond. I have never had much to do with grog at home. My father only drank at home on special occasions and perhaps this influenced me to be the same way. I prefer to stick to my favourite home brew of tea – country-style and strong.

In those days I drank at parties and sometimes, like most of my friends, got drunk. That was the way we were in a sport where the clubhouse bar and the next party were never too far away. But I watched myself in working hours – leading up to and during tournaments.

The routine the following morning was the same as the day before: pack up, book out of the hotel and hit a few practice shots in the park alongside the Old Course. The big difference was the weather. There was an even stronger breeze and the threat of rain, so it appeared conditions were not going to be pleasant for the play-off.

Many of the tournament trappings were gone from Carnoustie, but I was amazed at the number of people. There must have been fifteen or twenty thousand to see a little-known American and me in the play-off. You could have understood it if Nicklaus had been there. But I guess I did have something of a following. I'd had a bit of success in Scotland and the Scots seemed to have an affinity with me.

I didn't really know Watson. We went through the formalities of wishing each other good luck on the first tee, but neither of us, I am sure, really meant it. The Open championship was at stake. (Even so, golf is one of the few gentlemanly games left. You've only got to look at tennis and wonder what's happened to the likes of Newcombe and Laver and Rosewall, Tony Roche and Stan Smith. Pat Rafter and a couple of others have emerged, but basically tennis remains a sport where egos dominate.)

I was brought up to acknowledge a good shot, but I soon discovered that Watson was not. I acknowledged his good shots but there was no reciprocation, so I stopped doing it pretty quickly. I found out later that he was a psychology major and I was actually boosting his confidence by complimenting his good shots while he maintained a stoic silence. I'm fairly sure he was playing mind games with me, and I wasn't about to let it become a one-way street. Not many Americans, I have learned since, are strong on acknowledging their opponents' good shots. It is a tradition that has just about died out as the psychologists take over from the purists.

Watson birdied two of the first four holes to go a couple ahead and then I picked up a birdie at the 5th and he bogeyed the 6th and we were back on level terms – but a couple of things happened in that final round that suggested

I wasn't meant to win. Jackie, a fatalist if ever there was one, agrees.

We came to the 8th, which is a 174-yard par 3 and basically a 5-iron shot. The target is difficult: a long, narrow green with bunkers right and left, and on the left-hand side, just outside the bunkers, a gallery fence made of three strands of wire. Watson's tee shot actually struck one of those strands of wire to drop inside the fence. I've never been crash-hot on figuring the odds of anything, but this had to be 1000 to 1. A wire no more than the thickness of half your little fingernail had prevented him from going out of bounds and playing three from the tee.

Watson has a great short game and somehow managed to manufacture a shot in which he picked the club up, almost straight up, to avoid hitting the fence on his backswing. He knocked it on and holed the putt for par to match my 3.

We stood on the tee of the 482-yard par-5 14th and I was one in front. It was pouring with rain and everything was soaked. Still, we both hit good drives and followed up with good second shots. Watson was about 15 yards short of the green while I was about 20 yards behind him. Obviously I played first, a lovely pitch to a foot, and I was staring a birdie in the face. Watson then holed his sand wedge for an eagle 3 and it was all square as we stood on the 15th tee.

I dropped a shot at the 15th and then Watson dropped the 16th. We both made par at the 17th and standing on the 18th tee were square at one under.

As I stood there, those thoughts of the bogey at 15 and taking the wrong club at 17 came rushing back. 'If I hadn't messed up there, I wouldn't be out here getting drowned,'

I thought. Still, guts and determination have always been a Newton trait, and after coming so far I wasn't about to toss it in.

Watson hit a fine drive up the right-hand side of the fairway. I was satisfied with mine, which was just a fraction left and meant I had a shot over the burn and a greenside trap to the pin, which was set left. There was no doubting Watson was coming from a better angle than I was, from the right side of the fairway.

It was his shot first and I swear that after he'd hit the ball he thought it was in the burn. I know he didn't catch it as he would have liked and heard him call, 'Get up, get up!' He cleared the burn by just a couple of yards and his ball galloped up the front portion of the green, but still a fair distance from the pin.

He hit 1-iron and I hit 2-iron. The breeze was coming into me from the left and I had the corner of the bunker to contend with plus the wind blowing the ball away from the flag. My standard shot was basically a fade and that's the way I hit it. The ball appeared to be going straight for the flag, but it caught the lip of the bunker and rolled back down. Just 6 more inches would have done the trick.

Because of the rain, the sand in the bunker was compacted and the sand iron skidded on me a little. The ball came out hot, but it did have a lot of spin on it. It checked on the second or third bounce but was about 12 feet past the pin. Watson hit his putt stone-dead and then I studied mine. I was convinced – I still am, for that matter – that the line was left lip, but I hadn't taken into account the water on the green, which meant the ball wouldn't take as much borrow. But with the slope, I couldn't see it as a straight putt, so I hit it left lip and that's where it stayed. The championship was Watson's.

I shook his hand but can't recall my words. Later, many days later, I heard rumours that I had refused to shake, but it simply wasn't true. The evidence, for those who missed it, was in a photograph in one of the golf magazines, but the rumour persisted for a long time through the remainder of 1975. That sort of crap was the last thing I needed, especially as I planned to play the US circuit. I certainly didn't want to be known as the jerk who had refused to shake Watson's hand after he won the Open championship.

Watson came to Australia later that year for the Wills Masters at the Victoria Golf Club in Melbourne, where some bright spark drew us together for the first two rounds. As soon as I saw him I fronted him about the rumour, saying, 'Tom, it's disappointing to hear this rumour going round. It's got to have come from your camp.'

'That's not true,' he replied.

I took him at his word, but it does leave a sour taste in your mouth. 'Look,' I said. 'I intend to go to the States and it's not going to be a nice feeling if the Americans believe I refused to shake your hand.'

'Forget it,' he said. But how can you?

The night of the Open play-off I did have a few drinks – Dan Jenkins would have been proud of me. All my friends gathered around and tried to console me with comments like 'It was a great performance' and 'You'll do it some time in the future', but I didn't feel that way.

You don't get too many opportunities like I'd had, and

there will always be a scar. You control your own destiny in golf and I'd had the chance to establish myself for life. I could have planned my future but one putt, one shot, decreed I didn't. Forget the money I might have made, the big thing was the title and the manner in which I could have organised my life.

You can't put a price on that.

A golf course
made in heaven

'Y'know, it's a bit cold up in Augusta this time of the year. Could be still snowin',' said the man behind the counter as I checked my bags and clubs at the ticketing desk of New York's La Guardia Airport.

'What do you mean? I'm going there to play golf. Man, I'm going to play the US Masters,' I replied.

He'd been about to book me through to Augusta, Maine, which I didn't even know existed. I'd only been to the US once before, back in 1969 when I had stayed with Bruce Devlin after playing the British amateur championship, and I thought there was only one Augusta – and in golf there is.

My big moment had come. I was about to play my first Masters. The gilt-edged invitation had arrived from Clifford Roberts in January 1976, and though they never tell you why you're invited or, in some cases, why you're *not* invited, the reason was fairly obvious. I'd lost that 18-hole play-off to Tom Watson at Carnoustie the previous year.

'Augusta, Georgia!' the infuriating chap at the counter said. 'Well, you can't fly there.' He was right again. My path so far to the Masters had been Zambia, Johannesburg, New York and now we had to fly to Atlanta to change to a little commuter aircraft for the journey to Augusta's tiny airport.

Jackie and I hadn't even booked a hotel room at Augusta. We just rode into town like babes in the wood and took pot luck on the first hotel we saw with a 'Vacancy' sign out front. It gloried under the name of 'The Thunderbird' and a very ordinary little hotel it was, the sort you see in B-grade movies where sleep doesn't seem to be the main interest of the guests. Certainly there was no red carpet rolled out for someone who was about to play in the world's most exclusive golf tournament.

We arrived on the Sunday and the moment had come to set eyes on Augusta National for the first time. I hadn't actually thought much about it. I was more worried by a foot injury that had surfaced in Africa – and besides, I had never been deeply interested in golf's history.

But as I drove through those big green wrought-iron gates and down Magnolia Drive, I was affected just the same as any other first-timer. A chill went down my spine. You see the place on television, but it doesn't quite prepare you for the real thing. At the end of the drive, the white colonial mansion that is the clubhouse stands as a symbol to the elitism that is the US Masters. I could well understand why Lee Trevino had once said that even the car starts choking as you drive into Augusta.

Jack the lad: a terror with the soccer ball.

Goal-kicking full-back: Epping Boys' High School First XV.

Destined for big things: Rodger Davis (holding shield) and me (with cup) after the New South Wales schoolboys championships at Monash Golf Club in 1966.

New South Wales schoolboys champion, Bonnie Doon Golf Club, 1967.

The Golfing Newtons: with Mum and Dad in 1969, just before my first overseas tour.

First job, 1968, at the Dunlop Slazenger showroom.

With the great Norman von Nida (left) as my caddy, at
the Wills Masters in 1970.

Driving my pacer, 'Newt', during work at Kumeu in New Zealand, 1974.

Our wedding day, at Dulwich Village Chapel in London, 1974.

H. Campbell

Third round of the 1975 British Open and I leave the 18th with Jack Nicklaus after my course-record 65.

APWirephoto

After the tie, Tom Watson and I go through the motions as we hold up the auld claret jug for the media.

Playing for the rough on the 3rd fairway in the play-off against Watson.

A tearful Jackie offers consolation to me after the play–off loss.

Jackie, pregnant with Kristie, and Mum (left), with my grandmother, Isobel Newton ('Gam').

And then there were three: with Jackie and Kristie in 1978.

The photographs on the walls of the clubhouse were a catalogue of golfing history, with portraits of Bobby Jones, Ben Hogan, Gene Sarazen and the like. Then I saw Sarazen walking past, wearing the same clobber, his trousers stuck into his socks as in the photographs. It's like I was in a time warp – and Clifford Roberts was part of that.

You can ignore history for only so long, and that day I did think of the aura of Bobby Jones and his legacy to the world of golf. Roberts, a New York businessman who wintered in Augusta in the early '30s, was asked by Jones to find a patch of land where he could form a very private golf club at which his friends from around the world could join him. It was a golf course that he himself would design with the master touch of Scottish-born Alister Mackenzie, who'd abandoned medicine in his pursuit of golf and its architecture.

'Fruitlands', a former nursery, was the setting for Jones's dream and Augusta National was born. So too was the Masters, which started in golf's calendar as the Augusta National Invitational in 1934. Roberts was the first tournament chairman, and forty-two years later when I arrived for my first Masters, he still occupied that position.

Our meeting came immediately after I'd registered for the tournament. I even had to ask where to go to register, and I felt very alone, not knowing a soul.

'My name is Jack Newton,' I volunteered to the person staffing the registration office.

'Ah, yes. Welcome, Mr Newton. Mr Roberts requests an audience with you.'

There was a moment of panic. I hadn't even been in the place five minutes and the boss wanted to see me. Hell,

I hadn't even had time for one beer, let alone six. I shouldn't have worried. Roberts always asked to see any newcomer to Augusta, just to outline the dos and don'ts.

I'd imagined he would be a great big Southern man, smoking a fat cigar and wearing a large hat, so it was with some surprise that I was introduced to a bespectacled little man not unlike Norman von Nida.

Even sitting in his office, there was a mystique. In front of me was the man who, with Jones, had started it all. You got the impression that he could be both a tyrant and a gentleman – and the impression wasn't wrong.

I had already started hearing some of the stories about Roberts and the manner in which he upheld the unbending traditions of Augusta National. One thing you never, ever did was mention money, only the green jacket, and you never slipped into the vernacular when describing the Masters and the events of Masters week.

A piece of Augusta folklore relates to Jack Whitaker, who, in the early '70s, had the plum job of commentating on the 18th hole. Whitaker was describing play and after the second shots were hit to the green, the gallery was allowed to break the ropes and run up to the green's front edge.

Whitaker spoke of the 'wonderful sight of the mob' as the spectators rushed towards the green, and thought nothing more of his comment until he was summoned to Roberts' office. A Masters committeeman monitors everything said on television and had noted that Whitaker, shame on him, had used the word 'mob' in reference to the golf gallery. ' "Mob" is a word synonymous with the Mafia, not the golf spectators at Augusta,' Roberts said, adding that Whitaker's services for the TV commentary at the Masters were no longer required.

Extraordinary, isn't it? Whitaker was probably making $1 million a year with his contract to the US network telecasting the Masters, but such was the power of the Augusta National committee that they could choose who the network used in its commentary team.

Whitaker wasn't allowed back to Augusta until the early '80s and only then because another commentator, Vince Scully, got a throat infection a week or so before the tournament. The network asked for special permission to allow Whitaker back after his ten-year absence.

And now here I was in the director's office. Roberts said, 'It's nice to have you here. We've had a very good relationship with most of the Australians who've played here. I wish you well.' And then he told me in no uncertain terms that if I were caught giving away any of my tickets I would never be invited back to the Masters.

'Yes, sir,' I replied.

After the meeting I sought directions to the caddie master's hut. In those days you were assigned a caddie. Even if a player had a regular caddie on the Tour, he had to use the one allocated by the Masters. I did think it a bit strange that Nicklaus always seemed to end up with his regular man while others copped the luck of the draw, but then, there is only one Jack Nicklaus.

My caddie was 'Bull', an African-American who probably weighed around 125 or 130 kilos. His birth certificate gave his name as Charles Williams, but if you called out 'Charles' he wouldn't pause in his stride because it was a name with which he was not familiar. I discovered he was a great character with the ability to make you laugh, which isn't a bad thing in the heat of the moment.

'Jack Nooton. Man, I've heard about you. You're from Awstralia,' Bull greeted me in his Southern drawl. There was no doubting he'd checked out my credentials to discover whether he would be wasting his time that week. Of course, I hoped he wasn't.

Most of the caddies at Augusta have an uncanny ability to read the greens. That first year at the Masters I felt the greens were pretty grainy – they were a combination of bermuda and rye grasses, overseeded, I thought, with rye. There were three or four greens in particular where, when you looked at the putt and it seemed right lip, it was, in fact, left lip. On each putt, big Bull would crouch behind me and give me my instructions. 'Now, two balls left of the hole. Stroke.' With that, he would jump from his crouched position like a basketballer about to add a two-pointer to the scoreboard. Pity help the next player who came that way, given the indentations that Bull's bulk must have made on the green.

I was still having trouble with my foot, and was very shin-sore coming into the tournament. It was partly because I'd been favouring the foot and partly because I was wearing a new pair of Footjoy shoes that were a lot heavier than the ones I normally wore. The Footjoy man had handed the shoes to me (and I guess all the other players) on arrival and it seemed like the right thing to do to wear them.

People had told me Augusta was a hooker's course and I'd spent time in Africa practising the hook. It certainly does favour those who hit the ball from right to left, but the big problem is that most of the trouble is down the left. However, it is also an advantage to fade your iron shots at Augusta to get the ball to stop on the firm greens. Drawing your woods and fading your irons isn't easy to do, which is why it takes a great player to win there. You have to play every shot in the book. It's like playing a game of chess, positioning every shot. It's my favourite course in the world.

Another unique thing about Augusta is the Par 3 Contest, played on a wonderful small course adjacent to the championship layout. Nine par threes ranging in length from about 75 yards to 160–170 yards, and it's an open-slather day where you can actually buy a ticket to watch the action. I'm not sure how many were there that year, but it seemed like about fifty thousand were crammed in on the great little course. It was awe-inspiring.

All players were expected to play the Par 3 Contest; it was an unwritten law. In fact, you were told that if you didn't play and you were a fringe player, then an invitation to the Masters wouldn't be in the mail the following year. But I noticed that Nicklaus didn't play – yet another indication of the special relationship between him and Roberts.

The first tee shot at your first Masters is, without doubt, the scariest first shot in golf, even more scary than the first shot I played in the British Open play-off in 1975. My hand was shaking as I bent to tee up the ball. It's the only time in my life – with two arms anyway – that I've stood over a golf ball and just wished and hoped that I could hit it, never mind about finding the fairway. Just about everyone who's been there will tell you the same thing.

The first hole is a par 4 of 400 yards and a good driving

hole. There's a bunker on the right where if you push your drive you'll finish in the sand and it's a chip out sideways. On the left there are pine trees, so it's a pretty demanding tee shot and probably one of the narrowest drives on the golf course apart from the 7th and those at Amen Corner.

My playing partner, a veteran American called Doug Ford, did nothing to settle my nerves. He simply grunted to me on the tee when I introduced myself. Ford had won the Masters back in 1957, and if you win at Augusta, you get invited religiously year after year. He seemed a bit of an old crackpot and later I discovered he was one of a few older players who were dirty on the world because their time had been before the real money years. Another of Ford's bugbears was foreign players. He seemed to hate us, I guess because he felt that each new foreign name that appeared on the scene was going to put him a further rung down on the ladder. In truth, in 1976 he was finished as a player and would have been lucky to hit the ball out of his shadow on a late Sunday afternoon. You could see his growing irritation through the round, especially as I was a pretty long hitter.

He hadn't said a word to me all the way around until we got to the 14th, which is a slight dogleg to the left par 4. It should be remembered that Augusta is notorious in that if you can hit the ball far enough and carry it to the top of the hills, it will run down the other side. But if you can't quite carry it far enough, it pitches into the upslope and you get very little run at all. You're then confronted with a very awkward second shot because you're standing on the upslope.

Ford stood up on the 14th tee with the honour and blasted his Sunday punch only to see it pitch halfway up the hill, where it stopped dead. I then drove over the top of the hill and this prompted him to speak to me for the first time. He swung around and almost shouted, 'This goddamn course is made for you gorillas!' And that was all he said all day. He signed my card and I've never seen him again.

Unfortunately no one else saw much more of me at the Masters, either. I followed up my opening 77 with a 75 to miss the cut, and as I farewelled Bull I said, 'Mate, I'm sorry I played so badly, that you didn't get a good bag.'

He replied, 'Man, you'll be back here some time and I'll get your bag again and then we'll get these mothers.'

I let my hair down a bit on the Friday night with a few Aussie beers. It's been a tradition to hold an Australian party at the Masters since the days of the old Wills Masters tournaments in Australia in the '60s. Aussie beer, Aussie steaks, the whole shooting match. Dear old Phil May of Wills in Australia, who sadly is no longer with us, was the host and quite a few players would attend, as well as several officials associated with the tournament. It was May's annual shopping expedition for players for the Wills Masters event on the Australian circuit.

That night I met Clifford Roberts' secretary, who at first was quite daunting, but I guess knowing Phil broke down a few barriers. Over a few drinks it tumbled out that I'd played with a crook foot. I hadn't mentioned it to anyone through the week, and I didn't mean to mention it then, either. I guess it was one of those Aussie traditions of the time – among tennis players, cricketers, golfers – that you never complained. If you were in the combat area, you were fit. Nothing more, nothing less.

The modern trend is a little removed from that philosophy and money is the reason behind it. Doug Ford may have complained about the money we earned in the '70s compared with the '50s, but these days there is a three-million-dollar tournament every week, so we get a lot of reported injuries. What the hell if a player has to withdraw? There's another three million on offer next week. In the '70s, it was a case of 'make no complaint and hope to pay the bills'. You just backed up, week after week.

I thought nothing more of mentioning my injury until I went to the tournament office the following day to pick up my cheque for $1500. (Everyone got a cheque, whether they made the cut or not.) Again I was told that Mr Roberts had requested an audience with me.

There I saw his gentle side. 'It has come to my attention that you have had an injury this week and that is the reason you have played poorly. You've said nothing about it and I like that. I feel we can invite you back next year,' Roberts told me.

I could scarcely conceal my delight. It was as though I'd finished in the top 24 at that year's Masters. Apart from winning an event on the US Tour in the preceding year or another designated event such as the British Open, finishing in the top 24 was the only automatic entrance to the Augusta National.

The US Masters and Augusta were indeed Clifford Roberts' life and it was on the course that he died by his own hand in 1977. Roberts discovered he had terminal cancer and walked onto the 16th green and put a gun to his head. In his will, he asked that his ashes be strewn on that green, his favourite hole on the course. He had built the Masters into the world's greatest tournament, a players' tournament where you are spoiled to the core. It is an exclusive event, it is elitist, but it is the best.

I told no one but Jackie that Roberts had invited me back for the 1977 Masters. If I had, you can bet there would have been no invitation forthcoming. You don't tell the Augusta committee who they should invite, nor do you talk about it in the press. Rodger Davis certainly discovered that – to his eternal dismay, I'd imagine – when he criticised Augusta for not inviting him to play the 1987 Masters after he'd won the Australian and New Zealand Opens and another NZ tournament in 1986. He did, however, get an invitation in 1988, after a winless 1987.

Roberts' informal invitation fanned a burning desire in me to go back, because I knew it was a course that suited my game. Some golfers like particular courses and others don't, in much the same fashion as certain horses handle some tracks better than others.

The par fives at Augusta are a challenge. They dare you to take a shot and I like that. It's purely set up, there are no tricks and there's no rough. It is chess at Augusta; if the pin is cut on the left-hand side of the green, you have to drive down the right to get the best angle to the flag. The subtleties are similar to those at Royal Melbourne, which is not surprising given that Alister Mackenzie was involved in the design of both courses.

The other thing that struck me on that first visit was the immaculate condition of the course. Not a blade of grass seemed out of place. It always used to freak me out on the par threes that after you'd taken your divot on the tee, a guy in a Masters jacket would appear with a bucket of green dirt with seed in it to repair the patch. When the TV cameras next focused on the tee there would not be a brown divot to be seen.

Yes, if there's a golf course in heaven, I'm sure it will be a replica of Augusta National.

Clifford Roberts was true to his word, with my invitation to the 1977 Masters arriving around Christmas 1976. It really was a time of peace on earth for me. I had just played some of my finest tournament golf, shooting rounds of 67, 68, 68 and 66 for a 19-under total at Royal Sydney to win the 1976 New South Wales Open. Sadly I didn't carry that form into the New Year, which was to be my first full-time crack at the US Tour.

During those first few months I discovered just how tough it was playing the toughest circuit of them all as I went through the soul-destroying business of attempting to prequalify on Mondays for the right to tee up on Thursdays. It was an experience I had not 'enjoyed' since 1971. I missed prequalifying at Greensboro in the week before the Masters, and rounds of 76–77 at Augusta itself left me four shots shy of the 36-hole cut. Once more I went to Clifford Roberts' office to thank him for keeping his word. I vowed to return as a genuine contender in future years.

Jackie and I hit the road out of Augusta in our little rotary Mazda to drive the 650 or so kilometres to Tallahassee down in Florida for the next tournament. Not for us the luxury of airline travel, as I had no financial backer and our budget was approaching that of a shoestring. We drove in turn and Jackie was at the wheel when we went through a tiny little town that wasn't even a whistlestop. It did have a local sheriff, though, who was diligent when it came to enforcing the speed limit.

This sheriff could have doubled for Rod Steiger in the movie *In the Heat of the Night* as he jabbed his finger at us to pull over. You just didn't drive at 30 km/h over the speed limit and get away with it in his county. His invitation to follow him to his office – complete with lock-up – was compelling, especially given the howitzer that was slung on his hip. He settled his fat frame in the chair behind his desk, put his feet up and lit a cigar.

'Ma'am,' he drawled, 'that'll be 100 bucks. Cash or credit card. No one speeds on my road.'

Now that was a problem. We didn't have $100 cash, nor did we have a credit card. We'd transferred funds into an American bank account and we had a cheque book, but at that stage hadn't got around to applying for plastic money.

'No cheques,' came his staccato reply to our offer of payment in that form.

'Well, how are we supposed to pay the fine?' Jackie said.

'Ma'am, if you ain't payin' the fine my way, you're goin' to jail.'

It was Easter Sunday and the banks were closed. For the next forty-five minutes we pleaded rather than argued. Finally he relented. He would accept a cheque, but only if we left our passports behind. They would be forwarded to us after the cheque had been cleared. And so we continued on our way, very much chastened, not only because I had missed the cut in my second Masters, but also because of our meeting with a very large man who was hell-bent on throwing Jackie in jail.

––––––––––––

The 1978 US Masters was played – and won by Gary Player – in my absence, but just a couple of months later I guaranteed my return to Augusta in 1979 by winning my first tournament in the US, the Buick Open, which, as a PGA Tour co-sponsored event, satisfied Clause 13 of the qualifications for invitation to the Masters.

Unlike in 1977, I was playing much better when the azaleas and magnolias began blooming right on cue in April 1979. Again the Greater Greensboro Open was the lead-up tournament, and after finishing tied ninth in the Players' Championship and tied seventeenth in Heritage in the two preceeding weeks, I was pretty confident of a good build-up at Greensboro. The course was changed that year, being set up in much the same fashion as Augusta, and I was reasonably comfortable with my 73, 76, 73, 73, which gave me a tie for 44th spot.

At Augusta, Bull greeted me like a long-lost friend when I checked in at the caddie master's hut. So much for caddies being drawn out of a hat; he had manoeuvred his massive frame onto my bag and that suited me just fine. I was expecting pretty big things, so why not have one of the biggest blokes in overalls alongside me?

My opening round of 70 – two under – was nothing spectacular, but solid nonetheless given that Bruce Lietzke was leading with a 67 and nine other players shot either 68 or 69. I followed up with a second-round 72 on a day when scores were generally higher. I had achieved my first objective, to make the cut, and the next was to finish in the top 24 to ensure my return the following year. As well, I felt I had a chance of winning if I could put together a decent third round.

On the Saturday I made a bit of a charge to get my name on the leaderboard by the time we came to the 520-yard 15th, the most famous par 5 in golf, a make-or-break hole where eagle is possible but disaster will greet you if you mis-club. The small green is set behind a wide pond at the base of a gentle downslope, and more often than not it is rock-hard. If you pitch anywhere past the centre of the green, the ball will finish over the back and you can kiss goodbye to not only your birdie, but also your par.

I hit a pretty good drive and reckoned it was a 2-iron to the green. It is always difficult to get a flat stance at Augusta, and the 15th is no exception. The fairway slopes from right to left, and because your feet are below the ball, you can be prone to a hook.

I hit a rank bad shot, with the ball actually running into the pond. It was totally submerged and I weighed up the options. Where I could drop was quite muddy and I thought if I were to then attempt a delicate little pitch across the lake, I would have to land it absolutely perfectly to get it anywhere near the hole. It would have been so easy either to chunk it in the lake or chicken out and hit it too far.

'Man, you ain't thinkin' what I think you're thinkin',' Bull muttered.

'Well, look, Bull, this is what I think—' I started to say, but Bull was no longer muttering.

'Man, you're plum crazy. Get that ball in your hand

and drop it!' he shouted, with a few expletives thrown in to add emphasis to his concern. He stood horrified as I began to take my shoes and socks off. There was a collective sucking-in of air by the six thousand or so spectators in the Ben Hogan Stand to the left of the green, which also offers views of the shot from the 16th tee.

I've got to say, without a hint of modesty, that it was the most unbelievable shot. Absolutely perfect. The ball landed about 2 feet short of the pin and rolled on about 20 feet past the hole. I reckon I could have walked across the water to the green as my ears rang with the cheers and whistles of those thousands in the stands. Then, just for good measure, I rolled the putt in for my birdie 4.

Bull was still speechless – and I swear a tinge white – as I walked to the 16th tee. He reached for his cigarettes, which he carried underneath his cap, and lit one. Finally he broke his silence. 'Man, I can't believe the shot you just played. That was one of the greatest shots I've ever seen. I guess you were right after all.'

I signed for a three-under 69 and was five under, just two shots off the pace. Craig Stadler and Ed Sneed were leading at seven under while Lietzke and Fuzzy Zoeller were at six under. I considered I was in there with a second chance to win a 'major'.

———————————

A group of friends from Newcastle had made the journey to Augusta and we gathered that evening for dinner at the Hilton, where Dan Price, the manager, was a good friend. It was great to be surrounded by people with similar accents and talk of other things than golf. Dick Maclean, one of my best mates (with whom I've since raced most of my horses), has a particular party trick where he uses a straw broom as a mock guitar, and we thought we'd have a few laughs by asking him to perform. Straw brooms, it should be said, are hard to come by in US hotels, but one of the chefs managed to locate one. Dan Price introduced Dick, who then proceeded to sing 'Be-bop-a-lula, she's my baby' with rare gusto.

Just for a moment there were many creased brows from the Americans present, who felt we might in some way be demeaning such a serious week as the Masters, but in the end most of them joined in to make quite a party of it. My mind certainly wasn't playing every shot of the next day's round.

Another in the party was Dr Jim Graham from Myrtle Beach, South Carolina. He was actually the guy who diagnosed Bob Shearer's pancreatitis problems, and he became a pretty good friend of ours. Jim had had a bit of a drink problem a few years before and had sworn off the stuff, but that evening he broke out because I was doing so well in the tournament. I didn't even notice he went missing, but I later learned that Jackie's brother John had spent most of the night searching various bars for Jim without success.

We shouldn't have worried. He found us as I was standing on the first tee of Augusta about to hit off in the third-last group of the final round. The starter had barely said the words 'Mr Jack Newton' when Jim burst through the gallery ropes. It was obvious my brother-in-law hadn't looked in the right bars through the night. Poor Jim was as drunk as a skunk.

'Come on, my main man Newt the Brute! Show these goddamn Americans how to play this game,' he shouted, as two huge security guards materialised to tear him limb from limb.

It's just not done to disrupt proceedings on the first tee at Augusta in such a fashion. 'No, no. He's a friend of mine. He'll be all right. He's just had a few too many drinks,' I assured the security guys, who fortunately were a little easier to convince than Rod Steiger's double of the previous year.

It was, in fact, the second incident that day. Earlier, on the practice putting green, I had thought it might be me who would be torn limb from limb when I heard a voice saying, 'Hey, Jack Slazenger. You lying son-of-a-bitch.' A chill had gone down my spine. I had only ever been called 'Jack Slazenger' once in my life and that was earlier in the year when I had been involved in a hustle that saw me pocket $7000 for a couple of rounds of golf.

Myrtle Beach, Jim Graham's town, was renowned for its golf hustlers and one of them was a chap called Ed Martin, who was in his late fifties and had obviously been a very good golfer in his heyday. Ed was a former tobacco farmer in the town of Loris in South Carolina, who sold out to play a little golf for money. Mostly other people's money. He was also a partner in the formation of the Bay Tree Plantation, a 54-hole golf course and residential complex.

Ed called me one day and said, 'Jack, why don't you come up to Loris and play golf with me as my partner? You can take any part of the action you want. The only trouble is I'll have to introduce you as "Jack Slazenger, my cousin from Australia."' At that stage I was still using a Slazenger golf bag in the US, and of course, 'Slazenger' was emblazoned down its side. I told Ed I could only afford to play for a couple of grand and that was fine by him. My $2000, I suspect, was only a very small slice of the action he hustled that day.

The tobacco had just been harvested in Loris, all the farmers were cashed up and Ed felt he should probably relieve them of a little of their hard-earned. There were fifteen or so of them waiting at the course when Ed and I drove up and he duly introduced me as 'Jack Slazenger'. Out we went to play and the farmers were a little taken aback when I shot 66 to help Ed clean up. They reckoned I was lucky and demanded a second eighteen – an emergency eighteen – in the afternoon, as you're entitled to do in any gambling on the golf course. More bets were laid by Ed and out we went again. I got even luckier and fired a 64. As Ed collected his cash, one of the farmers came across to me and said, 'Goddamn it, Jack Slazenger. You can really golf your ball.'

On the way home that evening, Ed handed me $5000 on top of the $2000 I had won on my own investment. Hell, $7000 was eighth place in the Masters that year. To this day, I don't know how much Ed cleaned up.

So there I was, preparing for one of the most vital rounds of my career, when that tobacco farmer who had told Jack Slazenger he could really golf his ball bobbed up. If he had put a shotgun up my backside I would have had no cause for complaint, but he turned out to be one helluva loser. It must have been some tobacco harvest, I suppose.

That day at Augusta the wind really blew, getting stronger and stronger as the day went by, and it was a real struggle. I dropped a shot at the first and that became the pattern for the day. For a time I thought I had dropped so far off the pace that I'd be battling to make the top 24 for an automatic invitation the following year, but then I saw a leaderboard late on the back nine and realised the others were having their troubles as well.

I fired a four-over 76 for tied twelfth, while Fuzzy Zoeller, with a 70, forced Ed Sneed into a play-off after Sneed shot a 76 as well. Zoeller won with a birdie on the second play-off hole, but it was a day when the wind won, with only two players – Jack Nicklaus and Andy North – breaking 70, but only by a shot.

Seve Ballesteros, North, Trevino, Miller Barber and I all finished on the same score of 287, one under. I'm sure that, at that stage, the Americans didn't realise how good Ballesteros was, even though he had won the Greensboro Open in 1978. During one of my media interviews through the week I was asked, because I had played the European Tour, what my impressions of Seve were. I got the impression the American writers felt he was there under sufferance. I announced to all and sundry that they'd better learn how to spell his name as he was going to be around for a long time, adding that I felt he could actually end up as the best player in the world. My statement got quite a bit of press and the irony of those remarks will never be lost on me.

A couple of months later Ballesteros won the British Open at Royal Lytham and St Annes and again he didn't get due credit, with some saying he'd got lucky after visiting a carpark en route to victory. He silenced his critics, much to my chagrin, at Augusta in 1980.

I played even better at Greensboro in '80, finishing second to Craig Stadler, and all the problems of that lingering foot injury were behind me. I had won the Australian Open at Metropolitan late in 1979 against a class field and, importantly, I was hitting the ball from right to left, which is a key to Augusta. I felt in total control.

There was a feeling that I could take Augusta by the scruff of the neck and I was so obsessed by the thought that I went out to practise, despite officials posting a major cyclone warning that day. 'You're plum crazy,' Trevino told me, but I guess he had a greater fear of a threatening sky than most after being struck by lightning at the Western Open in Chicago some years before. I was well satisfied with my 67 in practice.

No one could have asked for a better start to the opening round. Five under after eight holes had the adrenaline running, and at the 9th I hit an 8-iron from about 150 yards which pitched 2 feet short of the pin but, dammit, sucked back off the green. I thought it was going to be stone-dead. I three-putted from the fringe for a bogey 5 to go out in 32, but I was certainly right in the thick of things.

An eagle 3 at the 13th put me back to six under, but then bogeys at the 14th and 18th – the latter from yet another three-putt – left me on 68, two shots off the pace set by Ballesteros, David Graham and the young Texan Jeff Mitchell, a newcomer on the scene.

I made another good start to the second round, going out two under, but then dropped four shots in the last five holes to card a 74. I was having trouble with my concentration. I guess all my career that was something of a worry, and looking back, it's the one area of my game I would like to change. It wasn't as if I was going walkabout, but rather I was pulling the wrong option at certain times.

In the light of what was to come, those four bogeys in the last five holes on the Friday cost me the US Masters title. That evening I was pretty disappointed. I wasn't about to jump off a cliff, just annoyed with myself. You have to cop those sort of things on the chin, but in golf, and life, it's a matter of grasping opportunities when they come along. That Friday I didn't.

On the Saturday, my front nine was nothing special: bogeys on the 1st and 9th and a two-putt birdie on the par-5 8th. Then, suddenly, things started to happen on the back nine. I birdied the 10th, one of the most difficult holes on the course, and then picked up three more birdies to come home in 32 for a 69. Again, it might have been better. On that back nine, I had four other birdie putts from within 15 feet.

Seve was the runaway leader after rounds of 66, 69 and 68, while I was in a four-way tie for third, seven shots back, with Ed Fiori the man in the middle but six shots shy of Ballesteros.

I was drawn with Ballesteros in the final round and went out with the sole intention of keeping him honest. We were quite friendly because of the days on the European Tour. In those early days he would ask me to look at his swing, and as far as I was concerned, the only thing he ever did wrong was to get slightly across the line at the top of it.

He had never felt really comfortable in the States, perhaps because of the early media criticism, and Jackie and I quite often had dinner with him. He would make comments about 'gringos' in relation to the Yanks, and I still have a sneaking suspicion that it was part of the history of feuding between the Americans and the Spanish. His Spanish flair and taste for the dramatic certainly didn't sit comfortably with the more genial nature of the Americans.

I felt that if I could keep him honest and perhaps make a slight inroad early in the round, Seve might crack a little. His Latin heritage is such that he is a great player when all is going well but when things aren't so fine he loses the handle a bit. Realistically, though, I was only playing for second place.

At the 9th, I three-putted for the umpteenth time in the championship while Seve made birdie. He was nine shots in front of me with just nine to play. You hear about Arnold Palmer losing PGAs from seven in front with nine to play, but nine shots was a pretty big ask. Everything should have been hunky-dory for Seve, but those last nine holes were the most amazing I have ever been involved in.

He dropped a shot at the 10th while I made par and it was eight the difference. Nothing to get excited about. Then, at the 11th, a very difficult 455-yard par 4 that begins Amen Corner, I holed a 15-footer for birdie while he made par. Seven the difference. Maybe, I thought, there was a chink in his armour.

At the 155-yard 12th, once described by Jack Nicklaus as 'the most demanding tournament hole in the world', the chink widened to a crack. Legend has it that Ben Hogan, perfectionist that he was, would stand on the tee for minutes before making up his mind which way the wind was blowing. That day, I took 7-iron and it came to rest just 12 feet from the hole. Seve then stood on the tee. Just as he was about to hit, the wind swung around, with the result that he backed off the shot. He changed club and as he struck it, the wind swirled again and his ball fell into the water at the front of the green. He made double-bogey 5; I made birdie 2. The difference was just four.

The 13th, a 465-yard par 5 and the last of the holes of Amen Corner, bends sharply to the left. My drive was right on target around the corner to give me 4-iron to the green. Seve hung his to the right a bit, which gave him a stance where the natural tendency was to hook the ball when what he needed to do was cut his second shot. He miscued and the ball was never going anywhere else but in Rae's Creek, which runs from the front of the 12th and meanders down the left of the 13th and across the front of the green. I knocked my second on to give myself a 20-foot putt for eagle while Seve dropped from the water and made bogey 6. I two-putted for birdie.

The difference was now just two. Incredibly, there had been a swing of seven shots in just four holes. It was a real ball game. As I stood on the 14th tee, I could tell Seve was getting really angry with himself. He could see the tournament slipping away from what had been a waddle in the park just four holes before. I'm not fluent in Spanish, but I know the swear words and they were certainly flying thick and fast. I thought, 'Just one more birdie, or one more loose shot from him, and I've got this.'

The drive at the 14th is difficult. The fairway runs away from you and there is a copse of pines on the left on the point of the dogleg, about 240 yards out. My drive was perfect, up over the hill, giving me nothing more than an 8- or 9-iron home on the 405-yard hole. Seve hooked his drive straight into the pines, and as we walked up the fairway I thought of places like Royal Canberra where, if you hit in the pines, the ball drops straight down as the pine needles grab hold of it and sling it down.

To all intents and purposes, I figured Seve was dead. He had lost the plot totally. Thoughts were running through my mind that if he made another bogey – which seemed inevitable after the tee shot – and I made birdie, we'd be tied with four to play. But as we neared the corner, I saw that the gallery had gathered some 30 or 40 yards left of where his ball had gone into the pine trees. It had actually been slung that distance to the left and he had room to get his second shot up over the pines. So from the potential to be in the deepest of deep effluent, he actually had a shot – and as we all know, Seve's a miracle man when in trouble. He played a great shot to the back edge of the green and we both made fours. Shakily, he had steadied.

We both had eagle putts at the 15th, but once more I three-putted while he two-putted for birdie and the difference blew out to three shots again. That was the end of the penny section. Ballesteros fired a final-round 72 to my 68, which left me in a tie for second place with Gibby Gilbert, who closed with a five-under 67.

Again I cast my mind back to those four shots dropped in the last five holes in the second round. That was the crucial difference. However, it was a satisfying tournament and really raised my image in the US because the Masters is the most watched event there. It also reinforced my view that I could play well at Augusta.

The 1980 Masters result certainly wasn't as devastating for me as it had been to finish second to Watson in the

1975 British Open. There, I had lost the tournament; at Augusta, Seve dominated for three rounds and it was simply a matter of playing catch-up all the time in a bid to pinch it from him, like Watson had pinched the Open from me.

I had great support from a couple of good friends. Richie Benaud, the former Australian Test cricket skipper, was there and we talked a lot about how well I was playing. Big Mac Briggs, the club pro from Arcadian Shores who was like a godfather to me, also came down for the final round. Throughout I could hear his voice above the others in the gallery, shouting, 'Come on, Fig!' There's a biscuit in the States called Fig Newton and he had hoisted that nickname on me.

That week I played really well, but I didn't win. There are times when you actually win a tournament and don't think you've played well, which is something I guess a lot of people can't understand. Greg Norman used to get criticised a lot because he would say, after shooting a 66, that he was playing badly. The average person would scoff and accuse Norman of being a big-head as they couldn't, even in their wildest dreams, imagine shooting a 66 themselves. Maybe Norman should have made a better selection of words, but I can understand exactly what he was saying. It's like Tiger Woods right now. He can shoot 66 and then earnestly tell the media that he didn't bring his A game to the course that day.

But I did play well that week. I was thirty years of age and my father had always said the best years in golf were between thirty and forty, so I reasoned I was coming into my decade. It was 1980 and I had just finished second in the US Masters. I felt I had matured a lot as a person and my golf had matured as well. I had nothing but optimism for the future.

Certainly the 1981 Masters was a giant letdown. I was having injections in my 'golfer's elbow' and golf is a difficult enough game without being hurt while you're playing. Rounds of 79–73 to miss the cut by four shots was a fairly inglorious result given the heady stuff of a year earlier.

Sadly, that was the last US Masters I played. But the memories linger on, and each year when I watch the tournament I get a lump in my throat as I recall the very special moments I had there. My home in Cardiff, just outside Newcastle in New South Wales, is called 'Augusta'.

Sweet victory at Metropolitan

Injuries plagued me throughout my professional career, and for that matter, before it even started.

At school during a rugby union match I was at the bottom of a ruck when it collapsed on top of me. I felt my leg going one way and my body the other. My meniscus cartilage was damaged and a cortisone injection helped me through the remainder of that year in football. It was thought time would mend the damage and all went well until a year or so later when I visited my grandmother at Lake Macquarie. She asked me to move a television set from her house to the place next door and in the darkness I tripped and smashed the same knee. The scar remains to this day and at the time I was rendered something of a cripple.

I had just turned professional and it was in the days of

the Vietnam War. The Liberal–Country Party government had ordered conscription and my birthday marble came out of the barrel. The stitches were still in my knee when I went for my medical examination and the army doctor said, 'We can't look at you now. Come back in three weeks when the stitches are out.'

I was receiving physiotherapy for the stiffness caused by the cartilage damage and went to my own doctor, who asked if I wanted to go into the army. I am as nationalistic as any Australian, but to many people this war was an unwanted one. Besides, I was just embarking on my professional career.

'No,' I replied, and my doctor wrote a report. I had to front a board of three other doctors to prove my case, but I did have a crook knee and it was confirmed.

My next major injury came in 1975 when I turned my ankle on a rabbit hole while looking for a partner's ball at a pro-am at Downfield, in Scotland, just before the British Open. I played through the Open with my ankle strapped, but it became progressively worse as the year wore on. I came home and consulted Dr Brian Corrigan, then doctor to the Australian cricket and Olympic teams, at a Test match at the SCG and he recommended a cortisone injection.

For the next few months I had no trouble at all. I went to Africa and played some of the finest golf of my career and was about to depart for my first US Masters when the injury flared again in early 1976. Back in England, Alan Ball, England soccer captain and Arsenal star, recommended I see the Arsenal medical staff, who were generally regarded as the best in English soccer. Their opinion was that I had a stress fracture. Although X-rays showed nothing, it was decided to place the foot in plaster for six weeks.

It seemed an eternity till the removal date and after that I had to go through a period of strengthening the foot before returning to golf. I will never forget the first day I went to the practice fairway. I spilled the contents of my shag-bag onto the turf, started with the sand iron and was in tears after just one shot. Nothing had changed. Six weeks and the rehabilitation period had been wasted.

I strapped the ankle and played the two tournaments at Royal Birkdale leading up to the British Open, for which I was exempt after the affairs of the previous year, and made regular visits to the physio. I opened with a 70, just one off the pace, and was in contention for a while until fading to finish tied for seventeenth. The following week I played in Sweden and then returned to London, where surgeons performed an exploratory operation, slicing the foot open on both the top and bottom. They found nothing. You can imagine the frustration. There I was with a foot full of stitches and then, to compound matters, the incision at the base of the foot became infected. I came home a little disappointed with the English medical fraternity.

When everything had healed, the pain persisted. My father suggested I see a chap by the name of Don Macbeth, who had been Dad's chiropractor for years and had treated him for a back injury. (Dad had lost the knuckles of the last three vertebrae in a shooting accident as a kid when he was climbing through a fence with a loaded gun.) Don reckoned my problem was scar tissue on the foot. In favouring it when walking, I had tilted my pelvis to the point where I actually had one leg longer than the other.

He felt I needed arch supports and casts of my feet

were taken to produce aluminium inner soles for my shoes. He also manipulated my back and for the first time in a year I felt no pain while playing golf.

My first tournament in Australia late in 1976 was the Queensland Open, where I played well but lost by a shot to Jeff Senior, then an amateur, after a very wonky decision by the tournament match committee.

I played the last round with Senior and an American, Art Russell, and the latter claimed my ball had moved while I played my second shot on the 12th. I had gone through my normal routine of looking at the ball, looking at the target and then looking at the ball again, and I didn't notice it move, but Russell swore it did. I was penalised a shot after we completed the round and that was the stroke that made the difference.

The following week I confirmed my good form by winning the NSW Open at Royal Sydney by ten shots. It was one of the best 72 holes of golf I have played. But on and off over the next couple of years I had swing problems associated with the original foot injury. As well, I always seemed to return to Australia feeling jaded after a long stint overseas. In hindsight, perhaps I should have got off the Tour to get the foot sorted out, but you live in hope that one morning you'll wake up and all your troubles will be behind you.

That happened during 1979 and the results were there. I was actually hitting the ball with a draw, which is the way I like to play although my natural shot is a fade. But I was in such total control of my swing and game that I felt I could hit the ball either way. That certainly proved to be the case in the NSW Open at The Lakes, where I won by nine shots from American Gary Vanier, Englishman Geoff Hall and Wayne Grady.

What a confidence builder! I was ready to take on the world, and the world of golf was assembling in Melbourne for the Australian Open at Metropolitan just two weeks later. Dunhill, the Open sponsor, had opened its cheque book to bring the hot shots to town and among them were three future champions of 1979: Seve Ballesteros (British Open), Fuzzy Zoeller (US Masters) and David Graham (US PGA). The only 'major' winner of '79 missing was US Open winner Hale Irwin.

As well as those players there was the 1977 US Open champion Hubert Green, and Gary Player, who had won the last of his nine majors, a third US Masters title, just a year earlier. It was a class field, perhaps the best ever assembled in Australia, and I certainly didn't begrudge them their appearance money even though the bulk of the Australians were playing for prize money alone.

Despite the credentials of those present for the Open, I wasn't the least bit overawed by the occasion. Mind you, I had rarely played well in Melbourne. In the early days I was probably too aggressive on the courses, which tend to play shorter in the summer months. I would hit driver off every tee instead of 2-iron or 3- or 4-wood. It wasn't a macho thing, rather a lack of course discipline, and you certainly paid the supreme penalty on Melbourne courses if you hit it off the fairway. We didn't have courses like that in Sydney. As well, the greens on the Melbourne sandbelt courses were faster than anywhere else we played, faster than we ever played in the States. I liked them quick, but not that quick. Royal Melbourne used to get me every year.

I certainly hadn't developed a complex about the Melbourne syndrome and felt I'd been more successful than some of the guys who were winning in Melbourne. I couldn't see any reason why I wouldn't triumph there one day, too. It was just a case of biding my time, not something to lose sleep over.

———————

Ballesteros, Zoeller, Player and co. were all staying at a five-star hotel in town. Invariably I stayed at the Beaumaris Bay Motel, where the owners, Nick and Dulcie Fermanis, made us feel totally at home and Dulcie was like a godmother to me. Dad was caddying for me, as he always did in Australia. It was his holiday, but it was rare for Mum to go to tournaments. The 1979 Open was an exception and she was with us, as of course was Jackie. It was like one very large, happy family.

I was off late on the opening day and a north-westerly wind got up, with the result that the greens firmed. While Metropolitan's greens are quick, they certainly aren't the speed of Royal Melbourne and that suited me. Even though I felt I played well, I signed for a relatively unremarkable two-over 74, which left me only four off the pace. They weren't exactly household names at the top of the leaderboard. Only the real trivia buffs could tell you that American Deray Simon, Englishman Tony Johnson and Sydney's Paul Hart led with 70. And the hot shots? Ballesteros had a 79, Zoeller and Green 76 and Player and Graham were on the same line as I was. So no great damage done.

I went straight to the practice putting green to work on a stroke for the remaining three rounds and then had a few beers with the old man under the big flowering gum tree outside the Metropolitan clubhouse. We'd developed a bit of a tradition each time I played in Melbourne, and that night it was dinner at Mario's. Dad reckoned they served the biggest and best flounder you could find.

Well fed, we went back to the Beaumaris Bay Hotel, just across the road from the motel, for a few more beers before calling it quits around midnight. Throughout my playing career I had my share of knockers who frowned on my lifestyle of enjoying a few beers, but I found it a great way to relax. The wowsers only ever saw me with glass in hand, not during the hours I spent on the practice fairway.

I birdied the first hole of the second round, but in the end signed for a par 72 and felt I hadn't been rewarded for my play. The set-up of the course was pretty tough. The rough was savage and it was always going to be a high-scoring tournament. No way was fourteen or fifteen under going to win. I figured if I could just get myself into a position to challenge in the third round, the course would eliminate the pretenders.

Greg Norman was leading on 142 after rounds of 73–69, two shots ahead of Graham Marsh and Deray Simon, a Californian who came out with a group of young Americans. I was four shots back and felt I was by no means out of touch, but the third round would be crucial. Naturally enough, the old man and I shared a few beers again before turning in about midnight.

I always tried to work my schedule so that I had plenty of sleep. Not for me waking up at 6 a.m. worrying about what I was going to do at 2 p.m. out on the golf course. By comparison, a guy like Billy Dunk was always up around 5.30 or

6 o'clock. I think that habit had a lot to do with many of his downfalls and his failure to fulfil his potential, though I must say he did pretty well on the seniors circuit in Japan in the late '80s. Back in the '70s, though, he used to become a nervous wreck before he hit off, especially in the big time. He was all right playing the pro-ams when the heavy artillery wasn't around, but as soon as the big guns arrived in town, especially in an Australian Open, he got very toey, and it may have been because he had more time on his hands.

I was drawn in the fourth-last group of the day with Americans Jim Nelford and Scott Simpson. Simpson was about as anonymous then as he is now, even though he won the 1987 US Open championship. He was typical of many of the college golfers, who are all cast in the same mould. They are mechanical men who play the ABC game: strike the ball, walk after it, strike the ball again. It was hardly the way I played.

Now Nelford, he was different. Like me, he enjoyed a drink and was a bit of a tearaway. Bob Shearer and I became quite friendly with him while we were in the States. He never did win on the US Tour, with his career virtually ended by a shocking water-ski accident in Phoenix in 1985 where he broke his right arm in nine places and needed a plate plus thirteen screws to put it together again. By the end of 1986 he was back on the circuit, saying, 'There's no place for negative thinking. I believe you follow the path in life that your mind sees first.'

Regrettably Jim didn't make it back, playing only three tournaments in 1989 and winning just a tick over $1000. But I now know exactly what he was saying.

Hitting off in the fourth-last group gave me a good position from which to make a move. Norman and co. were off later and I had the feeling there was going to be a mad scramble at the top of the leaderboard. I felt if I could break 70 it would get me right back in the thick of things – unless Norman shot the lights out, but that was going to be difficult given the way the course was set up.

At that stage, Norman was just setting out on his international career. I certainly wasn't afraid of him. I'd beaten him in the NSW Open just a couple of weeks earlier where we'd been in the last group on the final day with Wayne Grady. It was actually Norman who had fallen by the wayside first, with Grades hanging in for a while. Grades finished tied for second nine shots back, and Norman was twelve shots behind.

So he held no fears for me. But the media, even at that early stage of his career, had embraced him as the great white hope of Australian golf. The word 'shark' replaced 'hope' as the years rolled by, but a lot of the hype back then was generated by an Englishman, James Marshall, who was Norman's original manager.

Actually, Marshall had approached me in 1976 wanting to manage me. His brother, John, was involved in film-making, with his biggest credit to that point being *The Greatest* (the Muhammad Ali story), and James wanted to get into the entrepreneurial business by managing an Australian golfer. He said he felt he could make me a lot of money and promote me better than before.

I went home to think about it and talk it over with Jackie. The trouble was basically that James Marshall and I just didn't see eye to eye. He stood for a lot of things I don't like in people. He seemed a pseudo-rich, snobbish English gentleman and I felt there would always be a personality conflict, even though the guy could indeed probably have made me a lot of money. I couldn't see myself working under those circumstances and after a lot of discussion with Jackie decided to say no at our scheduled meeting in London a week later.

'What about this guy Greg Norman?' he asked after I had given him my answer.

'If you're going to take a punt on anyone, he's your man,' I replied. Next thing I heard, Marshall had fronted Norman and the contract was signed. Norman had done bugger-all except win the Westlakes Classic in Adelaide that year and still hadn't really set the world on fire during the next couple of years up to the '79 Australian Open. Sure, he won in Europe, Asia and at home, and Marshall had done a really good job in promoting him, but he was still very much a minnow in the grand school of golf.

Relations between Norman and me were becoming strained. I had roomed with him that year at the Double Diamond tournament in England and there had been no problems, but he was becoming more of a loner as the weeks went by. Maybe Marshall was attempting to instil in Norman a belief that he was superior to his fellow Australians.

I again birdied the first hole to start the third round and felt confident, but certainly had the stuffing knocked out of me at the 3rd, where my second shot covered the flag all the way only to hit the back of the green and shoot into the bush. It took three to get out and another two putts to get down, and a triple-bogey 7 went on the card.

At Metropolitan you have to set up your round in the first six or seven holes. The 4th, a par 5 of 486 yards, was a gimme birdie. I looked on the positive side and the hurt of the triple was forgotten in an instant. I duly made birdie and then another at the 6th. Then I knocked it on the 520-yard 8th for two and holed a 25-footer for an eagle 3. At the turn, I was one under with a 7 on the card.

Strange, that! Nothing bothered me on the course that week. It was almost as though I could accept anything that came my way, good or bad, and if it were the latter it wouldn't alter the nature of things to come. In short, I felt good. Call it destiny, call it what you like. Some suggested my biorhythms were right. Maybe. Biorhythms were the big go in those days and I'd done my share of reading about them. There was talk in the States that they wouldn't let airline pilots fly unless their biorhythms were right and company executives also placed a great deal of faith in them when it came to decision making.

As far as I was concerned, I felt good. When I took the 7, I simply got on with the job, whereas at other times it would have been the finish of me.

I made just one birdie on the back nine – at the par-5 14th where I two-putted – and signed for a two-under 70, which left me just one shot behind Norman, who fired a 73. I was delighted to be in that position. One shot is nothing coming into the final round.

Tied on the second line with me was Scott Tuttle, another of the young Americans, who had turned to golf after being a star basketballer at college. Marsh was one shot back and two shots back were Shearer and Player, who was looking to win an eighth Australian Open championship.

It was going to be a great final-round showdown, but I certainly wasn't thinking then about being Open champion twenty-four hours later. If you start counting your chickens, you only create unnecessary problems in your mind. There's enough pressure anyway. But the fact that this was my best chance to win an Australian Open didn't escape me, either.

That night I went to the Australian golf writers' annual dinner at a little restaurant in South Melbourne. Player, Norman, Shearer and Ian Stanley were among the other invited players and what should have been a relaxing night turned sour. I was sitting opposite Norman and somehow the conversation got around to his deal with Qantas. None of the other players were on the Qantas books and, in truth, it had been the likes of Shearer, Stanley, Stewie Ginn and me who had flown the flag for Australia through the '70s in European golf. Norman began throwing it in our faces that he was the one with the Qantas deal and it developed into quite a heated discussion.

At one stage I suggested I throw him out the first-floor window, to which he retorted, 'Just try!' Wiser heads prevailed, but on the way home, being driven by veteran Melbourne golf writer Don Lawrence, I was still white hot. 'Norman won't even walk in my spike marks tomorrow,' I declared.

———————

It was a good session on the practice fairway and then I moved to the putting green where I passed Shears. We wished each other well. 'Good luck. If I don't win, I hope you do,' I said and he reciprocated. Neither of us wanted

Norman to win because we both felt we'd paid our dues and deserved to win an Australian Open more than Norman did at that time.

I guess both Bob and I felt Norman would win the Open at some stage, but that day was one of our really good chances. I also felt a bit angry towards the media because of its obsession not just with Norman but also the overseas players. Maybe this was being a bit wet behind the ears, but that Sunday in 1979 was a chance to really slam the door on a very good field and prove something for Australian golf.

Shears was drawn with Norman, and I was paired with Marsh and Player. Player was notoriously tough, and Marsh is in the same mould, tough and dour, and one who'd been known to pull the odd tactic or three.

I made a solid par 4 down the 1st, and at the 2nd, which I'd birdied twice in the first three days, I hit it to 10 feet or so and holed the putt. Walking to the 3rd tee, I was conscious of the 7 of the previous day, but was happy to walk away with par to go to the 4th, where I duly made my birdie 4.

A bogey 5 at the 5th was a slight hiccup and then at the 6th, the second of the par fives, I missed birdie. At the 7th, which was playing into the breeze, it was just too far to get a 2-iron back to the flag. I could hit the green okay but felt I wouldn't be able to hold it, so instead I tried to hit a high 4-wood and fade it, attempting to land soft.

Instead of fading it, I actually pulled it left of the green-side trap onto a lie where people had been walking. I duffed the chip into the bunker but then holed out to save par. I had dodged my first bullet for the day.

I was out in 36, one under, and then dropped the 10th, a long par 4 and one of the toughest in golf because of its sharp dogleg to the left. It is a dangerous hole because you want to drive down the left to shorten it, but too far left and you hit the overhanging branches. That's exactly what happened. But the grapevine had told me the others were struggling. I was two shots in front.

At the short 11th I hit a good shot to the green, but it just trickled two or three paces off the back edge. I used putter and holed it for another birdie. I parred the next two holes and came to the 14th, where you look for birdie. After a good drive, I was looking to get home in two but blocked my second shot, taking some of the steam off it. Instead of getting in the greenside trap, I finished in the bunker short of the green and was faced with a 40- to 50-yard bunker shot that also involved a carry of the greenside trap. As well, I had to get the ball to stop. Some assignment.

It was a bunker that hadn't had much use and when I played the shot, the sand iron bounced on me and the ball went through the green and into the bunker at the back. Things weren't looking too flash. I was faced with another difficult trap shot, with my ball on the downslope of the bunker and downhill to the hole. There was no way I could get any backspin on the ball and it ran across the green and into the greenside bunker. I was in the sand for a third time on the hole and exploded out and two-putted for yet another seven.

Suddenly, I had left the door open. Marsh and Player saw a glimmer of hope and the bush telegraph arrived with the news that Shearer was starting to run hot. In fact, he birdied five in a row from the 11th through the 15th, but after I had played the 14th it had only been three in a row.

I had gone from cruising to being pretty jumpy and all the bad thoughts started flooding back. I thought I'd blown it. On the 15th, a long par 4, I hit a good second but again my ball just trickled through the back of the green. There was no chance of using a putter as I'd done on the 11th, so I chipped with a little 8-iron. While I reckon I had a pretty good short game, I wasn't thinking of holing it, particularly as I'd already holed a bunker shot and putted in from off the green.

In it went. Birdie. It certainly took my mind off the double bogey at the previous hole, which I confess had rattled me more than I cared to show.

At the 16th, a shortish par 4 where I had hit iron off the tee in the first three rounds, I took 3-wood and blocked it down the right-hand side where there's a group of bunkers right at the point of the dogleg. Sure enough, I was in one of them and facing a very difficult shot to a green with a lot of undulation, where anything past the hole is very definitely three-putt territory.

Strangely enough, I hit a very similar shot out of the trap to the one on the 14th, and it came out low and hot, pitching onto the green and running through into the back trap.

I knew I was dead as I walked towards the green. Out of that bunker it was all downhill to the flag and the greens were firm. I knew in my mind it was an impossibility to get up and down to save par. Things had gone from cruising to panic stations, and of course everything I was doing was only encouraging Player and Marsh, who were witnessing the whole sorry spectacle.

But as it's said, no one achieves the impossible unless they attempt it. When I got in the bunker, I reasoned I had 1 foot of dirt on which to land my ball. If I didn't hit it far enough it was back in the bunker, and if I hit it past that spot there was a good chance of not only going past the hole but off the green on the other side.

To this day, I think it's one of the greatest shots I've hit under the circumstances – any circumstances. It stopped just 3 inches from the hole and I had a tap-in for par.

Player, one of the best bunker players of all time, walked over to me and said, 'Man, that's one of the greatest shots I've ever seen.' Now that was pretty strong stuff coming from Player at that stage of the round, especially as he'd virtually said nothing all the way around.

I parred the last two holes to card a level-par 72. At the last, Marsh did add to the drama by holing a 25-footer for birdie, leaving me to hole out from about 18 inches for my 4 and a one-shot lead, with Shearer and Norman still on the course.

Shears' run of five birdies ended at the 15th and he then made bogey at both the 16th and 17th. But Norman was still in there with a chance of tying. I sat and watched from the back of the green as he played his second onto the front right portion of it. He needed two putts to force a play-off, but the first, which started uphill with a big right-to-left and then downhill to the hole, was one of the toughest you could get.

I certainly wouldn't have backed myself to two-putt it, and his first putt slipped about 3 feet past – a great putt under the circumstances. Then he lined it up to tie up the ball game. I was sitting right behind him as he hit it. It was left to right, but he hit it so firmly that the ball just didn't take the break. The championship was mine.

'Well done, Newt,' Norman said as he walked to the scorers' hut while pandemonium broke around me. Jackie, Mum, Dad all embraced me. There would be a party that night.

I didn't see Norman again that day. He didn't turn up for the presentation ceremony, which I thought was a touch rude, but for all I knew he might have gone to the locker-room and necked himself. It was only later that I discovered he was having a drink in the clubhouse with British tennis player Sue Barker. That still didn't excuse him for what I considered were bad manners.

It was a big drink with the old man and other friends, and though it is a cliché, what I'd done didn't really sink in until some time later. Then I sat down and reflected on all the hard work, ups and downs, different emotions, traumas, good times and bad. All those bad memories were suddenly gone in the euphoria and then the aftermath of victory in my national Open championship.

My mind raced back to 1975 and the British Open play-off with Tom Watson. Winning at Metropolitan was some consolation, but the especially satisfying aspect was that my father had been beside me as my caddie. It was Dad, after all, who had been so instrumental in my playing golf in the first place, and it was a unique moment.

We were always great mates – not just father and son – and to me it was one of the most special moments I've had in golf.

Postscript: Jack Sr passed away on 17 January 1996. I lost my best mate, my confidant, my caddie and my dad, who I loved having a beer with. He looked so fit and strong in death, but Alzheimer's disease had taken a toll on his mind that had been tragic to see. His funeral was a very sad day and yet a happy one as his four teenage grandchildren – our daughter Kristie and son Clint, and my sister Jan's two girls, Cassandra and Belinda – all spoke in their own way of the man who had loved them so dearly and played such a large part in formulating their lives.

The battle in the USA

Through the early years in Europe I became quite friendly with Doug Sanders, who lost the 1970 British Open at St Andrews in an 18-hole play-off with Jack Nicklaus. Doug missed a putt of no more than a yard on the 72nd hole and I doubt there was a soul there who didn't feel sorry for one of golf's most flamboyant characters. He then lost the play-off by a shot. As history now shows, there is every cause for Sanders and me to have empathy with each other.

Because of his style and the wave of sympathy that went out to him, Doug was very popular in both Britain and Europe. Promoters gladly parted with appearance money as he gave such good value both on and off the golf course. I recall a time he turned up for the Swiss Open at Crans-sur-Sierre, where he was met by limousine and driver at the airport. The driver had to call for another car just to transport all Doug's gear. He always travelled with twelve different-coloured pairs of golf shoes and clothing to match, six outfits for day wear and six for night.

In those days, Doug could aptly be described as a playboy. He never missed an opportunity, but there were occasional knockbacks. Once we were playing a tournament at Gleneagles in Scotland and Doug took a shine to one of the Benson & Hedges hospitality girls who did the rounds of some tournaments. It should be pointed out that these girls were all 180 cm plus, had blonde hair and wore chocolate-coloured uniforms with gold trimming. In short, they were stunners. Doug used all his considerable charm in a bid to persuade the girl to have dinner with him, but she rebuffed him and he had to settle for second prize: eating with me.

We walked into the Gleneagles Hotel restaurant and were seated at a table adjacent to the Benson & Hedges girls, who had almost finished their main course. He tried again, walking to the table to engage the girl in conversation, but returned moments later after she threatened to call the manager to have him thrown out of the restaurant.

Doug was now a man on a real mission. He called a teenage waiter over and said, 'Son, how much do you earn a week?'

'Twelve pounds, three and sixpence, Mr Sanders,' the kid replied.

'Well, how would you like to make quadruple your wages?' Sanders proposed. The kid's eyes lit up.

'What I want you to do is that when the girl over there orders her dessert, I want you to tip her ice-cream and chocolate sauce, or whatever she's having, over her head. You understand that?'

'Oh, sir. I canna do that. I'll get sacked,' said the youngster.

Sanders was reassuring. 'No, no. I'll make sure you're not sacked. You can make it look like an accident, as though you've tripped.'

And so we waited for events to unfold. Sure enough, as the kid brought the girl her ice-cream with chocolate sauce (and jelly, as it turned out), he tripped over, sprawling forward so that the bowl tipped over her head. As the contents started dripping down her hair and onto her immaculate clothes, Doug rushed across to her with his table napkin and attentively helped in the clean-up job while exressing his dismay that such an accident could happen. The kid got his fifty quid, and Sanders and the girl went out for a drink.

I spent quite a bit of time with Sanders in Houston, Texas, before heading to the US players' school in Brownsville in September 1976. He suggested the stopover so I could work on my game while acclimatising to the Texas weather. As fate would have it, the singer Andy Williams was staying with Doug at the same time. Like many American entertainers in those days, Williams had his name attached to a US PGA Tour event, in his case, the Andy Williams San Diego Open. I put the hard word on Mr Williams for an invitation the following year if, of course, I secured my players' card in Brownsville, and the deal was sealed over a glass of Tattinger champagne.

Weather conditions in Brownsville were atrocious but there was no point worrying about them. They were the same for all of us and the prize at the end was a passport to the riches of the US circuit. I shared a house with Graham Marsh that was located next to one of the holes of the golf course, and each night we calculated the odds of being one of the sixteen players who would win cards among the 250 starters in the eight-round school. Coming into the last round I was in 27th spot and knew a big round was needed in the rain and gales that prevailed. I shot a 72 to leapfrog a number of players and gained my card by a single shot.

Marshie secured his card, too, though his later career path led him to Japan, where he made millions. American Curtis Strange was another to qualify at the school and just a month later he came to Australia to finish second to Jack Nicklaus in the Australian Open at the Australian Golf Club in Sydney. Curtis has often said that the $17 000 he picked up as runner-up gave him the financial security in those early days to become the great player he was, winning the US Open in 1988 and again in 1989.

On my way back from the players' school I again dropped in on Sanders, who had spent the week in hospital for an operation to repair ligament damage to his shoulder. He tossed a telegram in my direction, saying, 'He'd try anything, wouldn't he?'

It was from Evel Knievel, the daredevil motorbike rider, who was at the height of his career of jumping over London buses and what have you. About the only thing he hadn't tackled was the Grand Canyon. Evel was loaded with greenbacks pushed by the barrowload in his direction by promoters, and Doug had been helping him get rid of it on the golf course. Evel fancied himself more as a golfer than a trick rider, but as a golfer he made a damn good trick rider.

My good friend Gay Brewer (leading US golfer) and I go fishing in Toronto, Canada.

Dad in his role as my caddy.

The crowd goes wild as I hole a putt from the back of the 11th green at Metropolitan on the way to my Australian Open victory in 1979.

Moment of triumph: I hold the Stonehaven Cup aloft after winning the Australian Open.

Caddy Charles 'Bull' Williams offers me some advice at Augusta.

With Seve Ballesteros in the final round of the 1980 US Masters.

Kristie gets into the swing of practice, but needs to work on her grip
(at the 1981 Australian Open in Melbourne).

Jackie faces the media as I fight for life in hospital.

Craig Stadler auctions a painting at a benefit tournament in Myrtle Beach, South Carolina.

Clint and Kristie with their Da (Jack senior), while I was in hospital.

Kristie looks on during my first post-operative interview.

Working on my rehabilitation with Bob Shearer (right) and Ian Stanley during the ABE PGA Jack Newton Classic at the Belmont Golf Club, Newcastle, in 1983.

Golf again: playing in the Jack Newton Celebrity Classic at the Tewantin-Noosa Golf Club, Queensland, with former Australian prime minister Bob Hawke, patron of the tournament.

Evel had heard about Doug's operation and the telegram issued a challenge for them to meet on the first tee the following day to play for $50 000 a hole. Doug's reply read: 'Sorry – I can't make it, but I'll send a substitute. You'll recognise his golf swing and his initials are JN.' Newton, that was, not Nicklaus. The reply worked out. Eight rounds of golf in Brownsville weather deserved a drink.

The sponsor's invitation to the 1977 Andy Williams tournament duly came through, so I kicked off my new American career in San Diego. The event was played on a public course, Tory Pines, which has two layouts with rounds alternating between the two. I had taken a break from golf for a few weeks after the New Zealand circuit before going to the States and my game wasn't as sharp as it should have been. As well, I was still having problems with my foot injury. The trouble lay in my weight transference and therefore my swing suffered. Rounds of 75–75 left me well shy of the 36-hole cut.

As I sat in the locker-room changing my shoes and feeling just a touch annoyed with myself, Bruce Crampton came in, clearly in a pretty distraught state.

'That's it. I'm finished.' His words were squeezed out of an emotional wringer and his eyes were glazed.

I sort of laughed. Quite often when they're at their wits' end you'll hear blokes say in the heat of the moment that they're quitting, and then the following week they're back out there on the practice tee.

'I'll see you next week,' I said to Bruce.

'No, you won't. It's over,' he replied. With that, the Iron Man of golf, who had finished second to Nicklaus in two of golf's majors in 1972, walked away from the game for a number of years. I subsequently learned he had admitted himself to hospital, where, as part of a bid to repair a marriage that was on the rocks, he was treated for a slight manic depressive syndrome.

My next tournament was the Hawaiian Open. I arrived there on Sunday afternoon and played a practice round. It was after six o'clock when I finished and I went to check on my time for prequalifying the following day. My name was not on the sheet and I discovered I was supposed to have committed for prequalifying by registering before 6 p.m. that very day. Wrongly, I had assumed my original entry was all that was needed. And so I learned my first lesson on the US Tour: know the rules.

The only thing was to make the best of a bad situation, so Jackie and I had a few days off before heading to California and the Bob Hope Classic at Palm Springs. On arrival, before anything else I committed for prequalifying. I might be stubborn, but I'm not stupid. While the Classic was unpopular with several of the leading players, it did draw a big entry of those exempt from prequalifying. As a result, just eight spots were on offer. I managed a 68 and was in.

There is now an all-exempt Tour in the US, but in the days of prequalifying it was a heartless affair. They were all damn good players in PQ and proved it by shooting 62s and 63s on a Monday. Then, in the tournament proper, it was not uncommon for them to shoot 78 in the opening round. The total relief in getting a start seemed to make it impossible to build yourself up psychologically for the second time in a week. It was also a numbers game, with up to 200 players trying for anything from four to twenty spots. In the end the powers that be felt it was detrimental to put players through that ordeal. Some bum writer in the States coined the term 'rabbit' for the players who had to hop from tournament to tournament hoping to prequalify, and I can tell you, none of us was that. It was a term I did not enjoy.

I had met Bob Hope during a tournament at Waterville in Ireland over a locker-room drink after the opening round. We talked of golf, which was entirely predictable, but during the conversation the subject of his wife, Dolores, came up.

'How long have you been married?' I enquired.

'So long that I'm on my second bottle of Tabasco sauce,' Hope replied.

The Classic was played over five rounds on four different courses, and after prequalifing it was impossible to practise on all four. I managed two on the Tuesday and felt my game was in reasonable shape for the Wednesday tournament start. It was a pro-am tournament with amateurs paired with the pros in each of the first three rounds and then a cut being made to the final 36 holes.

Mind you, this wasn't just any old pro-am. For openers, an amateur had to know somebody who knew Hope personally. Better, of course, if you were friends with the man himself. Then, you had to make a minimum donation of $7500 to the Eisenhower Medical Center, the tournament's major charity, and then pay a further $2500 entry fee. So it was, at the very least, a $10 000 deal. That was big money at the time and an ironic contrast to the pro-ams we had in Australia. In those days, if you asked an amateur to pay $100, you practically had to wrench his arm out of his pocket for the privilege of having a round of golf with a pro.

Through the years the Hope Classic has raised in excess of $80 million for the Eisenhower Center, which is one of the foremost children's hospitals in the world.

It was one big party for the entire week. The amateurs paid to have a good time while the pros had to remember they were primarily there to play golf. Some players – Nicklaus, George Archer, Frank Beard and Gene Littler among them – would always avoid the event. It just wasn't their scene and there were associated dangers in playing, as well. In 1970, Spiro Agnew was one of the amateurs, and the word amateur could be used in its strictest sense when it came to the then US Vice-President. He was paired with Doug Sanders and poor Doug was skulled by an errant shot from Agnew. The following year, Richard Nixon's offsider was at it again. On the first tee, he fired his shot from the toe of his driver and the ball slammed into the forearm of a woman spectator. After apologising and kissing the damaged spot, Agnew teed up again and once more managed to claim a spectator. Despite the pleading of a very game gallery, Mr Agnew had had enough. He jumped in his golf cart and sped off with his security staff in hot pursuit. Another US vice-president, Gerald Ford, was in attendance at my first Hope Classic, but his golf was not so dangerous.

Rounds of 72–69 left me in pretty good shape, but we'd played on the two courses on which I'd practised. It was unknown territory on the third day, but all went well for a while. That is, until I came to a hole where I had no idea of the line off the tee. I lost my ball and finished up with an 8 on the card along the way to a 74 – and that was very much the end of it all. I finished up with rounds of 76–73 to scrape into last money of $310, but it was a start, albeit a very meagre one. I was thrilled, though, for Bob Shearer, who finished in a tie for fourth behind Rik Massengale.

I knew it wasn't going to be easy getting a start in the US circuit. Not only did you have to find your feet with housing and transport, but you also had to familiarise yourself with the golf courses. The Americans had been playing the same courses for years and the scoring was unbelievable. The greatest example was the Sammy Davis Hartford Open, where one year a guy shot 25 under to win. When I played my first practice round there I thought, 'Hell, this course isn't that easy. How could anyone shoot 25 under?' Later in my career I knew the course and shot four rounds under 70, but finished only 35th. You can draw a parallel with Royal Melbourne. Once, we very rarely played tournament golf there and the scores reflected that, but in the '80s and early '90s we had one, sometimes two, events there each year and the guys were shooting lower and lower scores.

I again missed the cut in the next tournament, the Glen Campbell Los Angeles Open, and then Jackie and I caught the red-eye special to Miami, Florida. We arrived on the Sunday morning to begin preparations for prequalifying on the Monday for the Jackie Gleason Inverrary Classic. Naturally enough we didn't know a soul and discovered everything was booked out. Putting that trouble aside for a moment, we went to the golf club so I could at least play a practice round.

Jackie sat waiting for me in the foyer of the clubhouse and was soon engaged in conversation by an older guy. He heard her English accent and it wasn't long before she was telling him the story of our lives. As well, she took the opportunity of asking whether he knew where we could stay.

'If you haven't booked, you won't get anywhere. Why don't you come and stay at our place?' he replied.

Fred and Marlene were a lovely couple who had a home right on the water. He'd obviously been a very successful businessman and was semi-retired. With a roof over our heads, I came through prequalifying but then missed the cut with rounds of 77–73. It was becoming an all-too-familiar occurrence, but I still wasn't discouraged. Jackie and I were babes in the wood and with the hectic schedule, still hadn't done some of the important things in life – like establishing a base, securing credit cards, opening a bank account and, with all those things rolled into one, joining American society.

Marlene had just bought a new second car for her family and was still to dispose of her old car, a little rotary Mazda. We bought that car from Fred and Marlene and set off on the drive from Lauderdale to Orlando – these days the home of the likes of Tiger Woods, Mark O'Meara, Robert Allenby, Stuart Appleby and many other top golfers – for the Citrus Open.

I'm sure everyone thought, 'Who the hell is that?' as we drove into the Rio Pinar Country Club, but no one found out. I shot a 78 in PQ and yet another week was wasted. Things were looking far from good and I was starting to feel pretty frustrated. I had lost confidence and wasn't swinging well, but it was too soon even to think about crossing the Atlantic to return to where I'd felt so comfortable in my golfing life. We were fish out of water. We had gone from a situation where we knew everybody – and they knew us – to me being just another anonymous name on the draw sheet for prequalifying, and we still hadn't sorted out our banking arrangements.

Everything compounded, came tumbling down around us, and Jackie and I sat down one evening with both of us coming to the conclusion: 'Christ, we're not very well set up, are we!' That week at the Citrus Open I met a guy called Mickey Jordan who was in insurance but had a friend in the banking business. He took me to meet this friend and credit cards were arranged on the spot. With that, we were Americanised. Not so long afterwards, American Express became one of the major sponsors of the Tour and I signed up for one of their cards as well. I no longer had to argue with anyone about whether they took a personal cheque.

I knew a few guys on the circuit. Shears was obviously one of them and then there were the likes of Eddie Pearce, Tom Kite and John Schroeder, who I'd met on the Australian and New Zealand circuits. But in the early days, Jackie and I were very much our own company. The Americans tended to have sponsors who gave them around $40 000 a year to travel and so they flew everywhere. If they missed a cut, they simply got on a plane and went home to their wives or families or whatever. We basically didn't have a place to call home. We were stuck on the road week in, week out, living a gypsylike existence. With hindsight, I would probably do it differently.

Jackie wasn't one of those wives who went shopping every day, but rather walked the golf course. She was terrific, able to see that I was battling with my game and fully aware of where we were meant to go and how we were going to get there. She kept the lid on the whole thing, kept us sane, as she could see I was getting entirely pissed off with the situation.

After six tournaments I had collected a grand total of $310 while making a hole in the $50 000 we'd budgeted for in our first year in the States. We solved the housing situation by renting a small place in Myrtle Beach, South Carolina, in the same area in which Shears had based himself. It gave us a place to leave our excess baggage and somewhere to throw our hats when I had a week off. It would have been stupid to buy a house, because at that stage I was still prequalifying and my long-term future on the US circuit was far from secure.

In May 1977 there were two invitational tournaments – the Colonial and the Memorial – in which I couldn't get a start. We decided to go back to England to play the Benson & Hedges and matchplay events, both of which I'd won before, and the British PGA title. Then we'd return to the States to take up the battle again.

It was the same miserable story in the B&H and match-play, but in the PGA at Sandwich I started to hit my straps and worked into contention playing the 17th in the third round. I hit my drive into the left rough and as I played out, the light heather wrapped around the hosel of the club. I felt something going in the fatty part of my left thumb and in the base of my wrist. I made par at the last for a share of the lead and went in search of treatment.

Dr Sam Riddell worked on the injury with laser beam, manipulation and hot and cold water and then strapped it up, saying he felt I would be able to finish the tournament, but on the practice fairway the following day I couldn't even hit a shot with a sand iron. I had to pull out of the final round and was really up the creek. Not only was I not where I was supposed to be – in America playing golf – but I was injured yet again.

Jackie and I began the drive back to London. Just outside Sandwich I saw a little travel agency with a sign advertising holidays to the Greek Islands. 'Pull in here,' I said to Jackie. 'We just might get away from it all.'

Why not? The doctor had advised I shouldn't play golf for two weeks and a break was perhaps the tonic I needed. 'What trips do you have available immediately?' I asked the girl behind the counter.

'There's a package leaving tonight to Corfu,' she replied. I didn't have a clue where Corfu was, but anywhere would be paradise compared with the hell my golf had become. We drove straight to Gatwick Airport, got on the plane and went to Corfu, where I didn't pick up a club for two weeks. We spent the time fishing and swimming and declined an opportunity to become extras in the film *The Greek Tycoon*, about Aristotle Onassis' life and starring Anthony Quinn. I guess it might have paid a bit more than I had earned from golf in those recent months.

We returned to England, rather than America, after the holiday. The original plan for three weeks in England had become three months, with Corfu thrown in, and I returned to golf in the Uniroyal International at Moor Park and finally got my hands on another cheque, if only for £168.

Rounds of 75–80 are not the stuff of potential British Open champions and I missed the cut at Turnberry in that most memorable of championships, in which Watson beat

Nicklaus by a shot after each had opened 68–70–66, with Watson shooting 65 in the final round to Nicklaus's 66. If only I hadn't taken the wrong club on the 17th two years earlier and it had been me instead of Watson who had claimed the auld claret jug, who knows what might have been. But you can't live in the past.

––––––––––

It felt like a breath of fresh air to return to America. There had been so many twists and turns in just a few short months and I had made a few decisions. Deep down I hoped to do what Tony Jacklin had done: go in and get out of both the US and European circuits. I now see this as being indecisive. Having made the decision to go to the States, I should have stuck to it instead of having two bob each way.

My best result in '77 was tenth in the Colgate Hall of Fame Classic at Pinehurst late in the year, where I shot 73, 66, 68, 70 to win $5500. Without that finish I would have lost my card. It was a tough initiation; I had not had to qualify for any tournament since 1971 and that took a bit of coming to terms with.

The first half of 1978 was much the same. I picked up cheques in the Greater Greensboro Open, the New Orleans Open ($3400 for that one paid a few bills) and the Atlanta Classic. Obviously I wasn't exempt for the US Open and I chose to try to prequalify at the Atlanta Athletic Club in Georgia, which is one hell of a tough course. A field of 180 was playing for eighteen spots in the Open and I missed by a shot. But there was a consolation that year for Tour players who didn't make it into the Open. US PGA Tour boss Deane Beman decided to schedule the $100 000 Buick

Open at Warwick Hills Country Club in Grand Blanc, Michigan, for the same week.

While they may have preferred to be at Cherry Hills for the Open, there were some pretty handy players going around at Warwick Hills, among them Jim Nelford, Craig Stadler, John Mahaffey, Orville Moody, Jerry Heard, Frank Beard, Bobby Cole and D.A. Weibring.

Jackie found us a very convenient motel near the course. None of the other golfers were staying there and later in the week we realised perhaps why. Jackie was seven months pregnant and spent a fair amount of time at the motel because she was tired. She noticed a lot of coming and going, cars arriving and departing throughout the day, and it wasn't long before she discovered that the Skylark Motel was aptly named. She saw that a lot of the blokes from the nearby car factories were bringing their girlfriends, or what have you, to the motel for a sly Billy Galoot, and that the rooms were let by the hour as well as by the day and week.

Rounds of 72, 67 and 70 gave me a one-shot lead over Cole and American Rex Caldwell, but I was feeling terrible. I had a heavy cold for much of the week caused by the air-conditioning in the motel, and on the morning of the final round I had a really belting sinus headache. I teed off and by the 5th hole was really doing it tough. I had taken medication through the week for the cold, but it got to the point where I thought I would have to pull out of the tournament even though I was leading.

Jackie was walking the course and had teamed up with another woman who was very pregnant as well. I told Jackie I was considering quitting at the 9th if I didn't feel any better. I had gotten to the stage where I couldn't even bend over to tee up the ball or pick it up on the green. On the 1st, Jackie had told her companion about my sinus headache and the woman had offered to go home and get her medication as she suffered from the same ailment, but Jackie declined because she didn't want me mixing my pills.

But at the 5th she knew I was in real trouble and it was at that point she asked the woman if she would mind fetching the medication after all. She lived quite a distance from the course and I had played the 9th hole, going out two over and surrendering the lead, before she turned up again. She told me that the pill, Teledrin, would take fifteen minutes to have an effect. I birdied the 10th and by the 11th the headache was completely gone. Further birdies at the 12th and 14th took me to eight under and I came to the last hole needing a four to tie American Mike Sullivan. I pulled my drive damn near out of bounds and then had to play my second over trees to the green. Two putts later I was in a sudden-death play-off.

The first play-off hole was the 16th, a par 5, and I drove into a fairway trap. Sullivan's drive was perfect, but he pushed his second into trees just off the green while I played an iron out of the bunker and down the fairway. My third shot gave me a 15-foot birdie putt while Sullivan came out of the trees and then knocked it to 4 feet, giving him a putt for par.

He didn't need to attempt it when I rolled in my birdie putt for my first win on the US circuit, a victory which meant a cheque for $20 000. It was the sixth play-off in which I'd been involved, and the only one I had lost was to Tom Watson.

It was certainly a great feeling. We had done it tough since settling in the States and it was a good win on a good golf course. It also meant I had a year's exemption from pre-qualifying. You couldn't put a price on that.

There was, however, a moment of real unpleasantness through the week. During the second round I was paired with an American, Brady Miller, and a third player whose name time has erased. At the 9th hole we were warned for slow play. It was Miller who was the problem. He was battling to make the cut and was one of those annoying players who started to do his yardages and put on his glove only when it was his turn to play. I turned to him and said, 'Listen, Brady, we're not the slow players. You're the one who's holding us up, so get your arse in gear. None of us wants to blow the tournament because of a two-shot penalty.' He picked up his game and I thought nothing more of the incident.

Next stop on the circuit was the Canadian Open at Glen Abbey. I was drawn to play with Johnny Miller and Danny Edwards in the first two rounds, but Miller was a late withdrawal and, bugger me dead, it was Brady Miller who turned up on the tee as first alternate.

It blew a gale that day and we were late off. Best score in the clubhouse was a 67 by Jeff Hewes, but no one else broke 70. Ben Crenshaw and Arnold Palmer both had a one-under 70, while only three players, Shearer among them, fired a 71. I was more than happy with a 72 in the hurricane-like conditions. Miller opened with a 77.

Our tee time the next day was 8.06 a.m. and I went through my usual routine on the practice fairway followed by a session on the practice putting green. As I was walking towards the first tee, PGA Tour official Jack Sterling came over to me and said, 'Jack, you're disqualified.'

Sterling, who had surely had a personality by-pass somewhere along the line, was known as something of a policeman on the Tour and during my short time on it I reckoned he had given me a couple of dud rulings. But this was something else.

'Disqualified! What do you mean I'm disqualified?' I thundered back at him. The blood was very definitely rising to my head.

'On the first hole you played yesterday [which was actually the 10th], your caddie stood on your line when you were putting,' Sterling replied.

I was dumbfounded and searched the memory bank to remember what had happened on the 10th green. My caddie was the son of a lawyer who was one of the committeemen of Glen Abbey. I was going through a few problems with my putting that week, having trouble in getting the putter back, so I wasn't taking any practice strokes. Just line it up and hit it.

The pin on the 10th was set back left on the very long green, 40–50 yards long, and my second shot just made the green. My first putt finished about 6 feet short and I walked up and told Miller and Edwards I'd finish out. My caddie had been standing next to the golf bag where I had hit my first putt from, and thinking he had time for me to have a couple of practice swings, he hoisted the bag over his shoulder and started walking around the circumference of the green, believing he had time to get past my line of vision before I putted. Suddenly he saw that I was putting and stopped. He was maybe 35 yards away from me and off the green and

I hadn't noticed him at all. I holed the putt and away we went to the 11th tee.

Someone had gone to the PGA officials and told them I'd used my caddie to stand on my putting line. It was a pretty hot rule at the time. Johnny Miller used to get his caddie down behind him and line up his putter blade, saying, 'Yes, that's right', and the caddie would remain there as Miller putted. The rule had then been changed to say a caddie could not stand on or near the line while a player made his shot.

God damn it! My caddie had been 35 yards behind me. 'How far back is the line? Does this mean that someone 200 yards away could be classed as on a player's line?' I said to Sterling.

He said, 'The way the rule reads, it means infinity', to which I replied, 'Bullshit.'

The incident had been reported and I was, indeed, disqualified. Edwards, whom I always regarded as a wimp, had, according to Sterling, said 'Maybe' when asked whether my caddie had erred.

'What the hell is going on here? Surely you should have given me the opportunity to put my case. You've taken the word of one man and another bloke who said "maybe" and disqualified me out of the golf tournament. In any court of law, you've got the right to defend yourself,' I shouted at Sterling. I was steaming and began accusing him of bias against foreign players.

'That's the decision and it's final,' he said.

I gave Deane Beman a serve when he arrived at the course as well. To me, it all smelt of a slight to a foreign player and finally it was agreed I should have been given the right to defend myself. Chi Chi Rodriguez, Lee Trevino and Raymond Floyd all went to bat for me over the incident and I guess it was the turning point of my acceptance on the US Tour.

I later found out that Brady Miller had told some of the Americans he would get me for the slow-play incident – and it hadn't taken long. But his dues were that he was ostracised by many of those players who are real sticklers for the rules. And so they should be. Golf remains the one self-regulatory sport we have.

It was a very sour week. The Canadian Open was a tournament I'd earmarked because it was a course you couldn't chip and putt your way around. You had to be a good ball-striker and par on that course really meant something. I thought it was my sort of course.

Jackie decided to have the baby in Sydney because we really didn't have a permanent home, or doctor, in the States. So after the Canadian Open, it was time for her to depart. My parents, particularly my mother, were keen to be around, but I felt I should stay in the US for several more tournaments with my newly won exempt status.

Kristie Newton came into the world on 16 August 1978. Jackie and I had already decided that if it was a girl she would be either Kristie or Kim, and I made the final choice. We didn't want two names, nor did we want a name that could be shortened. It was pro-am day of the Westchester Classic and I had finished playing and practising when the news came through from Sydney mid-afternoon. I was staying with Bob Cooney, a Wall Street banker, and his wife, Marlene, whom I had first met with Bruce Devlin on my trip to the States in 1969. They'd planned a dinner party that night with me and Bob and Kathie Shearer, but we got into the celebrations at the golf club instead, along with US Tour pro Roger Maltbie.

The champagne and cigars came out and it became a right session. It's fair to say I was feeling no pain as the evening wore on. At one stage I had the palm of my hand outstretched on the table and Roger, without looking at what he was doing, mistook it for an ashtray and stubbed his cigar out on it. I barely noticed at the time, but it sure as hell hurt the next day, and the scar remains today.

I opened the Westchester with a 69, four off the pace set by Barry Jaeckel but in a tie for 12th. After that I dropped down the board with rounds of 73, 71 and 71 for a cheque for $1230. I was in the money again the following week at the Colgate Hall of Fame Classic at Pinehurst, but then missed the cut at the BC Open a week later. There were still five tournaments remaining for the year but I decided to call it quits and head home immediately. I had a wife and baby daughter to see.

The plane arrived at Sydney Airport just after 6 a.m. and I grabbed a cab for the journey across town to my parents' house in Carlingford. As we pulled into the street I asked the cabbie to stop and lugged my baggage the last 100 metres or so to the house. I hadn't told anyone I was coming home and I wanted to surprise them. Surprise them I did.

My performances on the 1978–79 Australian circuit were nothing to write home about. I tied for seventh in the Victorian PGA championship, which was won by a fired-up

Lanny Wadkins, who'd been accused by promoter Doug Mason of not trying in his opening 75. I was tied fourth in both the New South Wales Open and, in early 1979, the inaugural Australian Masters at Huntingdale.

Back in '76 we had bought a house at Warners Bay on Lake Macquarie near Newcastle, and on our return to the States in 1979 we felt we needed a more permanent home than a rented unit. Jackie was none too keen on Myrtle Beach because, as a golfing resort area, it was pretty much male-orientated, but the male prevailed. A small block of units was being erected at the back of a little lake and we knew the builder, so we put in our order with colour schemes and other specifications we wanted. We'd taken another step towards being Americanised and the process was almost complete when we reluctantly parted with the rotary Mazda in favour of a Buick. The arrival of Kristie brought new responsibilities and a proper home and larger car were part and parcel of that.

My golf started to pay our way. The Nicklaus-designed Glen Abbey course, venue of the Canadian Open, was indeed my sort of course – well, for a round anyway, when I fired a 64, knocking three shots off the course record, to open the 1979 championship. Despite rounds of 74–73, I was still in contention going into the final day. I was paired with none other than Tom Watson in the last group. Neither of us played well – Watson shot 78 and I had 79 – and Trevino came from behind to win.

Tom and I played a few practice rounds through the years but were rarely drawn together in a tournament. The first time after the British Open play-off was in the first two rounds of the 1976 Colgate Champion of Champions at Victoria GC in Melbourne, where organisers obviously had a sense of the dramatic. It may have been the alphabetical thing that we weren't drawn together more often, as I regularly met Johnny Miller on the first tee of a tournament.

Trevino was another who seemed to be a regular companion. Most of the guys preferred not to partner him because he liked to talk along the way. But having played many practice rounds with him I knew his weakness was a good dirty joke. If he was getting in my ear and driving me nuts, I'd scan the gallery and say, 'See that girl over there? She's hot to trot. Jeez, we had a great night last night.'

I then had control of the conversation and Lee would hang on every word as I gave graphic details of a fictitious night of lust.

There were some guys I hated being drawn with, like J.C. Snead and Leonard Thompson. They were whingers, grizzleguts, but also very tough cookies and very fiery. They were the sort of blokes who always reckoned it was them who got the bad breaks, that this putt should have gone in, that it was always their ball coming to rest in a divot mark. They would get to you. I don't say it was intentional, just part of their character, their make-up. You had to be prepared for them and keep away so you could concentrate on your own game.

In England I'd always found it hard to play with Brian Barnes. He's a good mate of mine, but always gave me the impression he wasn't trying. If he got a bad break, it would be a shrug of the shoulders and the words: 'Oh well, I'll be fishing tomorrow.'

Next thing you'd know he'd be dragging you down to thinking along the same lines, especially if it was you who had the bad break or missed a putt. Then he would make three birdies in a row, and while he was no longer thinking about fishing the next day, you were.

Nor did I enjoy playing with the likes of Peter Croker in Australia. He used to stuff around all day and get you to the point where you wanted to take him by the throat and shake him, saying, 'Hurry up!'

It's all a personal thing. Some can handle it; others can't. That's where the psychology of the game has changed so much. The more a player is educated not to let outside influences distract him, the better he'll play. The greatest example of a blinkered approach was at St Andrews when I was playing with Jack Nicklaus with the hydrofoil going across and back over the Firth of Forth. He didn't even hear it. It's all related to what Bobby Locke told me before the 1975 British Open: it's the 15th club, the one between your ears.

Take the week I won the Australian Open. All sorts of things happened that week that under normal circumstances would be distracting, but I was in a zone where nothing anyone said or did bothered me. It's the same with most sportspeople I know who have had their moment of triumph.

America is, of course, famous for its hustling, both on the golf course and on the pool table. In the early days Shearer and I fell victim to a couple of blokes at the pool table. Shears is an excellent snooker and pool player and we were at his club, Baytree, having a few beers and shooting a little pool one afternoon when we got into a challenge. Bob and I held the table, playing for $5 a game, and two guys kept challenging. We won five or six games with the stakes rising in each to a stage where it was $50 a game, and Bob and I were about $150 each ahead. Suddenly the standard of the opposition rose dramatically, as did the stake, which became $100, and we were cleaned out in no time.

We had a friend, a good two-marker from Florida, who each year in early spring would start down south and work his way up the eastern seaboard, playing golf for cash. In each town he had between eight and twelve guys whom he played each year and bets according to handicap were arranged. He was so good that he could score in a manner where some of the guys maybe won a little or lost a little, but he would really take one of them to the cleaners. The next day, and for several days after that, they'd play again and it would be the same situation. By week's end everyone had been taken for what they had, but they all reckoned they'd had a good time. So good, in fact, that arrangements were inevitably made for the following year. Our mate always had $100 000 cash on him and his clients were always eager to see him. At nights he proved equally proficient on the pool table. He was making around $250 000 a year in cash money by following the sun, which didn't seem a bad way to make a living.

A guy known as the Turk was another who liked a big bet, and one day at North Myrtle Beach he took on another big punter, Tyson Leonard, owner of a local nightclub, for $10 000 a hole. The Turk turned up with his money in a brown paper bag and carrying a sawn-off shotgun, while his opponent brought his accountant, who had his cash in a briefcase. Shears and I followed them around in a buggy for the full eighteen holes, just wishing we could get a slice of the action. Neither player broke 100 and there were just a couple of holes the difference at the end. And by the way, the shotgun wasn't necessary.

The guys on the Tour notorious for playing for money were Ray Floyd, Wadkins, Watson, Tom Weiskopf, Lon Hinkle, Arnold Palmer, Moody, Trevino and, to a degree, Nicklaus. Tuesday practice was always betting day, with the $100 Nassau and one or two down presses being played.

We were playing $100 for each nine and $100 for the match, but the two presses meant you could press the opposition for a new game for $100 to cover what was left of the nine. All other bets carried on as before. It could get awfully expensive. One such game was against Trevino and Moody. My partner was Frank Conner, a former US junior tennis champion who'd turned to professional golf, and he arranged all the bets. I barely saw him all day, as he spent most of his time in the bushes, and I made a birdie 3 at the last for a 65 after pressing to save $2000, but it still cost me $1000. Moody and Trevino were awesome when the cash was on.

They don't have legal betting on tournaments in the US but they do in England, and there have been times when players have helped themselves to the bookies' cash. Not only could you bet on the tournament result but also player against player in a particular round. During a John Player Classic at Turnberry one year, Tony Jacklin had shot 69 in the first round and Harry Bannerman 81. Next day, Bannerman walked into the betting shop and enquired the odds of his beating Jacklin on second-round scores. He was quoted 12–1 and had 500 quid on it.

Sure enough, Bannerman picked up his game – plus £6000. I'm not suggesting Harry played dead in his opening round, but six grand was a pretty big spur for him to better the former US and British Open champion's score in the second round.

One of the biggest bets I ever heard of was relayed to me by Brian Jones, who these days has stopped counting his millions because of a lack of form. (He's hanging on for the Seniors Tour, which he'll be eligible for in late 2001.) It happened during the Asahi Glass Four Tours event, in which the US was playing Australia with third and fourth places at stake. As Jonesy tells the story, the players were on a bus on the way to the course when Greg Norman said to American Hal Sutton, 'I want to play you in today's matches.'

'Fine by me,' replied Sutton.

'Not only do I want to play you, I want to play you for what we make,' Norman said. Given that third money was $30 000, it was a not inconsiderable bet, and Norman duly beat Sutton.

The stories of Trevino hustling for a living before joining the pro tour are legendary. Not so well known is that Calvin Peete did the same thing. You could imagine the well-heeled chaps who fancied themselves at golf stumbling over each other to get a slice of the action against a little black guy who had a deformed elbow. Calvin had eighteen brothers and sisters and when he wasn't hustling drove a station wagon crammed with watches, jewellery and clothing to sell to migrant workers.

When he finally did turn pro, he became well known for his big-money bets, especially with Palmer. Calvin was a fascinating character, an original. He never carried much cash, but as a safeguard against any unknown expense that might crop up along the way he bought two diamonds and had them inserted in his front teeth.

There was never much danger of his running short of a dollar. He had a big black travel van with all the home comforts built in, which was capable of doing 200 km/h, and not to put too fine a point on it, he had as travelling companions a few ladies of the night. With his percentages, it didn't matter if he missed the odd cut or three.

Jackie Gleason gave every appearance that he probably didn't need a stand-in to play the shots in the movie *The Hustler*, in which he played Minnesota Fats. One year at the Houston Open, played on Doug Sanders' home course of Woodlands, Gleason and the real Minnesota Fats put on a great exhibition for the players and guests on pro-am night. That night we also had a player–celebrity pool competition and I discovered, when two thousand people booed me, that you shouldn't beat Palmer at anything. I didn't reach the final, but Shearer did and played Bunkie Henry, who was one of the knockabout guys on the Tour.

I became Shears' manager – brought him the drinks, in other words – and when he put the eight-ball in, we claimed victory. But all hell broke loose because the Americans play a nine-ball game, with the ninth ball having to be railed in instead of played straight into the hole. Henry was declared the winner, but Shears and I always reckon Shears won.

Our son, Clint, was born on 18 June 1981 in Myrtle Beach and quite fancied himself as a Yank in his youth. He does have an American passport as well as an Australian one, but these days he is a true-blue Aussie.

It was at the Southern Open in San Antonio in 1982 that I decided to quit the US. I was playing badly and fired an 81 in the first round. I just packed my bags and walked away; I'd had a gutful. Jackie was already back in Australia with the kids and I was sharing a flat with Buddy Gardner and Bill Calfee. Just as Crampton had said some years before, it was my turn to say, 'Stuff it. That's it – I'm finished.'

I flew to Dallas and then Los Angeles, where I got the first flight back to Australia. It was a spur-of-the-moment decision and I hadn't given a lot of thought to what would come next, but there was an enormous sense of relief. I'd taken a giant weight off my shoulders. I hadn't been successful in America, apart from two reasonably good years, and it's the sort of place where if you're a little bit off your game they'll kill you. It's a numbers game. If you're playing well it's the only place to be, because it just flows, everything is easy. But it can be hell if you are down.

I'd had the injury problems, firstly with the foot and in '82 a 'golfer's elbow'. This is the opposite of a tennis elbow, which is on the outside; the golfer's elbow is on the inside. I'd started off having an injection every six months from early 1980 and it had got to once a week by the time I walked away. It wasn't like it is now, with a big-money tournament every week. These days you can quit for six weeks, like the doctor advised, but then you couldn't afford to. You had to keep grinding it out.

I needed time to regroup and get rid of the injuries.

I never felt I was at the crossroads of my career, but rather that I needed to get my game back. I was 33, still young and strong enough to handle it, but had to sort out my swing problems and there didn't seem to be anyone who could help me.

I hadn't said goodbye to America forever. I was quite prepared to go back there, but needed to get away from the place to sort myself out. I honestly believed that my best years were still in front of me. I felt mentally stronger than I'd ever been and had myself more under control, and felt I was a more stable person because of my family responsibilities.

My last tournament as a professional was the 1983 Western Australian Open. I shot 68 to tie Terry Gale, who was already in the clubhouse, and it was near dark when we went out for the play-off. After three holes we were still tied, and as we walked to the 18th tee it was so dark that I knew it would be the last hole we could play that day. I hit a good drive down the left side of the fairway, where most of the gallery was congregated, and reckoned it would leave me with a 7- or 8-iron to the green. My ball hit a guy on the leg and went straight left underneath a bush, and all I could do was chip out sideways.

Terry knocked his second onto the green while I played my third to the green. I missed my putt and he two-putted for his par and victory. That was my final hurrah and the rest, as they say, is history. Save, that is, for one small detail.

Some months after the accident, when I was back on deck and doing television commentary, I was on the same flight to Perth as Terry. He sat opposite me across the aisle. Over the Nullarbor he handed me a cheque. I said, 'What's that for?' and Terry replied, 'I've worked out the difference between first and second in that play-off, and that's what the balance is. I haven't put any money into the other things and I just wanted this to be between you and me.'

It was typical Terry Gale. He can be blunt, but he is genuine. That touching gesture I will long remember.

The accident – and a fight for life

After the accident, in July 1983, I lapsed in and out of consciousness. My recollection of the waking moments is vivid to this day, but I knew nothing of what was occurring in the outside world, so in this chapter I'll let Peter Stone take up the story.

I remember seeing Jackie by my side constantly; I heard the priest at the end of the hospital bed giving me the last rites; and I saw our kids, so vibrant and young, their lives still ahead of them. I am fortunate to be alive – I had a very good team on my side and thank them for their care. I fought for my life and they fought for it, too. I'm eternally grateful for the outcome.

The decision by six mates from the Newcastle area to fly to Sydney to watch the Sydney Swans clash with Melbourne in the Victorian Football League competition on Sunday 24 July 1983 was made on the spur of the moment.

Jack Newton, Frank D'Arcy, Neil Gaudion, Rod McPherson, Greg McCallum and pilot Ron Lake had made the trip in the past in Lake's Cessna 210 and it seemed the perfect way to spend a murky winter's afternoon.

They left Belmont airfield on the outskirts of Newcastle around midday, and on arrival at Sydney Airport, Lake parked the plane at the Flight Facilities Terminal for light aircraft and helicopters. The men then walked 100 or so metres to hail a taxi.

Though the cab was only licensed to take five passengers, the driver agreed to take the six and they were dropped off at the Sydney Cricket Ground forty minutes before the first bounce. They ate and then settled back to watch the Swans beat Melbourne by thirteen points. Through the match they had half a dozen beers, a shout each, with Lake, of course, on soft drink, and later joined the after-match entertainment in the supporters' club section at the back of the ground. They telephoned for a taxi and a couple of beers later it turned up. This time, the driver refused to take all six.

Lake, McCallum, Gaudion and McPherson took the cab while Newton and D'Arcy rang for a second car. They waited. There was no particular drama as it would take Lake some time to submit his flight plan to the authorities. But it was a cold, wet night, the sort to keep taxi drivers busy, and the SCG is never an easy place to get a cab. A second call to the cab company was made and Newton and D'Arcy were given the stock reply: 'First available'. Thirty minutes passed from the time their mates had left and there was still no sign of the second cab, at which point one of the promotional girls on the Swans' staff offered to drive them to the airport.

The Swans were new to Sydney. A year earlier, the old South Melbourne club had been dying and the VFL, in its wisdom, had aided and abetted the transplant of the Swans into rugby league's stronghold. But the need was there for promotion – and cash. On the way to the airport, Newton and the girl from the Swans began discussing a golf day for the Aussie Rules team and they were still sifting through the possibilities on arrival at the Flight Facilities Terminal.

The Cessna 210 was not where it had been parked and D'Arcy offered to go and find their mates while Newton continued his conversation. D'Arcy was back within two or three minutes, saying, 'I've found them.'

'Fine. I'll be there in a second,' Newton replied. Five minutes or so later he left the car and walked through the cattle-gate side entrance to where the planes were parked. On previous trips the friends had not walked through the main building, but rather took that side entrance.

JACK • *The lights were on the plane as I walked through the gate and as I reached the edge of the tarmac, with the plane maybe 40 metres away, it started to move off, but only very slowly. I ran after it, a bit like chasing after a moving bus. Just instinct. I was on the right-hand side of the plane and tried to attract the attention of the pilot, but he was on the left and didn't see me. I ran towards the left-hand side, waving, trying to get his attention.*

Then Frank D'Arcy was pushing me down to the ground, saying, 'Stay down, stay down.'

*I tried to get up, saying, 'I'm all right, I'm all right,' but he
wouldn't listen and continued to hold me down. The last thing I
remember is the paramedics putting a balloon-type thing around
me and placing me in an ambulance.*

Jack Newton's right arm was severed on impact and thrown
15 metres into the air. D'Arcy, a trained lifesaver, was by
his side within seconds and pressed his body against Newton's
in a bid to stem the flow of blood pumping from his mate's
body. They talked as they waited for the ambulance and
talked some more on the 45-minute journey to the hospital.
The propeller of the aircraft had sliced at a 45-degree angle
through the entire right side of Newton's body, from the
hip to the shoulder and the eye.

Jackie Newton was sitting at home in Warners Bay, near
Newcastle, sewing up a pair of her husband's trousers in
preparation for his brief trip to Europe the following week
for the Irish Open at Royal Dublin. It was around eight
o'clock, maybe a fraction later, when there was a knock at
the back door. She was expecting Jack home from Sydney
at any time, but it wasn't him standing in the doorway.

Two of her girlfriends, Denise Maclean and Toni Hayes,
were there and they were ashen-faced. The words came
tumbling out: Jack had been involved in an accident on the
plane in Sydney. All the other boys were fine; it was just
Jack. They didn't know much, only what had been relayed
to them by an Aero Pelican pilot who had telephoned to say
Jack had been taken to Sydney's Prince of Wales Hospital.

Jackie picked up the phone and spoke to a doctor in the

emergency room at the hospital. 'Come as quickly as possible. I don't think Jack is going to make it,' were the chilling words. There was little time for detail, save for the fact that her husband had lost an arm and was critically injured.

While Jackie spoke on the phone, her girlfriends' husbands, Dick Maclean and Brian Hayes, arrived. Kristie and Clint were asleep and after throwing a few clothes in a bag, Jackie quietly went to their rooms to kiss them without waking them. Denise and Dick took care of the children while Brian and Jackie set out on the two-hour drive to Sydney.

JACKIE • It was one of the longest drives I've ever had. Would I see Jack again? He might be dead by the time we arrived. A million things ran through my head and Brian left me to talk if I wanted to. He was great. It was the not knowing – not knowing whether by the time I got there it would be too late.

———————

Mr Jim Nield, consulting surgeon to the Prince of Wales Hospital, was on call on the evening of 24 July 1983 and was reading at his home just a kilometre from the hospital when the telephone rang. Someone had walked into the propeller blade of a light aircraft and was being taken straight to the operating theatre. Similar calls were received by the late Professor Fred Hollows, world-renowned eye specialist, and plastic surgeon Michael Baldwin; the three eminent doctors made haste to the hospital in Randwick. Nield arrived within two minutes of receiving the telephone call and after scrubbing up went to the theatre, where the anaesthetist and resuscitation team were already assembled.

'It's Jack Newton,' Nield was told. As a keen golfer and member of the Australian GC in Sydney, Nield needed no further information. The injuries were horrific, the like of which he had not seen before. Apart from the severed right arm, half the liver was mutilated as was the small bowel. There was generalised bleeding and the patient had lost a considerable part of the abdominal wall. The gall bladder was a lost cause.

It was immediately assessed that nothing could be done to save the arm. It was far too mutilated even to consider surgery to reattach it to Newton's body. As Nield worked on the abdominal injuries, Baldwin grafted skin from the severed arm onto the gaping wound on the stump. While he wasn't involved in the surgical procedure, Professor Hollows worked on the right eye. Six hours later, their work was done and not one of the three doctors knew whether or not it had all been in vain.

Newton's parents, Jack and Meg, were at the hospital when Jackie arrived. So, too, were the other men from the aircraft and they all sat and waited as the life-and-death struggle continued in the operating theatre. There was little talk. What could be said? All that could be done was to hope and pray.

Shortly before 3 a.m., Nield and the operating team emerged. Nield spoke with Jackie and with Jack's parents and gave his honest assessment of the chances of survival. The odds, he said, were 50–1. Jackie, accompanied by a nurse, went into the intensive-care ward.

JACKIE • *It is hard to see the man you love in such a horrific condition. I could hardly see Jack for bandages and tubes. I looked in hope to where his arm had been; it was gone. A sense of helplessness and despair went through me. How could this be? The fight for life was on. That was the dearest thing. Whether it had been saved, only time could answer.*

After just a few hours' sleep, Jim Nield was given a report on Newton's condition before going to another hospital on the Monday morning to do the rounds of his patients. Jack was in a relatively stable condition and his chances of survival had marginally improved.

Later in the morning, as Nield drove to the Prince of Wales, he saw a newspaper poster: NEWTON SURGERY FAILS. He was deeply upset. The six hours of surgery had *not* failed and Newton was clinging to life. The newspaper told of him losing his arm, which was justification for the screaming banner.

Jackie did not leave her husband's side for almost forty-eight hours as he fought for the life he had so enjoyed. Decisions were made. The children would remain at home in the care of Denise and Dick Maclean, but Kristie was withdrawn from preschool to protect her from the inquisitive questioning of youth. Newspapers were kept out of the house and the television was turned off at news time.

Jackie decided to remain at the hospital in one of the rooms provided for relatives of patients instead of going across Sydney with Jack's parents to Carlingford, or to one of the many hotel rooms that were offered. She wanted to be close to Jack and away from the press and public. The hospital provided that sanctuary.

Two days later, Newton had improved dramatically and his father told the media, 'Jack has been incredibly courageous. Doctors told me that at one stage they thought he had gone.'

JACK • I woke up dazed and aware I was in hospital, but not really sure why. I knew I had all these tubes in me and felt a sort of pain in my shoulder and arm. I reached for it, but there was nothing there. A nurse said, 'It's gone.'

My mind screamed, 'No, no, no!' and I lapsed back into unconsciousness.

Jackie sat with her husband from 8 a.m. to ten or eleven o'clock at night. She talked, but Jack couldn't as he was still on a respirator. He scrawled notes with his left hand, awkward and barely legible. One of the early ones said, '1. You write. 2. I can't. Still in intensive care. 3. Many disappointments. 4. My golfing finished.'

Another read: 'I feel well within myself; however, with my guts so sore it's difficult both physically and mentally to say, "Right, I'm in control of this."'

Later the resolve was there: 'It's all a mental thing. I've got this thing beaten.'

Jackie took each note with her and to this day they represent a resilience in the man she loves.

'We should go for a walk together,' said a later note, and Jackie still smiles at that. Through the first nine years of their married life, Jack had hated going for walks.

JACKIE • He was sort of trying to apologise to me for what had happened, and he didn't need to. I found it hard. I didn't want to show any weakness and if I felt I wanted to bawl my eyes out

I normally left the room. I was in a little shell. No one else, save for his parents and his grandmother, was allowed to visit him, and I was in a cocoon as I sat beside him.

When I walked out the doors of intensive care, there was the world. I had to talk openly when I faced reality and a lot of people found it hard, maybe harsh in some ways, when I spoke freely about the accident. Some people walked away and I thought, 'Maybe I'm saying too much,' but then I reasoned, 'That's not me. I have to keep talking about it.' The only way to cope with any situation is to talk about it.

Five days after the accident, Jackie felt ready to face the media. To that point Jack Sr had faced the brunt of the press interest, which was considerable. After all, Jack was a winner on the US circuit, a multi-winner on the European and British circuits and the 1979 Australian Open champion. He'd lost a play-off to Tom Watson for the 1975 British Open championship and tied second behind Seve Ballesteros in the 1980 US Masters.

The hospital public-relations person, Liz Shaw, organised a general media conference at which only one guideline was laid down: Jackie would not answer specific questions on the accident itself. The doctors, the nursing staff and all who had come in contact with her in the hospital were starting to marvel at her qualities and the media was captivated, too.

'I'm going to be his caddie. Jack is so courageous. We're going to win this one,' she said.

JACKIE • I had always stayed in the background whenever Jack won a tournament. All of a sudden I was pushed to the fore and

*had to find the strength to get up and say what had to be said.
I found it difficult, but must have been given the inner strength
to do it. I had a feeling that the media were genuinely worried
about Jack and they didn't ask me too many hard questions.*

Others were worried about Jack as well. Bob Shearer, his
mate for so many years, along with Jack Nicklaus, Gary
Player, Ballesteros and Greg Norman, taped a television
message of encouragement during the Canadian Open on the
Glen Abbey course, a course that Newton had always felt he
could conquer. Phone calls swamped the Prince of Wales
Hospital, with Nicklaus, Shearer, Lee Trevino, Bruce Devlin
and many more ringing, including the then prime minister,
Bob Hawke. Jack's play-off this time was with death and he
had a worldwide gallery on his side for the fight.

In Australia a fund was started at the instigation of
Graham Lovett, managing director of Slazenger. Among
those on the organising committee were Australian PGA
Tour executive director Keith Sillett, former Australian Test
captain Ian Chappell, Newton's solicitor and former Shield
cricketer Michael Hill, and Greg McCallum, who had been
on the plane that fateful night. Newton was still fighting for
his life and the trust wasn't so much for him as for Jackie
and the kids should Jack die. But the odds were getting
better.

The improvement in Jack's condition was such that after
a week he was taken off the respirator and moved to a less
critical intensive-care ward. Jackie decided the children
should stay with their grandparents in Sydney, which would

allow them to be brought to the hospital each day for a couple of hours to see their mother. The time was still not right for them to see their father.

On Kristie and Clint's first visit, Jackie drove to the cliff at Coogee, to a children's playground, and there she explained what had happened to their father. Clint, aged two, was too young to really understand, but Kristie, soon to turn five, was not.

JACKIE • I felt I needed to talk to them on my own. 'What's the matter with Daddy?' Kristie asked.

'Daddy's had an accident, he's very sick and he's lost his arm,' I told her.

'What do you mean?'

I said, 'Well, his arm is no longer there.'

'But Mummy, he won't be able to cuddle me any more.'

'Don't worry. He's got one big arm to cuddle with and he'll give you a cuddle with that.'

'Mummy, has it really gone?'

'Yes, it's gone to heaven.'

'Will it grow again?' Kristie asked, and she looked like she was going to cry. I hugged her as I tried to explain what had happened. The children were both young enough to accept it and not try to look into it in any great detail.

Jackie continued to sit with her husband in intensive care for up to sixteen hours a day. They talked. She read the hundreds of messages of support, but it wasn't a time to start planning for the future. He was no longer on the critical list, but the healing process had only just begun.

JACK • I don't know how long it was, but I started to feel all right. I mean, I was pretty knocked around, but I didn't feel in any great danger. I felt halfway okay and remember them changing the bandages and actually getting me out of bed and putting me in a chair, taking me around the side of intensive care to sit me in the sun. I dreaded them pulling me out of bed and putting me in the chair as it was agony. 'You've got to do it,' they said.

Suddenly, Newton fell dramatically ill again. Originally the large bowel had appeared quite viable, but it had begun failing and Jim Nield had made the decision to remove a large portion of it. After that operation, septicaemia, a virulent blood poisoning, took over Newton's body to threaten his multi-organ function – the heart, kidneys and lungs. He also contracted pneumonia.

His condition deteriorated to such an extent that the doctors again warned Jackie and his parents that he might not live. The next ten days, they said, would be crucial. It was literally a matter of waiting while Jack lay attached again to a respirator. His kidneys were failing.

But as each day dawned he was still alive, and that was at least something. Jackie maintained her bedside vigil but didn't talk much. Looks and holding of hands meant far more.

JACKIE • The important thing was for Jack to fight for life. He had to want to live and I couldn't show any weakness. He needed strength and love. He was on death row and I could tell he knew it. One thing that helped me was that in the bed next to Jack was a young man called Craig Hazell, a garbo who had had an accident with the garbage truck. There appeared to be nothing wrong with him. He didn't have one bandage on him, but he was lying there in a coma. To this day he is still in a coma and years of his life have been lost.

As I watched Craig lying there it made me realise how lucky I was, even though the man I loved was lying there with an arm missing, without the sight of one eye and with horrific injuries, fighting for his life. At least I could talk to Jack and he could acknowledge me holding his hand, whereas that boy, without a mark on him, lay there with his parents and friends unable to communicate with him. It made me feel lucky.

Jackie spoke often with Warwick Thomas, the hospital chaplain. He was a neutral person and she found it easy to talk to him as talking with relatives and friends was always an emotional experience. She also sat alone in the chapel, where she found inner peace as she prayed.

JACKIE • I do believe in God, but I am very much a fatalist. I really believe that when it's your time, it's your time, wherever and whatever you might be doing. I didn't believe it was Jack's time, and thank goodness for that.

Another thing that helped Jackie greatly was the letters. There were suitcases full of them, some from people the family had never heard of, and she sat in the hospital cafeteria reading them. Again she drew strength from them and was able to transmit that strength to Jack. She took all the overseas telephone calls that came into the hospital, but it was physically impossible to answer the local calls.

Day became night and then day again and still there was no sign of an improvement in Jack's condition.

JACK • *I remember being in a ward with three beds and I saw a priest walking around my bed. It was at that point that I guessed things weren't all that good. My next recollection was of a bunch of doctors standing at the base of the bed looking at charts. I guess they were all putting their two bobs' worth in, trying to decide which was the best way to go.*

The two things that were to affect Newton for the rest of his life – the loss of an arm and an eye – were relatively unimportant in the scheme of things. Whether he would live or die would be determined by the abdominal injuries.

Jackie didn't count down the days, but rather took each one as it came. On the tenth day the crisis passed and Jack showed enough improvement to be taken off the respirator. Perhaps the greatest indication that he was on the road to recovery was when he started swearing again. Part of the respiratory assistance was an endotracheal tube inserted down his throat. It stayed in for ten days and was agony, particularly when it came out. It also had the effect of drying his mouth and tongue.

JACK • *I felt like I had bloody sandpaper on my tongue and one of the doctors told me I could suck some ice. I asked a nurse for ice and she refused. I went off my brain and swore at her horribly. She didn't want to come near me again but eventually it was sorted out and I got my ice. The morphine was having side effects, making me aggressive and angry. They took me off it and put me on pethidine instead.*

Kristie and Clint still hadn't seen their father since the accident. On their visits to Jackie the kids always wanted to see him, but the time still wasn't right. As they left Clint would cry, his screams echoing through the hospital corridors, and Kristie would stare at the big doors to intensive care and ask her mother, 'Why can't I go through?'

There were times when the intense emotional pressure of coping with the situation took Jackie to the brink.

JACKIE • Some nights, maybe ten or eleven at night, I would walk from the hospital across the grounds to the room where I was staying and in the pitch-black would scream to release the tension of the day and of the whole thing. Or I would have a good cry. The pressure would build up being with Jack all day; I could see his pain and he would get agitated, and then there was the problem of the children, who wanted to see their father. I needed to release the tension to continue to support Jack.

The doctors said he would go through a mourning period before he took on the next hurdle. To lose a limb is like losing a mother or father, or a divorce; you have to go through a death in the family to reach out to the next stage. Jack would get very agitated and swear at me a lot and the nurses would raise their eyebrows, saying, 'Does he normally talk like this?'

'No,' I would answer, 'but I'd rather him swearing than saying nothing at all.'

Sometimes I had to bite my tongue and say nothing, but given what he was going through, I think I would have been swearing too.

There was another operation to be performed, a colostomy, which would be reversed further down the track when Jack's large bowel was repaired by nature. But in the days following that ten-day period his recovery was dramatic and it became clear he was going to live. What sort of life he would have depended on the man himself.

It was time to see Kristie and Clint and the big day was 16 August, Kristie's fifth birthday and 23 days after the accident. Meg Newton was a little dubious about her grandchildren going into the intensive-care ward to see their daddy in his condition, and also because of the other people there, but Jackie felt they would be so excited at being reunited with their father that they would be oblivious to everything around them. The nurses organised a present for Kristie, a hippopotamus moneybox, and when the moment came it was exactly as Jackie had thought. The kids only had eyes for their dad. Nothing else mattered.

Clint tried to crawl all over Jack and there wasn't a spot he touched that didn't hurt. His father's smile belied any pain he might have felt and at that point Jackie realised that, no matter what happened, the children still had their dad. They could cope with everything.

JACK • *It felt like months since I'd seen them and I remember looking at them thinking how innocent they were and how unaware of what had happened. It was just so pure and it made me more determined as I thought to myself, 'If I cark it, they've got no father.'*

I didn't want them to go and was sad when they did, blubber-

ing like a deprived brat, but their visit left me with two thoughts. Firstly, I knew the severity of my injuries and secondly, I realised how important I was to three people in my life. Jackie was terrific from the word go, but the kids emphasised it even more.

That evening there was a little birthday party for Kristie at the home of Col and Annette McGregor, Kristie's godmother. As Jackie and the kids were leaving the party to return to the hospital where Jack's parents were sitting with their son, Clint caught his left eye on a brick wall and gashed himself quite badly. They ended up in Casualty at the hospital, where three stitches were inserted above Clint's eye.

As the doctor stitched, Clint hollered, and the doctor turned to Jackie, saying, 'Do you want to go out? You're not going to faint or anything, are you?' He hadn't recognised her.

She replied, 'After what I've seen in the last few weeks with my husband, I don't think this is going to make me faint.'

Mother and children then went to see Newton, where Clint proudly displayed his bad eye. 'Look, Daddy, I have a bad eye too.'

JACKIE • Seeing the children was just the tonic Jack needed. It made him realise that he had two little children who desperately needed him, and he fought for them. He once said to me that if it had not been for Kristie and Clint he probably would have said, 'Pull the lifeline. I don't want to live.' We gave him the will to live.

A short time later Jack and Jackie renewed their marriage vows, with the hospital chaplain, Warwick Thomas, conducting the ceremony. Jack's wedding ring had been mangled in the accident and given to Jackie, who'd had it remade.

Apart from the strength he gained from the love and support of his wife and children, Newton was also deeply affected by a young girl who had been admitted to intensive care after attempting to take her life by overdose. There he was, desperately wanting to live, and all she wanted was to end it all.

———————

Six weeks after the accident Jack was taken out of intensive care and placed in a normal hospital bed. It was like coming out into the world again, returning to civilisation, where he could shave himself and take a shower on his own.

Jackie often took the kids to nearby Centennial Park and soon after his discharge from intensive care Jack went with them. 'Slow down, slow down,' Jack barked at his wife as they drove the short distance to the park.

'I'm only going 40 kilometres an hour,' she said.

'Rubbish, you're going 150 an hour!' he replied.

JACKIE • I think it was probably because he had been in hospital so long that the speed sensation was heightened so dramatically. He was also scared that people would see him in Centennial Park. It is hard to imagine Jack being scared, but he was, basically because he was so frail and had lost so much weight.

No one noticed the Newton family in the park. If they had, a horde of photographers would surely have descended. Throughout the ordeal there were almost daily requests from newspapers seeking a photograph of Jack in hospital. One photographer rang Jack's father offering money for an exclusive picture. Jack Sr was never one to mess with words and there were no further attempts, with the high security of the hospital ensuring Newton's privacy was maintained.

Jack and Jackie slipped out of the hospital on another occasion as well, going to dinner at the Woollahra home of Col and Annette McGregor with the permission of one of the doctors. No one else knew, and the pair felt like criminals as they slipped out of the hospital through the kitchen and drove the ten minutes to the McGregors' home, where roast beef and red wine were on the table. On their return, none of the hospital staff knew they had been absent – or if they did, nothing was said. Suffice to say Jackie was very careful when driving. Imagine the newspaper headlines had they been involved in an accident.

The appeal for Newton and his family gathered momentum. Ian Stanley, former golf promoter Peter Williams, and Bob Shearer's accountant John Hoare ran the Melbourne end, where the major function was a benefit dinner at the Southern Cross Hotel. Ultra-distance runner Cliff Young, former Richmond VFL star Kevin Bartlett, former Test wicket-keeper Rod Marsh and leading trainer Bob Hoysted made up the sports forum.

In Sydney, one of the big nights was at the Coachman restaurant, where an auction of various donated items was held. A car, a service from one of John Singleton's horses, big-screen televisions and many more expensive items were sold at the primarily men-only night. Jackie was the only woman present, and she spoke to them from her heart.

In the US, Bob Shearer organised an extraordinary pro-am at Bay Tree Golf Plantation with the help of club pro Sam Timms. Newton had many friends in the North Myrtle Beach area and in American golf generally. As Jack Nicklaus later remarked, 'I can't understand how Bob Shearer played golf in the World Series a week earlier. Every time I turned around, he was talking to somebody about the Newton benefit tournament. He did a super job, an incredible job.'

A total of 56 US Tour players played in the event, along with 224 amateurs, with the list of pros reading like a who's who of golf. Only two of the top twenty players on the 1983 money list were missing: Tom Watson and Calvin Peete, who apologised because of engagements that couldn't be put off and sent hefty donations. Evonne Cawley and her husband played an exhibition tennis match, which was a stunningly successful day with players and a host of big-business people arriving by private jet and also a chartered jumbo. That single day at Bay Tree raised almost $300 000 of the overwhelming total of $670 000 that was raised for Newton.

From the window in his hospital ward Jack looked down longingly at the Royal Hotel across the road and thought to himself, 'One day I'm going to slip out of here and have a drink.' On 23 September, when he stepped into the bright Sydney sunshine on his discharge from hospital two months after the accident, he did just that. He held a press conference at the Prince of Wales and afterwards, instead of going out the front entrance where some members of the media were still waiting, he and Jackie ducked out the back and crossed the road to the hotel to join several of their closest friends. A couple of middies later and Jack Newton had resumed life as he knew it.

Does Jim Nield believe in miracles? He says, 'The bottom line is that Jack is still alive.'

Jackie maybe does.

JACKIE • As I sat with Jack day after day, it was quite amazing to see the power of the body to heal. Given the state his poor body was in, it was incredible to see the healing process and an experience I will never forget.

JACK • Here's where I take up the story again.

I owe my life to the Prince of Wales medical team who were on duty that night. I would be a hypocrite if I said any differently. Not that I was aware of it at the time, but they did an incredible job and I believe I was very lucky that they had their 'A team' on duty when I was brought in – guys like Jim Nield, Fred Hollows and Michael Baldwin. I'm certain in my mind that had they not been available, I would not be here today.

The Scottish nurse, Jackie Hain, who was head of intensive care, was terrific, as was the sister in pathology who took my blood. The doctors and interns couldn't get blood out of me but she never missed, and at times I would think, 'Christ, I wish these doctors would go away and just let her do it,' because I felt my one arm was becoming some-thing of a pincushion. There were times when I was irritable and for that I am sorry. My respect for the medical and nursing profession could not be greater.

I owe a great deal, too, to the live-in rehabilitants at the Mt Wilga Centre, a great eye-opener for me. After my discharge from hospital we stayed with my parents and each

day I was picked up by bus and taken to Mt Wilga for rehabilitation. It was like going off to school again, with my lunch-
box packed. To see the camaraderie between all these people
with mental and physical problems, those who had been dis-
membered by car or motorbike accidents, those with Down
syndrome and cerebral palsy, was quite amazing.

As a sportsperson I had tended to give a wide berth to
people in wheelchairs because it was a side of life I didn't
want to know about. I discovered that not only were these
people with problems very friendly, but they all had a great
sense of humour. That was the common denominator and
I soon realised my problems were minimal compared with
many of those at Mt Wilga.

There was a young boy there who had cerebral palsy. He
was mad-keen on golf and had seen me on television. Everywhere I went, he went. He would sit beside me at lunch, which
was the central meeting point for all the patients. It was a very
humbling experience to see his idolisation of me.

There were two further major operations to come: the
reversal of the colostomy and the repair of the stomach wall.
Because my abdomen had been severed, the wall and muscle
had been badly damaged. A protective gauze had been
installed to replace them and hold in the abdominal facilities.
(This is why my stomach looks distended. I find it quite
humorous when some guy, often with a beer gut, gives me
stick about my weight, referring to my stomach. If only they
knew. Quite often I feel like saying, 'What's your excuse?',
and sometimes I do.)

At Mt Wilga I attended classes in hand–eye coordination, typing and writing with my left hand, and I also had
to get fit for the coming operations. I played a lot of table

tennis – excellent for hand–eye coordination – with one of the instructors and worked fairly strenuously in the gym each day. The fitter I was, the less time I would need to spend in hospital for the next operation. I just wanted all that over, so I could get home to Warners Bay.

The overwhelming memory of my time at Mt Wilga is of the people there. I will never forget them. It should be compulsory for some people to go to a rehabilitation hospital and witness the result of so many horrific accidents. You would never ride a motorbike if you did that. What kept them all going at Mt Wilga was their will, their strong desire to succeed. It was quite staggering to see someone who couldn't walk struggling like all get out to take just one step. It was a very touching experience.

But it is the humour, above all else, that I will never forget. Part of the Australian heritage is a sense of humour and it is rare that a news event goes by without the associated jokes flying within a day. I was no different. Soon jokes like this were doing the rounds:

'Did you hear that Jack Newton has bought the plane involved in his accident?'

'No.'

'He's had his eye on it for some time.'

Jokes like this don't bother me. Life – and believe me, I know how precious it is – would be pretty dull without laughter.

Speaking of laughter, my friends and I have had our light moments when my prosthetic eye has gone missing. Once, Dick Maclean, Brian Hayes and another mate, Peter Neilson, came with me to Paleface Adios country at Temora in the south-west of NSW to look at some horses and also race three of our own in Sires Stakes races. We booked into the local hotel, where Keith and Sandra Dobson were mine host and hostess. Obviously enough, we gravitated to the bar in the evening, and as it often does, my eye socket became irritated by the glass eye. I removed it and shoved it in my pocket, thinking nothing more about it.

All – and a lot more – was revealed the next morning. Piecing together the available information, I had gone to my room in the pub, where the only washing facility was a hand basin with a tap that automatically shut off if it wasn't being turned. I placed the plug in and filled the basin to wash my face and hands and clean my teeth. I then hit the sack, rejoining the waking world some time after nine the next morning. I looked for my eye in my jacket pocket, but in vain. As well, I noticed the basin was full and there was water on the floor.

At that moment I heard voices in the street outside and poked my head out the window to see the other boys returning from working the horses at the track. I called to them and almost in reply heard a voice from the kitchen downstairs. 'Is that you, Newton? Are you awake?'

It was my host. Apparently my basin tap had not flicked off as it was designed to and in the kitchen immediately below pots and pans had been spread out to collect the falling water. Keith and Sandra had eliminated all other sources of the sudden precipitation save for my room.

That worry solved, there was the problem of my missing eye. I could only assume that in taking cash from my pocket to buy a round of drinks the eye had fallen on the floor. The trouble was that the cleaners had already done the rounds. A search of the garbage bins began and in the last of several there was my missing eye, among the cigarette butts, tomato slices and chicken legs.

Another occasion when the eye went missing was during the final of the 1985 Australian Indoor Tennis Championships at the Sydney Entertainment Centre, when Ivan Lendl and Henri Leconte were doing battle. Again the eye became irritated and I started rubbing at it, with the result that it fell out during a crucial stage of the match. While all other eyes were watching the passage of the ball across the net, I rummaged around on the floor on all fours searching for my missing eye, to the point of distracting those around me. A woman a couple of rows back asked the nature of my search, and on being told I was looking for my eye, her reaction was such that I felt she was about to send for a straitjacket. The errant eye finally turned up inside my open-necked shirt – and Lendl won.

One night I was at Ian Stanley's house for a barbecue and had a port at the end of the evening. I had taken one of my prosthetic eyes, which was an awful-looking thing – bloodshot and with the inscription 'Ignore me, I'm pissed' written on it. After all those years of Stanley's practical jokes I got even by dropping this eye into his port glass. On nearing the end of his drink he nearly died when he saw the eye glaring at him from the bottom of the glass.

––––––––––

The humour and somewhat awkward moments aside, I am forever grateful to all those involved in the appeal and those who gave so incredibly generously. It was something that was started without my knowledge and I was quite staggered, almost to the point of embarrassment, at how much was raised. The money did help to stabilise our lives when there was none coming in and enabled us to buy our present home at Cardiff. The rest has been put into a trust should anything happen down the track.

I know there were people who thought, 'Why raise this money for Newton? He'll only blow it at the Harold Park trots', but statements like that don't come from your true friends.

I am aware, too, of all the innuendo that has flown around about the accident. The popular conception is that I was drunk, with the argument being, 'How the hell can anyone get run over by an aeroplane if they're *not* drunk?'

I am not the first person to suffer a tragic accident with a propeller blade, but because of my reputation as a drinker and the fact that in my early days I enjoyed the company of women, people jump to conclusions. Their 'evidence' is that I had undeniably been drinking that day and I was in a car with a girl from the Sydney Swans. So they've put two and two together and come up with four.

The bottom line is that I had around eight beers that day and I do not constitute that as being drunk, and that the girl had offered to drive Frank D'Arcy and me to the airport when the taxi didn't turn up. The innuendo really sickens and annoys me. I know in my own mind the events that led to my accident and I can live with them.

Throughout the hard times after the accident, my mind would go to a poem that had always helped me get into the right attitude in my sporting life. I still get a lot out of it.

THE WINNER

If you think you are beaten, you are
If you think that you're not, you aren't
If you'd like to win, but you think you can't
It's almost a cinch, you won't.

If you think you'll lose, you've lost
For out in the world you find
Success begins with a fellow's will –
It's all in the state of mind.

If you think you're outclassed, you are
You've got to think high to rise
You've got to be sure of yourself before
You can ever win the prize.

Full many a race is lost
Before e'er a step is run
And many a coward fails
Before e'er his work's begun.

Think big and your deeds will grow
Think small and you'll fall behind
Think that you can and you will –
It's all in the state of mind.

Life's battles don't always go
To the stronger or faster man
But soon or late the man who wins
Is the fellow who thinks he can.

Anon.

Getting down to business

I was barely out of hospital after the accident when Murray
Ashford and Bill Pritchard, the backroom boys of golf tele-
casts for the ABC, asked me if I would like to do a stint of
commentary during the 1983 NSW Open at Concord.

I had only ever worked in TV a couple of times before,
back in the mid-'70s when Ben Wright was just starting to
branch out from his work as a golf writer for the *Financial
Times* into television commentary with the British ITV
network. Along with the likes of Britain's Peter Alliss and
America's Jack Whitaker, Wright is now one of the doyens
of the craft, though he has a mid-Atlantic accent by virtue of
the fact that he is an Englishman living in America. It was a
bit of fun working with Wright at the John Player Classic
and he, like me, didn't mind a gargle at the end of play.

The offer from Murray and Bill came out of the blue
and though it wasn't said in so many words, the inference

was that if I scrubbed up there would be more work to come. Obviously I had done a bit of thinking about my future as I lay in hospital, but had made no firm decisions about how to reshape my life. The one thing I knew was that I couldn't look back, only forward.

My on-air partners at the NSW Open were Peter Thomson, the late Brian Crafter and, believe it or not, former Australian cricket captain and former coach of the Australian team Bob Simpson, who is a member of the Concord Golf Club. Both Murray and Bill were very encouraging. I asked them to be supercritical of my performance on air because through my life I have always had a perfectionist streak. Maybe I was a little rough in the early days, but Murray kept saying that I was a natural and to continue doing it in the same way.

As a player I hadn't particularly enjoyed some of the television commentary on golf because I felt it was boring and that, in some cases, the commentators assumed that everyone watching at home was an expert on the game. They weren't relating to the average bloke and his wife sitting in their lounge room. Right from those early days it was my intention to be more informative, to try to include a few tips and give some sidelights into each player's background.

The arrangement with the ABC at Concord was to do the first couple of days and see how it went. I was still very weak, but I enjoyed the work. For the first time since the accident I had the opportunity to think about something other than myself. Murray and Bill were so pleased they ended up asking me to work at the weekend, and despite the fact that I'd been tired each evening on the first two days, I was delighted.

Jackie came to the golf with me each day, of course, and on the Sunday went walking the course with Kathie Shearer, following Bob, who was very much in contention on the final day. I was on air with Graham Marsh, who was doing a guest spot, when Shears came to the par-5 17th, actually the 7th hole as the members play the course, and carved his drive out to the right. The cameraman followed the ball wonderfully well as it hit the ground and bounced up to hit a woman's forehead.

'Oh, my goodness! I hope that woman is all right,' Marsh said, then remarked, 'Isn't that Kathie Shearer with her?'

'Yes, Marshie, and that's my missus on the ground. It might have knocked a bit of sense into her,' I said.

Well, do you think that remark in jest didn't create a furore? I copped flak from each and every way, with the ABC switchboard receiving calls about how heartless I was towards the marvellous woman who had been by my side in the weeks and months after the accident. Jackie and I still laugh about it and we still have the golf ball, signed by Shears, who finished third. Let me assure all those who were concerned that there has been no lasting damage, but I still maintain that the surprise was that the ball didn't go into Jackie's mouth, given the way she and Kathie yap each time they meet up!

A strong influence on my television commentary career has been Richie Benaud, who now splits his TV work between the Nine Network in Australia and Channel Four in Britain. We became very good friends through my association with Ian Chappell and other Australian cricketers, and Richie's passion for golf is such that he turns up at all the major golfing events as part of the gallery. Quite often

I've spoken with him after tournaments for his critical appraisal, starting when he rang me shortly after the '83 NSW Open and invited me to lunch. He had written out a list of dos and don'ts for golf commentary that he had converted from what he described as the bible on cricket commentary, given to him by E.W. Swanton years before. Swanton played a handful of first-class games nigh on seventy years ago in English county cricket and later became a respected newspaper and television commentator.

Some of the points Richie mentioned I was aware of; others not. He told me never to talk over the action and never to answer other commentators' questions. And I should always remember that every viewer is an expert and let the pictures do the talking.

———————

After that initial tournament for the ABC, I started a free-lance commentary career that ran from 1984 to 1989. I guess I must have set some sort of record when I worked for all four Australian networks in the one year. I must say there were times when I didn't enjoy the work at all. I didn't feel comfortable with what I perceived as a lot of back-stabbing and instability within the industry and suspected that people were saying things behind my back.

I felt particularly uncomfortable in the early days sharing the commentary duties with Thomson. From his point of view it was understandable – I was the new boy on the block and, just as he did to rookies on the golf course, he was going to put me through the wringer.

His approach to commentating was to sit in front of the monitor with his arms folded and to talk, totally ignoring everyone around him, until he found himself in a situation where he really didn't know which player or which hole it was. At that point, he would sit up from the monitor and expect you to take over. Communications, it should be said, weren't as good as they are now and it was possible to lose track.

Peter also tended to be supercritical of players who were confronted with awkward shots, and I felt some of his comments were totally unjust. For example, say a fellow missed a green and had a lie where thousands of people had trampled the grass down, with his next shot over a bunker. Instead of setting the shot up for the viewer and emphasising the problems, Thomson would say things like, 'This is a relatively straightforward shot.'

Then, if the guy screwed up and put the ball in the bunker or skinnied it through the back of the green, he would say, 'Now that's a terrible shot.' It was as though everyone was a schoolboy to Peter and that as a five-times British Open winner he had all the answers.

As well, I thought he was a boring commentator for a man with such knowledge and such a great playing record.

It all came to a head one day during the 1984 Australian PGA championships at Monash in Sydney. Thomson was playing the US Seniors circuit at that stage and I had taken over from him in writing a column for the *Age* newspaper in Melbourne. He was back in town and ready to work at the PGA title and I was none too keen to work with him.

I felt I worked well with Brian Crafter, that we had built up a rapport where I knew when he wanted to talk and he seemed to know when I wanted to contribute to the commentary. An absolute sin is to talk over the top of one another, and among the tricks of the trade is one commentator taking one group through a hole and the other doing the same with a different group.

So it was at the PGA that Thomson and I found ourselves on air together. The tension grew and I felt he was talking down to me, which he had a tendency to do at times. The final straw came when he was sitting there, arms folded as usual, watching the monitor. With no warning, the producer cut to a shot that I admit baffled me for a second or two. Peter obviously had no idea where or who it was and he promptly sat up and jabbed his finger in my direction as if to say, 'It's your turn.'

Not on your nelly. I stuck my thumb in the air, put the cans on the table and walked out. Enough was enough. Later that afternoon I had a discussion with the powers that be and said, 'Look, don't put me on with Peter Thomson ever again. I've had a gutful of him. I'll work with Brian. Let Thomson work with Brian, but not me.'

The directors refused to budge, saying they were happy with the way it was going and if I felt Thomson was talking down to me or his commentary was wrong I should say so on air. 'No,' I said. 'It's a totally unsatisfactory arrangement.'

Next morning Thomson came to me and said, 'Look, I'm sorry if I offended you.'

I replied, 'Peter, it's the same old story for you. You ride into town and everybody else is a dumbo. But I accept your apology. Really there is no need for it, but you know I don't enjoy working with you.'

'I'm sorry you feel that way,' Thomson said.

Amazingly, I didn't have too much trouble with him until the following year's Australian PGA title at Castle Hill in Sydney, when Greg Norman hit his tee shot to the 2nd, a par 3, where his ball finished flush against the fringe. It was a shot you could play with the leading edge of a sand iron because it can slide through the long fringe grass, whereas a putter would get hooked up in it.

I said in commentary, 'This is a shot for the viewers at home to practise. It's a shot that is not difficult if you turn the sand iron up as Norman is doing here. You'll find the sand iron will slide through the fringe grass and the ball will roll just as though it's been putted. It's a shot that Lee Trevino invented, and now many of the top players employ it.' I said in commentary.

Thomson interrupted, 'It wasn't Lee Trevino, it was Fuzzy Zoeller.'

We then proceeded to have a massive disagreement on air. I knew damn well it was Trevino who had first used the shot, back in the early '70s when Zoeller wasn't even on the scene, and I said so. I was furious. Firstly, Thomson was wrong in fact, and secondly, he was trying to make me look bad. Unless it's a blatantly obvious mistake, which it wasn't on my part, another commentator should never interrupt to point out an error. I felt he had attempted to make me look foolish that day.

The final major incident between us occurred at the Australian Open at Royal Melbourne that same year, 1985, when Norman won his second title. I always got the feeling that Peter loved to be doing the commentary on the potential winner and there were times when he would jump horse and change the grouping of commentary duties.

He did just that on this particular day. Norman had just holed out at the 6th and it was my turn to take up the commentary at the 7th, the short par 3. Peter barged in, saying, 'Now, here's Greg Norman at the 8th—'

He proceeded to say that Norman had hooked into the rubbish on the 8th the previous day while attempting to drive the green on the 305-yard par-4 hole. Blind Freddie could see that Norman had a 7- or 8-iron in his hand for this tee shot on the par-3 7th, but Peter continued, 'Today he is taking an iron from the tee and this is the right play. He is going to play it safe.'

Next moment, Norman went whack and knocked the ball to within 2 feet. 'Oh no. I'm before myself. He's actually on the 7th,' Thomson said. I could have told him in the first place he was wrong, but I remained silent and just let him go, let him wallow in it.

In 1984 I was on the BBC team at the British Open at St Andrews. Alex Hay and Bruce Critchley were doing the commentary while my job was to make expert comments. For those who don't know Hay, at times he comes out with some quite extraordinary statements. This was never more evident than when he asked American Mark Allen, winner of the 1989 Scottish Open, if he could point out Mark Allen to him in the bar at Gleneagles just half an hour after Allen had won the title.

Well, in 1984 Alex was commentating when Fred Couples, John Bland and Ian Baker-Finch came to the 18th, where the pin was cut back left with the Valley of Sin in front for an orthodox approach to the green. The wind was blowing into the players' faces with a touch of right to left in its direction. Couples got on the tee and smashed the ball up on to the first fairway adjoining the 18th with a controlled hook.

'Ooh, nooo,' said Alex in his Scottish accent. 'He's come over the top of it, he's hooked it. What a terrible swing he's made there.' I sat biting my tongue. Never contradict. Next up was Bland, who hit it on exactly the same line but about 40 yards short of Couples.

'Ooh, nooo,' said Alex again. 'That's another bad swing from John Bland.' Then Baker-Finch did exactly the same thing, knocking his ball out onto the first fairway.

'Ooh, nooo,' Alex began, and I could remain silent no longer.

'Alex, have you considered the players are *trying* to put the ball up there so they don't have to come over the Valley of Sin? It gives them a shot directly into the wind and it's the best angle to the flag,' I said.

Hay went haywire. 'I don't agree. The replays show they were bad swings,' he stated categorically.

'I don't care what you think of the replays. That's what they were trying to do,' I replied.

Bland hit his second shot to 6 feet and Baker-Finch knocked his to 8 feet. Then Couples holed his second shot to give the trio two threes and a two on the par-4 hole.

Former English professional Clive Clark was doing the on-course interviews and had obviously heard the disagreement between Hay and myself. He approached Couples and said, 'There's been a bit of discussion, quite heated discussion, in the commentary box about the way the three of you have played the last hole. Can you tell us?'

'The pin was back left and I tried to hit a low hook so I'd be out on the first fairway to avoid coming over the

Valley of Sin—,' Couples began. For a moment there was dead silence in the commentary box, but I couldn't resist another dig.

'Well, I guess that's why I was a tournament player and you're just a bloody teaching professional,' I remarked. I have not worked for the BBC since.

———————

It got to the stage where I was doing something like sixteen tournaments a year and wasn't enjoying it at all. I felt I was getting stale jumping from network to network, not sure of which blazer I was wearing. I was also starting to get involved in golf-course design and this was taking its toll on my time. So when Christopher Skase approached me in early 1989 offering a very big contract to work exclusively for the Seven Network, the timing was perfect. It was a three-year deal to do eight tournaments a year, including the Australian, NSW and Queensland Opens, the Australian Masters, the Test match between Australia and Britain and the Skins at Port Douglas. Skase told me the network was also attempting to get the rights to the British and US Opens, the US Masters and the US PGA, but that never occurred.

I've since renegotiated that contract and, while I'll continue to work with Seven, it also enables me to work with any non-commercial network, the ABC or SBS, or pay TV providing it is not re-shown on an opposition commercial network or overseas television. It also frees me up if I want to get involved in production-company coverage of tournaments in Asia or New Zealand.

Minor disagreements with fellow commentators aside, TV commentary can be rewarding, particularly as it affords

me the opportunity to stay involved with a side of the game
I loved – playing tournaments – and with many of my mates.
I'm gratified to have had the full support of golf professionals,
who believe I give them better representation. There have
been some quite frightening moments on the way, though.
I saw the tragedy of spectators being killed in lightning
strikes at the US Open and US PGA tournaments in 1991.

We very nearly lost a player and a cameraman in similar
circumstances during a violent electrical storm at the 1988
Palm Meadows Cup. It was the final round, when the
tournament had developed into a dogfight between Greg
Norman, Bernhard Langer and Jet Ozaki.

One cameraman was doing a close-up shot of Langer
as the German walked towards a green when lightning
struck some nearby scaffolding and rebounded onto the
camera. The lightning then bounced over Langer's head. He
could consider himself lucky; the cameraman was knocked
to the ground and suffered some burns, while those of us
in the commentary box received an electric shock through
our headphones. It was a moment of considerable panic and
play was immediately suspended while the storm passed.
There were some very nervous people around that day, and
ever since, there has been great deliberation as to when
cameramen should be withdrawn from scaffolding when a
storm is approaching.

Not so life-threatening, but equally disturbing, was the
moment during the 1988 US Open at the Country Club in
Brookline, Massachusetts, when we were working off Amer-
ican ABC coverage and suddenly our monitors went dead.
We were assured the pictures were still being seen on
Australian TV screens and our producer, John Ormsby,

came to our aid by giving us a description through the headphones as he watched on his monitors in the outside-broadcast van, which we then relayed to our viewers. Somehow we flummed our way through, but if there had been a practical joker in the pack we could have been sunk.

My other excursion into the media was my work writing for the *Age* and the Sydney Sunday paper the *Sun-Herald*. I must say it was terribly satisfying to write what I felt and thought. But it didn't come easily and there were times when I slaved over the articles, particularly those for the *Age*, which were written on each day's play after I had been on television for up to six hours. Although TV isn't tough, it does take a lot of concentration, and it was mentally demanding to then front up with pen and paper.

I will always remember the British Open at St Andrews in 1984, when I went to the press tent after doing the television to write my *Age* pieces. Trevor Grant, also of the *Age*, the late Don Lawrence of the Melbourne *Herald* and I were always the last to leave and Don would tell me, 'Don't slave too hard, Jack. It'll be tomorrow's fish-and-chip wrappers.'

I must admit I became more respectful of the press after that experience. Writing, even for the best of them, doesn't come easily. I continued the *Age* work for quite a time until Peter Thomson finished his years on the US Seniors circuit and reclaimed his spot. The newspaper wanted me to continue writing a weekly gossip column, but that's not my cup of tea, or pint of lager.

Of all the media work I've done, none has been more enjoyable than being a member of the television commentary team at the Irish Open between 1986 and 1990. Most of my best friends on the European Tour were Irish – Christy O'Connor senior and junior, John O'Leary, Eamonn Darcy, and many more – and we had a great affinity both for golf and a good time.

In 1984, after the British Open, I went over for Christy O'Connor Sr's pro-am and was made an honorary citizen of Ireland during a civic reception in Dublin. There will always be a place in my heart for the Irish.

———————

After getting out of hospital and back into mainstream life, I was amazed by the number of offers I received to do after-dinner speaking. I wasn't really aware that people could make a living out of this at times self-indulgent activity, but there is no doubting they do – and quite handsome livings, too.

My first appearance was at a sports writers' dinner at the Sydney Hilton and I was nervous. It just wasn't my forte to stand in front of three or four hundred people and talk – I'd rather stand around a bar yarning with a few mates.

But I soon discovered there was a routine to it all: tell a few jokes, talk about a few adventures in life, name my favourite golf courses. Basically I discovered I could, after all, talk for forty minutes. I guess some could criticise me because I haven't really changed my repertoire all that much over the years, but it's the same with most entertainers. There are people who could tell you comedian Brian Doyle's submarine joke word for word, but it's all in the manner of the telling.

Within months I found the speaking engagements were taking far too much time for something I didn't really enjoy doing, so I lifted my rate from $1500 to $2000. I was still getting knocked down in the rush. I boosted it to $2500 and the result was the same, so I now charge $3500 to speak for forty minutes, which is a bit of a joke, but I make no apology for it. I have found the right level, speaking once a month or every six weeks if time pemits, which is all I want to do. I may not be the best speaker in the world, but by setting a figure of three and a half grand, it's a case of supply and demand and the level of speaking I now have is comfortable.

It's a touch ironic that of all the sportsmen's nights I've agreed to do I have only had to withdraw from one, that of the Sydney Swans. Periodically my inside workings get blocked up and I have to go to hospital for repair work. One such occasion prevented me from fulfilling the Swans obligation. Those who believe my absence was because of some deep-seated psychological reason can think again.

––––––––

Another major involvement I have today grew out of a hot but friendly argument in 1985. It is fair to say that Graeme Grant, then course superintendent at Kingston Heath Golf Club in Melbourne, which is generally regarded as one of the best-conditioned golf courses in the world, does not take kindly to criticism. Perhaps the trait runs in the family: his brother, Trevor, one of Melbourne's leading sports writers, has been known to get a little hot under the collar if anyone ventures to express disapproval of his work.

Graeme and I were in the bar of Melbourne's Yarra Yarra GC in February 1985 when a discussion began over the nature of the Kingston Heath greens during the Australian Open played just a couple of months earlier.

Graeme Grant always presented very firm and fast greens, believing that if a player hit a good shot they should be rewarded but if they hit a poor one they should suffer the penalty. During the Australian Open I felt he'd gone a little over the top with greens that went blue and were so fast and firm they made putting a nightmare. John Spencer, course superintendent at nearby Huntingdale, home to the Australian Masters, was also involved in the argument and I got as good as I gave from them both.

'You golf pros are all the same. You want trenches into the holes so you can make every putt,' Grant observed.

It was, I repeat, a rational discussion and out of it all came the formation of the Newton, Grant & Spencer golf-course design and construction company. Few of the existing design companies had the construction and turf management expertise that John and Graeme could provide. We felt if we could pool our thoughts we might make an impact on the business. Certainly we expected it to be tough early because we were bidding against some more fashionable designers, such as the Peter Thomson–Mike Wolveridge combination, Pete Dye and Robert Trent Jones, and Graham Marsh. Interestingly enough, David Graham tried to persuade us to split up in the early days, asking Graeme and John to leave and join forces with him. But loyalty was born from that lively discussion at Yarra Yarra and they chose to stay with the fledgling company.

It has been tough getting a toehold in the industry and much of our time is spent on redesign and construction work at courses like The Grange and Kooyonga in Adelaide; Riversdale, Kingston Heath and Commonwealth in Melbourne; and the NSW Golf Club at La Perouse, Castle

Hill and The Lakes in Sydney. Some of it is redesign of greens; some is redesign of layout. At The Lakes, for example, we changed the 4th, 5th and 12th holes because of boundary problems.

Our biggest break came when Stewart Ginn telephoned and asked if we were interested in a job in Juo, Japan, where a friend of his wanted to build a golf course and country club. Graeme and I flew to Japan on spec and bid against the American duo of Trent Jones and Dye. We were fortunate: the head man of the Japanese company wanted an Australian flavour to his course and we won the commission.

Juo is in the prefecture of Ibaraki, about two hours' drive north-east of Tokyo. Land is obviously at a premium in Japan for golf courses and it had taken the owner ten years to gain approval from the local council to build the course. It is hilly country, the type of terrain that if you saw it in Australia you would think would be mostly rock, but in Juo we found a coarse, loamy type of sand that wasn't too hard to push around. Believe me, we had a lot to move. All up we shifted 9 million cubic metres of earth with the help of the Kumagai construction firm, which also constructed the tunnel under Sydney Harbour.

The usual Japanese client philosophy is for a course with a par of 72 and with water and bunkers that don't really feature or come into play. Not so in this case. The chairman of the Juo Golf and Country Club, Mr Kazuo Fujita, wanted his course to be one of the toughest in Japan, so tough in fact that he wanted to see Greg Norman come off the golf course in tears. That to me is a pretty sadistic attitude and I can assure you that Norman, if he ever does play the course, will not be crying after playing it. I believe we came up with a blend of fair yet difficult holes.

Graeme, John and I were pretty nervous awaiting the verdict of Raymond Floyd, Tom Weiskopf, Jerry Pate, Bill Rogers, Johnny Miller, my little Aussie mate Brian Jones and all the top Japanese players, including Jumbo Ozaki, who played in the $880 000 36-hole tournament held in conjunction with the official opening in September 1991.

'Diabolically great,' declared Miller. I'm not too sure what he meant, but I took it as a compliment.

Weiskopf was lavish in his praise, saying, 'Many golf-course designers have spent a lifetime trying to emulate Alister Mackenzie's work. This is some of the best I've seen.'

And Japanese legend Ozaki felt it was time his home country had a golf course of this nature, though he thought it might take time for amateur players to come to terms with it. He predicted it would be ranked in the top five courses in Japan within three years.

The Juo course cost $35 million to build. We tried to employ the Melbourne philosophy of the way we think a golf course should play, featuring the bunkering and not having tiered greens with rollercoasters or slippery-dips, which were being created by so many designers in the mid to late '80s. Our greens are rather big, with more gentle slope and undulation along Melbourne lines. The emphasis is on putting your iron shots in the right place and on fast greens, which are fairly unusual in Japan. There, all bunkers tend to look the same, but we tried to give ours different shapes as well as walkways, to eliminate the Japanese practice of walking straight up the face of a bunker to gain exit.

I think some designers, the Americans particularly, have lost the plot a little in what a golf course should offer. My idea of a good course is one that offers a good player a challenge from the championship tees, and off the forward tees gives the mug golfer a chance to go out and enjoy a day of golf. The last thing you need is for a fellow who plays maybe once a week, more than likely on a handicap of somewhere between 20 and 27, coming off the course absolutely distraught because he has lost half a dozen balls. Basically he hasn't enjoyed the game at all because the designer hasn't offered an 'out' shot – an alternative route or a soft option.

The greens should be able to hold a good shot but not a bad shot, just as they do in Melbourne's sandbelt. In Sydney, I feel the course superintendents put too much water on the greens and thus make them too soft, giving the same result for good and bad shots. People in NSW are generally poor putters because normally the greens are so slow that you have to take a big backswing to get the ball anywhere near the hole. There is no technique, no feel.

I also think that on some of the newer courses in Australia, particularly in the Surfers Paradise area, the designers have gone overboard with water. Much of the land there is low-lying and it reduces construction costs if you build lakes to get your topsoil and fill. You don't have to mow lakes, either, and, aesthetically, if you've got a very ordinary-looking piece of dirt, water is probably the easiest way to give it a feature. Nor, by taking that route, do you have to wait for trees to grow.

Water can be a very nice feature on a golf course but its use has been exaggerated. It's no fun at all to play a golf course with water down both sides of the fairway. In truth,

many of the courses in the Gold Coast area are pretty much
forgettable when you compare them with the Melbourne
sandbelt courses.

For a few years I was involved in the Newton Golf Company,
which was formed about a year after the accident. Tony
Steele, a NSW Sheffield Shield cricketer of the late '60s and
early '70s, had the Adidas agency for NSW at the time and
wanted to get involved in a golf company but needed a
'name'. We worked together on the design and selection of
a golf-club range and used the infrastructure of his Adidas
agency to market the clubs. We purposely went after the
middle to lower end of the market and enjoyed considerable
success with the JN1000 and JN2000 models. We were able
to sell the JN1000s to the pro shops and bigger stores for
under $200 for a full set of golf clubs, while the JN2000s
were under $300. We felt the former were the perfect clubs
for beginners and the latter were being used by the middle
range of players as well as a surprising number of better
players. We also put a Newton signature model in at the
top end of the market that, for a time, was used by Brett
Ogle and the 1991 Australian Open champion, Wayne Riley.
Ken Trimble, the 1990 NSW Open champion, also used
them.

Tony sold his share of the business in 1988 to another
group and I added an Aussie One model to fill the gap in
our price range. One of the problems in the golf-club industry
is that you can sell, say, 200 sets to Grace Bros or Kmart,
who because of their turnover may be able to sell them at
a 10 to 15 per cent mark-up, while the pros at the golf club

have to look at a mark-up of between 50 and 100 per cent simply to make a living. It is understandable that the pros get annoyed when the big stores down the road can in some cases sell the same set of golf clubs $150 cheaper.

After starting from nothing, we gained around 10 per cent of the golf-club market, which wasn't bad for a pretty small company, but unfortunately friction began to develop within the new partnership and it was decided that it would be in the best interests of all parties if we wound up the business. However, I still retain the trademark of the Newton Golf Company.

I guess one of the interesting things for me these days is the number of frustrated designers and inventors who call up about or send literature on weird and wonderful concoctions and contraptions they've come up with. One such was John Dumphy, the agent for Shimano fishing reels in Australia, who approached me with the idea of a putting trainer that could be used on the carpet in the office or home. I was a bit sceptical at first, but I've got to admit the product has done extraordinarily well.

The difference between our gadget and others like it is that ours has a tiny computer chip in the regulator that activates the slinging of the ball back to the player's feet. It doesn't break down like other models and is far sturdier as well. I had it at home for about a month before I decided to put my name to it. What convinced me was that I let Clint, who was then aged eight, play with it, and if a kid couldn't wreck it, surely an adult couldn't either. In truth, Clint did destroy it, but only after he held the ball in the hole until it burned out the mechanism. Outside of that, it's pretty foolproof!

John Dumphy is now a very good friend and when I get calls from excitable inventors I pass them along to him. But the putting trainer has been a nice little earner. The recommended retail price is still around $25, just as it was ten years ago, and we've sold about 300 000 units.

Another gadget that came our way was the Driving Partner, which was invented by Neil Russell, the publican of the Aberdale Hotel in Weston on the coalfields outside Newcastle. The Driving Partner operates by striking a specially constructed golf ball that oscillates on an axis. A small computer responds to the speed of oscillation to determine the distance the ball would travel. If John Daly ever comes this way again, I'll get him to give it a whirl.

Playing golf again – with a handicap

'I'm going to hit some golf balls. Why don't you come with me?' My mother had probably said the same words to me a hundred times and more in the past, but never had they had such an impact. I was gripped by fear: fear of the unknown and fear of failure. I wasn't ready, or so I thought, either physically or emotionally. I still wasn't strong following the series of operations. There were more to come, including the colostomy reversal that would rid me of the wretched bag.

It was just before Christmas of 1983, just a tick under five months after the accident, and I was staying at Mum and Dad's house in Carlingford in Sydney's west. My days were spent reading, watching television and walking. The first time I tried to run I lost my balance, stumbling about all over the place. Coordination – it's something you don't think about when you have two arms. When I was on the US circuit there was a Californian guy, Allen Miller, who used to practise playing with one arm, but he was the only one I had witnessed. It wasn't something I had ever contemplated.

My mother's words were so sudden. I suspect part of my confusion was the fact that I didn't want anybody to see me try to swing a golf club for the first time. Mum was okay, but there would be others around the Muirfield GC practice fairway and it was pretty obvious that I might attract a fair amount of attention. And it was the stepping into the unknown, like swimming for the first time. I didn't know what would happen. In everything I'd done I had tried to give it my best shot. To do that, I thought, might no longer be possible.

She is a very persistent, determined lady is my mum, so I decided to go with her to test the waters. I felt I could try it. If it didn't work, well, that would be the end of it. I wouldn't play golf again.

There was no one around, which suited me fine. The last thing I wanted was to make a goog of myself. I've since learned that this was probably a silly thought, because even now when I hit a bad shot and get angry, the reaction from those around is that they are amazed by how well I play.

My mother handed me a 5-iron and I teed up the ball. I felt I could get to it better that way than playing it from the ground. The next thing I wanted to make sure of was not to hit it too hard. I just wanted to hit it.

The thing I noticed straight away as I stood over the ball was that my depth perception had been distorted because of the loss of my eye. It was a weird feeling; I really didn't

Fostering young golfers at a junior tournament in Camden, south of Sydney.

Junior golfers, including a young Karrie Webb (far left), at the International Junior Tournament at Cessnock Golf Club, 1991.

With Mum and Dad at a Muirfield Golf Club awards night.

Tom Weiskopf was one of the great players who took part at the opening of the Juo Country Club course in Japan – my first overseas golf course design and construction assignment.

An obligatory public address as Chairman of the Australian PGA Tour, in Canberra.

Channel 7

In my Channel 7 commentator's clobber at the Australian Masters in Melbourne.

Tennis champion Pat Rafter had a stint in the 'dunking machine' at my Celebrity Classic, Novotel Twin Waters Resort, 1998.

Wearing the colours of my beloved Newcastle Knights rugby league team in 1998.

Two of my honoured guests at the Celebrity Classic in 1999 were young champion Aaron Baddeley and my old mentor, Norman von Nida.

Clint played State of Origin rugby league for the New South Wales Under 19s in 2000.

Kristie celebrates her graduation from the University of Newcastle with brother Clint.

Kevin Brown Studio Space

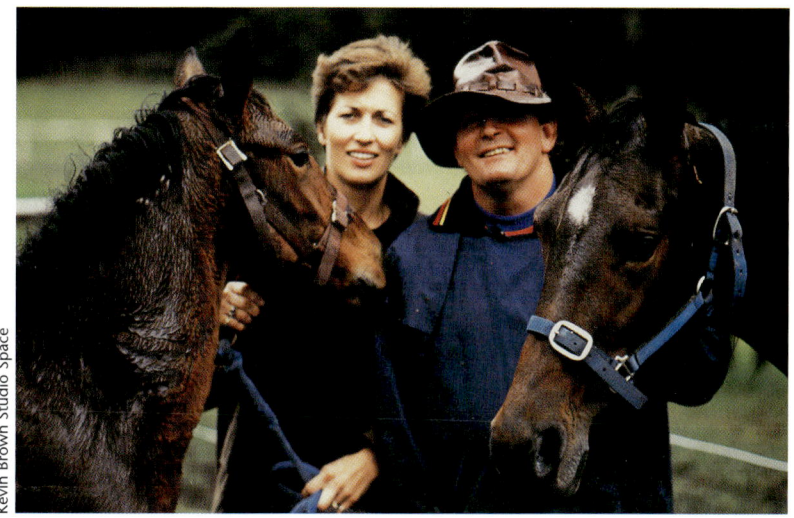

At home with Jackie at 'Augusta'.

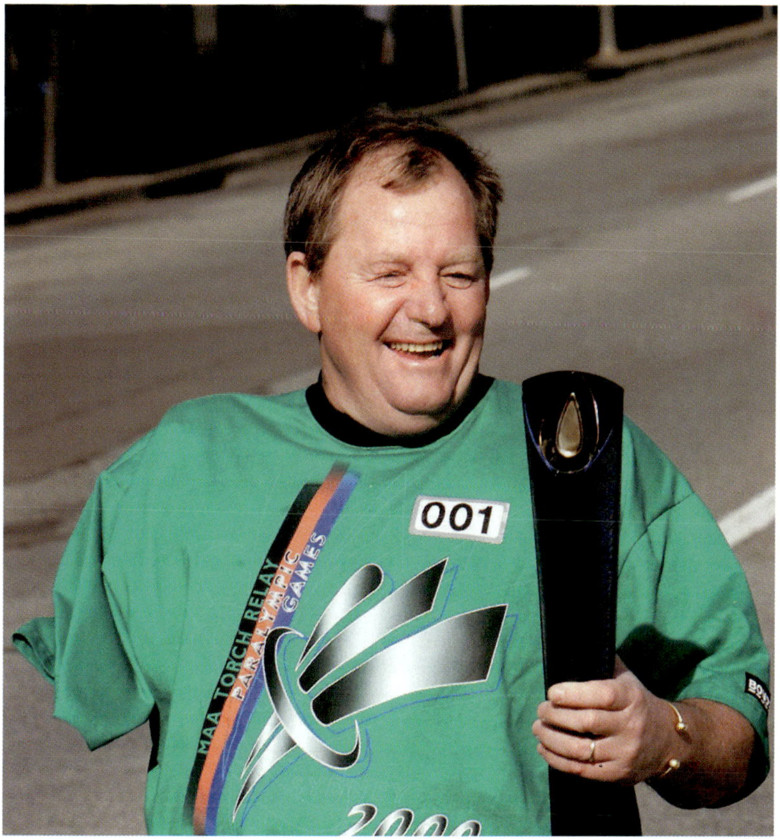

Newcastle Herald

Proudly carrying the Paralympic torch in Newcastle, 2000.

Back again at Carnoustie, standing on the same spot as I did in the British Open play-off all those years ago.

know what was going to happen. You could liken it to diving off a 10-metre board for the first time, looking down at the water and saying, 'Gee, that's a long way down.'

I tried to apply the same principles I had used all my golfing life: the same grip, the arm straight and a good shoulder turn. With my first swing I missed altogether, the club face going over the top of the ball. On my next attempt I hit it right on the top and it dribbled a few yards along the ground. I tried again, taking more time to look at the ball, and the swing felt smoother. The ball took off in the air, maybe 70 or 80 yards down the fairway, and it felt great. Everything's got to be in perspective, but I suspect it felt as good a shot as any I've hit, because I knew at that point it would be possible to play again. When you've played the professional game it becomes a 'feel' game. Simply getting the ball airborne gave me the feeling that all was not lost.

I hit about fifteen balls that day before I had to call it quits. I simply wasn't strong enough to stand there and hit a shag-bag full of balls. But it was a beginning and life was looking pretty positive. Everything was blending into one – the next operation, the rehabilitation, learning to write left-handed and playing golf – and it would mean I'd be able to get on with living life.

After the colostomy reversal operation in February 1984 I went home to Lake Macquarie and Mum and Dad came up to visit. Dad organised a game at Belmont Golf Club outside Newcastle with club professional Paul Robertson and another mate, Greg McCallum, and I went along for the walk. I was still very weak but they talked me into playing a hole, my first since the accident. I suspect it had been planned that way all along.

I played the 10th, which is a par 5, and topped my way up the fairway before two-putting for a ten. I was frustrated simply because I couldn't get the ball up off the ground, but I reasoned it was basically the depth perception that was causing the problems, as well as the feeling of a complete lack of strength, which prompted me to attempt to hit the ball too hard and therefore top it.

Playing golf again snowballed from there. Not so long after, I played three holes at Belmont and my mates were terrific. There wasn't any kowtowing to me; it was rather a case of getting out there and not feeling sorry for myself. Gradually I built up the number of holes I played, graduating to six and then nine.

At Noosa in December that year I had absolutely no intention of playing in my annual celebrity pro-am (which had been set up a few years before and now raises funds for the Jack Newton Junior Golf Foundation for the promotion and development of junior golf in NSW), but I agreed to do the television commentary for Channel Nine.

There was a lot of behind-the-scenes work with Dianne Henshaw, who was running the tournament with me. At the last moment, Sydney jockey Malcolm Johnston was a late withdrawal. With the same suddenness that my mother had suggested I go and hit a few balls, Dianne said, 'Well, why don't you play?'

I was temporarily taken aback. I really wasn't ready to play golf with five or six thousand people standing around. There's a big difference between playing a few holes with your mates at Belmont and teeing up in front of a large crowd – the sort of feeling I suspect the average amateur has when they play in a pro-am. It's all right playing at club level in the local four-ball or Sunday medal, but when you get out there with a sea of faces around it's a pretty nerve-wracking experience for most people. As a pro you don't tend to think about it, but you see the amateurs' gut-wrenching actions. You tell them, 'Just relax and enjoy yourself,' but one look at their faces tells you they're not. It's an unfamiliar environment for them.

It's the same with celebrities. They are consummate performers in their chosen career, but put a golf club in their hands with a crowd around and it can be awesome for them. Fortunately, through the years at Noosa, the celebrities have learned to relax and treat it as it is – a fun tournament.

I decided to take the plunge, and suddenly found myself cast in at the deep end again. My partners were Bob Hawke and Rodger Davis. My hand shook as I teed up the ball on the first tee. I was suffering the same excruciating attack of nerves I had seen so often in the past. There was also the matter of pride.

The words of my grandfather echoed in my thoughts: 'If you're going to do something, give it your best shot.'

I thought, too, of the famous lawn bowler I had met at a function, who had suggested I take up bowls. 'I'll give you a few lessons and you'll pick it up in no time. No problem at all.'

And here I was, about to play golf again in a tournament. I thought of those who had questioned why I would ever want to play again, having played at the highest level and experienced its giddy heights. Why turn around and play basically mug's golf?

All that was past, gone on a dark evening at Sydney Airport in July 1983. My whole life had changed and I had a new set of values, different priorities and things I wanted to do. It was a case of 'suck it and see'. I couldn't take the attitude that I'd had a semi-successful professional career and now I was going to play golf to a standard that was unfamiliar to me. It was a new challenge and for the first time in my life I understood the problems most mug golfers have in trying to put together a respectable game.

I only played nine holes, firing 49, and was pretty proud of what I'd done. Had someone asked me before I'd gone out, I would have gladly copped a 49. I really hadn't spent much time working on my short game at that stage and was having trouble with chipping, pitching and bunker shots, all brought about by the depth perception thing. I was also gripping the club too tightly. All the things you shouldn't do with two hands, I was doing with one. It wasn't until I relaxed the grip a bit and really concentrated on looking at the ball, then let my left wrist work through the shot, that that part of my game turned around.

But I had no time to work on those things that day at Noosa. I did hit a couple of shots that actually felt as though the ball ran up the clubface. As a pro, that was the feeling I had always sought and practised for. So I guess it was a pretty exciting day in my life.

Bob Hawke was a tremendous encouragement. He had witnessed first hand the way I was in hospital. He'd visited me twice, once when I was in intensive care and the other time in the ward, and I think he marvelled at the transformation. He was quite ecstatic, even though he reckoned I was a burglar, snipping $10 off him in a side bet that day.

It wasn't one of his better days and his score was well over 100, with me beating him on the nine holes we played.

Davis, too, was terrifically encouraging. We go back a long way, to school days in Sydney when he went to Normanhurst High while I was at Epping Boys', and there was a pretty fierce rivalry between us. I suspect he got quite a shock when he saw that I could hit the ball so well after such a short space of time, and he threw a few well-meaning digs at me on the way round.

After that I started going to the Steelworks Golf Club at Shortland, outside Newcastle, about fifteen minutes' drive from my present home in Cardiff. It's a club that basically started from the BHP Recreational Club and the blokes there were no nonsense and good fun. I started work on my short game on the practice pitching green, going there three times a week to work through the old shag-bag of practice balls I had carried with me on the pro tour.

I felt that this was the area which needed work, to build up my strength, and it was a natural progression to become a member of the club. I submitted three cards – 90, 92, 94 – and received a handicap of 19, which seemed to me a bit like going over old ground some twenty-five years after I'd started playing. But it was a starting point, a yardstick to work from and something on which to improve.

I must say there was a lot of room for improvement. At that stage I really didn't have my future planned, apart from television commentary. I figured at the time that I was going to be playing a lot more golf than has actually panned out. I imagined I'd be playing two or three times a week, leading a life of semi-retirement in a way, but down the track other business activities have intervened.

There was a time I felt I could get down to single figures again and, with my obvious limitations, play to the best of my ability. I still think I could, but my career path has changed and I'm playing less and less. I'm lucky these days if I play once or twice a month. I did get the handicap down to 15 and the best round I shot, numerically speaking, was a 79 at Noosa in 1989 when I played for money with my father against a couple of other guys.

But the 81 I had over the Royal Melbourne composite course in the pro-am for the 1988 $1.5 million Bicentennial Classic would have to be the most satisfying round I've played since the accident. It was a fairly windy sort of day, so conditions weren't easy, but I guess a bit of the old adrenaline came back through playing at a venue I had played many times in tournament golf and with a partner like Bruce Crampton. I actually drove it past him on the last hole and he just shook his head in disbelief. I hit a 6-iron into the green while he hit 5-iron, and I experienced the buzz that mug amateurs do at times.

Hindsight is always great. I had experienced some very serious swing problems just before the accident and I think there is a lot to be said for one-arm practice. The big problem most golfers have is that the right side is dominant – the right arm, hand and wrist – and inevitably the right side overpowers the left. I believe that, from the point of view of strengthening your left side and getting the feel of the way your left arm and side should work in a golf swing, it must be a good way to practise. So maybe all those years ago, Allen Miller had it right.

A good drive for me these days is between 220 and 240 yards, compared with the old days when it was between 255 and 270. I no longer carry 2-, 3- or 4-irons in the bag, preferring instead to use a 5-wood and a 7-wood, which are much more user-friendly. It's quite weird if I'm playing a course for which I still have a yardage book. I work out what I would have hit and then work back from there, sometimes adding one club but mostly two.

My enjoyment in golf now comes from the partners with whom I am drawn. For a number of years I played in Christy O'Connor Sr's pro-am, then stayed on and did the commentary for the Irish Open. That was one of the really fun tournaments because of the Irish hospitality involved. I played the pro-am with a mate, David Lavin, whom I first met back in the early '70s. I've always stayed with him in Dublin and he made the trip out to Australia for my fortieth birthday in 1990. I still see him and speak with him regularly.

During the early days as I got back into golf I received tremendous encouragement from the late Artie Devlin, Bruce's father. Artie lost his right arm in an accident when he was driving with it out the window and a truck travelling in the opposite direction sheared it off. Artie was B-grade club champion at Goulburn at the time and within two years won the C-grade title playing his brand of one-armed golf.

He came to see me in hospital and later tried to persuade me to play golf his way. He had adopted a left-handed swing, whereas I chose to use a right-handed swing using my left arm. I tried to swing left-handed a few times, but after you've hit literally millions of balls right-handed it just seems unnatural. If I play tennis now, my backhand is great because it's a repeat of the golf swing and I can see the ball coming on that side of the body, but I'm bloody useless on the forehand, especially if the ball comes quickly.

It's the same when I play cricket with Clint; I find it very hard to throw a ball left-handed because I can't develop any snap from the wrist. The movement feels like it's all coming from the shoulder.

Artie was great, a knockabout bloke who said it as it was, no messing around. He told me bluntly what life would be like with one arm and his support, plus that of my mates and my family, really helped me. My kids were particularly honest and didn't pull any punches. It's very easy to feel sorry for yourself, but when it gets down to the nitty-gritty you just have to get on with life the best you can.

There was a small-minded attitude to my return to playing golf from some quarters.

A mate, Neil Gaudion, and I entered the 1985 Jaguar–Rover competition, an Australia-wide contest in which the winners won a trip to Spain to contest the world title. I played off nineteen and Neil was off eight and we won the Newcastle section to go into the national final at Sydney's Oatlands course.

Before the final there was a lot of hoo-ha about my status. How, it was asked, could a professional golfer be playing in an amateur event? We played in the final and on the front nine I shot one over par to accumulate 27 points by myself. But on the back nine we had a small hiccup in the office, both failing to score on one hole, and we had 47 points for the round.

Again the question was asked about my status, but it

didn't matter. We were beaten on a countback and it was then that the Australian Golf Union stepped in, saying the event was unauthorised and anyone who took the trip would lose their amateur status. A raffle was held and the guys who won on countback went on the trip to Spain.

The whole business begged the question, how can anyone with all their faculties intact possibly say I am a professional golfer? I am, but in name only. I still pay my dues and I'll never relinquish my membership. I'm proud to have been a professional.

I struck the same prejudice in 1990 when I lodged an application to become a member of the Newcastle (or Stockton, as it is known) Golf Club. It wasn't that I was unhappy at Steelworks (now known as Shortland Waters), but as a semi-public course it suffers from massive overcrowding like every other similar course around the nation. The golf boom was with us then, as it is now, and at Steelworks a game became a five-hour ordeal. These days I haven't the time for that, nor the patience.

Stockton is a very fine golf course that doesn't get used all that often and I felt if I could join the club I'd be able to duck out there late in the afternoon and maybe play twelve or thirteen holes. The net result was that my application was turned down because the club has a by-law which precludes golf professionals from becoming members.

I wasn't asking for any favours. I wanted to pay my way. If the golf club had been going brilliantly in a financial sense I could have understood their not wanting my subscription. By the same token I would have thought it might have been something of an advantage to them for me to be a member. I received a letter back from them saying I was welcome to play there any time but couldn't become a member. That sticks in my craw. I guess it's a hand-me-down policy from the old days when golf professionals, bookies, jockeys and Jews were all banned from private golf clubs. It smells of pseudo-bloody-sophistication, elitism if you want. I've always found the good people in life are those who are down to earth and genuine. The pretenders are not in the same league as the people they would aspire to be.

The fact that Stockton knocked me back was reported in the newspapers in Melbourne and Sydney and the decision astounded a lot of people. Today I remain a member of Shortland Waters and Belmont.

A lot of people have asked if I'll ever play in the amputee championships around the world, like Sydney golfer Geoff Nicholas. He lost part of his right leg at birth as a thalidomide victim, and has won the British and US amputee championships each year for the past eleven years. He's to be admired for his courage and perseverance.

Maybe I'll play one day, but it's not high on my list of priorities. I don't have the time to go to Britain or America for a one-off situation, whereas Geoff goes because he wants to win. Without making too fine a point of it, a guy who has lost a leg, or part of it, has a much better chance than a one-armed golfer – but I'll give it a crack one day and if I get lucky and win the US title, I could find myself playing the US Open one more time. There's a push on from the National Amputee Golf Association in the States for the winner of its title to qualify automatically for the Open.

Another thing I'd like to do is to have a hole-in-one in some form of comp. I've only ever had two in my life, but they were in practice rounds. I did go close with one arm at Royal Melbourne during a social game with former Test wicket-keeper Rod Marsh. It was on the 16th of the east course – a lovely par 3 that is not played on the composite course – and the ball hung on the lip, giving me a tap in for birdie. And I've had two putts for eagle, both from about 25 feet, but missed them both.

A few of my mates have called me the Poker Machine, the one-armed bandit, but I wouldn't go that far. Maybe I could be, but so far I just haven't had the time to work on my game. One day, perhaps!

Of Tiger Woods, appearance money and other concerns

The newspaper story early in 2001 that reported that Tiger Woods was being offered A$6 million to play two tournaments in Australia later that year stopped me in my tracks. Phenomenal player that Woods is, no one is worth that much money. It's both ludicrous and obscene, and proof that the whole appearance-money question in this country is now totally out of control.

Obviously the weakened state of the Australian dollar was partly to blame for the grossly inflated sum being offered to Woods, as all appearance fees are paid in US dollars, but nevertheless it was an outrageous figure for a player who already reportedly earns around $100 million a year on and off the golf course. It is the continuation of a trend and has become an ever-tightening noose around the neck of golf in Australia and in other parts of the world outside of the United States.

In the late '80s and early '90s, Greg Norman was receiving $300 000 per tournament to play at home, which is roughly equivalent to the winning cheque in a $1.7 million tournament. Some argued that Norman was worth it, but I wouldn't have a bar of it. Leading radio personality John Laws called me up for his program as a supporter of Norman and the amount he was being paid. Laws attempted to draw a comparison with the opera singer Luciano Pavarotti, who as an entertainer – just as Laws suggested Norman is – was being paid $1 million to come to this country to sing. Where's the difference, he asked? Laws had little comeback when I pointed out that Norman (or Woods), as well as receiving a ridiculous sum of money to tee up, then had the chance to play for a slice of a further $1 million or $2 million in prize money, which Pavarotti did not.

My contention is that as purses in golf continue to rise, appearance money should go down – but try telling that to management agents. Another big factor these days is that the Americans are now playing for such vast sums of money on the US PGA Tour that most of them play fewer than thirty tournaments a year. In contrast, Bruce Crampton, the Aussie Iron Man of the '60s and '70s in the US, played in excess of forty events a year. These days, because of their inflated pay packets, some golfers can ask the earth. If they don't get it, they simply won't play.

The game gives the leading players of the world a very comfortable living – some could possibly solve the budget deficits of developing countries. I believe they have an obligation to develop the game all around the world and be ambassadors for golf and role models for the kids who, after all, are the future of the sport.

Had someone listened to a few voices in the wilderness during the '70s and early '80s, we might never have been in the position we are today. I first became outspoken on the appearance-money issue in 1974 when a number of Americans were flown into town for the old Wills Masters at the Australian in Sydney. They included the likes of Jerry Heard, John Schroeder, Danny Edwards, Tom Kite, Eddie Pearce and Allen Miller, who were all young and, as far as I was concerned, no better players than, say, Bob Shearer, Stewart Ginn, Ian Stanley or me. Yet they were paid to play because the seemingly all-powerful 'USA' appeared alongside their names.

The situation became totally out of control when Tony Charlton, one-time radio and television sportscaster, revitalised the Victorian Open in the '70s with a philosophy of centring the entire tournament around just one player. Johnny Miller, Arnold Palmer and Gary Player were among those paid exorbitant fees to play. The $90 000 received by Miller in 1977 was outrageous given that the entire purse was only $40 000 with $8000 going to the winner – who, ironically, was local club pro Geoff Parslow, playing on his home course of Yarra Yarra in Melbourne. Another crazy example of the emerging appearance-money syndrome was the $50 000 paid to Lee Trevino to play in the 1973 Chrysler Classic at The Lakes in Sydney when that tournament, then the richest in the land, was worth just $50 000. Trevino got first money through to last money just by showing up.

A lot of the Americans did want to play our great courses, particularly those in Melbourne's sandbelt area, and if prize money had been escalated in those early days with perhaps a fishing trip thrown in for the visitors, the appearance-money monster might never have been created. One man did get it right, and there are those who would suggest he always gets it right. Australia's richest man, Kerry Packer, became involved with the Australian Open in the mid-'70s. He spent $2 million on a redesign of the Australian course by Jack Nicklaus, and boosted the purse each year to what was then an incredible $220 000 in 1978. (By way of comparison, the US Masters that year was worth just A$260 000.) Packer also adopted the theory of 'equal pay to play' instead of throwing appearance money around like confetti. Each 'name' player was paid $6000 and in 1978 these players included Nicklaus, Ben Crenshaw, Bruce Leitzke, Lon Hinkle, Bruce Devlin, Jerry Pate, Ed Sneed, Miller Barber, Bob Byman, Bobby Wadkins, Lou Graham, Bill Rogers, David Graham, Heard and Kite. My old mate Bob Shearer also received $6000, but I did not. I had no gripe about this, because I felt that the appearance-money question was being tackled properly for the first time.

Golf in this country stagnated for seven or eight years when Packer withdrew his sponsorship after the '78 championship. The circumstances of his departure still amaze me. There was an argument with the Australian Golf Union over the trifling matter of 2 per cent of the gate receipts (around $2000) and the big bloke simply walked away. I suspect it was at that point that I started to question the direction in which the AGU was headed. It just didn't make sense to alienate a benefactor over such a ridiculous and petty issue. In my opinion, that was when the Australian Open started going backwards. I'm not sure it's ever recovered. Packer had the course and the television network, and he was sent on his way over the trivial issue of the split-up of the gate takings.

That same year, Shearer conducted a one-man campaign against appearance money being paid to visiting players in the Australian PGA Championship at Royal Melbourne. He withdrew from the event, which was a considerable personal sacrifice given that it was his favourite course and he had won two Chrysler Classics there. Again the tournament organiser was Tony Charlton and the cheque book had come out for Johnny Miller, J.C. Snead, Hale Irwin, Lou Graham and Nick Faldo, who at that stage had only won the British PGA Championship. Shears, by contrast, had won twice in Europe and had had eight other tournament victories in Australia and New Zealand. I'd won three times in England, once in the US and at half a dozen other tournaments in Africa, Australia and New Zealand. The Australia PGA was attempting to enforce a rule that its own players could not receive appearance money. This was crazy, given that David Graham was receiving around $15 000 every time he stepped into the country. It was considered that Graham was domiciled in America and thus was eligible for a hand-out. Shears and I played overseas for ten months every year but still called Australia home and as a result we were denied appearance money.

The issue came to a head in 1980, when I was the reigning Australian Open champion. A group of Australian players met and we decided to make an issue of the fact that overseas players, less credentialled than we were, were being paid appearance money in the Australian PGA tournament, which Charlton was still running. We made a pact not to play unless we were paid, too. As it happened, the other guys, each for his own reasons, backed off and in the end I was the only one who sat on the sidelines that week. Had we managed a mass boycott, we might not have the problems that exist to this day.

What made my battle over appearance money worse was that John Lindsey of Dunhill, which was sponsoring the 1980 Australian Open, came to the US and asked me to introduce him to some of the players he didn't know. He asked me to set up meetings and find out how much certain players wanted to come to Australia. There I was, the current Australian Open champion, helping him out and yet at that stage he wasn't paying me to play. I wasn't playing the PGA title that year because of appearance money, and I was also quite prepared to miss the Open. All I wanted was $5000 – a drop in the ocean – because of the principle at stake. Eventually I did get paid, and this was one of just two occasions where that happened. The other was the NSW PGA title, also in 1980. Through the years I did quite often receive airfares and accommodation, but generally speaking, that is now par for the course for 'name' players.

Mixed up in the whole vexed question of appearance money was – and is – the International Management Group. They still run three of our major tournaments – the Open (in conjunction with the AGU), the Australian Masters and the Johnnie Walker Classic – and not by coincidence, they also manage many of the world's top players, including Tiger

Woods. Greg Norman was on their books until the early 1990s when he established his own company, Great White Shark Enterprises. Invariably, it is IMG clients who are paid appearance money to play in IMG-controlled events. And, of course, the company does get its percentage of those hefty fees.

IMG once had an extraordinary stranglehold on Australian golf. Through their association with the AGU and the state amateur golf associations, the company commandeered events like the NSW Open, the Queensland Open and the Australian Match Play championship, all Order of Merit tournaments and significant events. Where are these events now? Dead in the water!

As well, IMG had a deal with the Seven Network that they liked to call 'leveraging'. They had control of Seven's coverage of golf, which prevented the network from televising nationally any event that was not run by IMG. For example, the Heineken Classic at The Vines in Perth was covered in Western Australia but not nationally, because it was run by independent promoter Tony Roosenburg. This fact was denied by IMG for years but has recently been confirmed to me.

The IMG influence on golf both perplexed and annoyed me. How could a management company with a conflict of interest as a tournament promoter and manager of players, justify going to a television network and doing a deal with them that included tournament dates and players they had no control over?

After 11 years as a board member of the Australasian PGA Tour, I became its chairman in 1991, a position I held until 2000. My chairmanship followed that of Graham Marsh and Terry Gale who – albeit with their hands tied behind their backs – had done great work. When I became chairman, I was determined to get to the bottom of the IMG issue. James Erskine, then IMG's Australasian managing director, and I had a tremendous love–hate relationship and I told him I would pursue the matter, which was my right as chairman of the Tour. I believed it was time for the PGA Tour to stand up for its rights: total control of professional tournament golf in this country, including dates.

The other major issue was television. We couldn't do anything about the Channel Seven/IMG events – watertight contracts had been signed in the days when Christopher Skase headed up the network before the collapse of his Quintex group – but we could tackle the others. Huge costs – as much as $700 000 – were involved in mounting television coverage of any given tournament. Promoters paid these amounts to the commercial networks (Channel Seven excluded) and lesser amounts to the ABC. Sponsors demand television and it had to be done, adding considerably to tournament budgets.

Out of this situation was born in the late '90s Australasian PGA Tour Productions. I had serious discussions with a number of ex-Channel Seven employees about how we could go about setting up a production company, and had also been approached by Seamus O'Brien, a unique character based in Hong Kong who is a television negotiator. Under the banner of the Oceanic Sports Group, he had the rights to Asian soccer and basketball plus a role in the new Davidoff Asian PGA Tour.

With O'Brien's help, we formed our own production company and contracts were signed with the Ten network and Fox Sports to deliver a fully packaged television coverage of eight tournaments per season. Ten traditionally had an under-25 age demographic and was looking for a profile at the other end of the market, which golf could give them. They also needed an extra sporting entity after losing the rights to rugby league and basketball, to go with their coverage of motor racing and the Melbourne Spring Racing Carnival.

The arrangement is doing quite nicely and without doubt has raised the profile of golf in Australia. We were able to 'do an IMG' by packaging eight tournaments to give sponsors a greater spread across the board. At the same time, we signed a massive five-year deal with the ANZ Banking Group for overall sponsorship of the Tour. The payments from Ten and Fox cover production costs with a little bit left over and the Australasian PGA Tour is now on a very sound financial footing. Mind you, we're still way behind the US PGA Tour, which recently signed a television agreement that boosted its annual TV earnings from $80 million to $200 million. This has contributed greatly to the massive increase in prize money in the States, where they are now playing for between $US3 million and $US4 million a week.

———————

The huge increase in American TV rights can be attributed directly to Tiger Woods. Because of this Afro-Asian American, groomed for stardom by his father Earl while still in nappies, golf has never been more popular. Tiger has shown that golf can be 'cool'. He is very young in what was once considered an old man's game and his influence is wide-reaching. Never has there been a player as good as he is at such a young age.

I do, however, wonder about Woods' longevity. Will he last as long as Jack Nicklaus, the yardstick of all golfers through the decades? Probably not, because of the financial rewards now available and the pressures, both on and off the sporting arena, that confront top-class sportspeople these days. But Tiger has certainly proved himself to be unique and he is already a legend. I believe his desire should not be to set new records when it comes to appearance money, but to leave a legacy to golf, play around the world, play the great courses and the championships that have meaning in the history of the game, and be an ambassador for golf with his extraordinary talent. Already I rate him, behind Nicklaus, as the second-best player ever to grace the fairways. He is the complete package.

Greg Norman's role in popularising the game should not be overlooked. For a time I was critical that we were too 'Normanised', that everything revolved around him, with the media preferring to write, say, about his sore big toe rather than about some other Australian doing well in the US, Europe, Japan, anywhere. But Norman set the benchmark for other Australians. He began the snowballing effect, with both Ian Baker-Finch and Wayne Grady believing that if Norman could win a major, so could they. So too Steve Elkington, with his victory in the 1995 US PGA championship. These players were inspired by Norman and now, in their turn, are inspiring others.

Our mix of Australian talent now has a 'middle-aged' bracket around the age of thirty, such as Stuart Appleby and Robert Allenby. Michael Campbell, surely an honorary Australian, lives in Sydney's Bondi as many New Zealanders do, and has one of the best swings in golf. Then we've got the youngsters – Greg Chalmers, Brett Rumford, Adam Scott, Scott Gardiner, James McLean, Geoff Ogilvy and, of course, Aaron Baddeley. As a teenager, Aaron won the Australian Open in successive years – as an amateur in 1999 and then as a professional in 2000. It was a marvellous achievement. In my mind, there are no better young players in 2001 than this group of Aussies, with the exception of Spaniard Sergio Garcia. The Australian approach may be a bit warts and all, but we must be doing something right to be producing such outstanding young players, and spies from the US, Sweden, Asia and Britain have been coming our way to see how it's done.

Let's not forget Karrie Webb. For my money, she is the best player, male or female, Australia has ever produced. By the time she retires, if her desire and fitness levels are maintained, she will be recognised as the greatest woman player the world has seen. She has one of the best swings in the game – men's or women's – and relishes the competition. Karrie is one hell of a tough cookie when it comes to golf. Basically she is a fairly quiet country girl, but her determination is second to none. She cops criticism and she shouldn't. Sometimes we can be too hard on people who don't smile all the time and don't look the way we want them to look. We can't all be Lee Trevino, laughing and joking his way round the golf course. Everyone has a different disposition, and Karrie has hers. She has given women's golf in this country a much-needed shot in the arm. Behind Karrie is the ever-improving Rachel Hetherington.

While we're on the subject of great players, just who are the greatest male players in golf? I'll give you two lists. One includes the players with whom I played in two decades of the game, and the other is my all-time list. The latter is purely subjective, based on what I've read through the years, and is, of course, open to argument.

IN MY YEARS	ALL-TIME
1 Jack Nicklaus	1 Jack Nicklaus
2 Tom Watson	2 Tiger Woods
3 Gary Player	3 Ben Hogan
4 Lee Trevino	4 Bobby Jones
5 Seve Ballesteros	5 Sam Sneed
6 Raymond Floyd	6 Arnold Palmer
7 Nick Faldo	7 Walter Hagen
8 Hale Irwin	8 Tom Watson
9 Johnny Miller	9 Gene Sarazen
10 Greg Norman	10 Gary Player

I like to think – no, I'm certain – that the success Australian golfers are now experiencing is due to the significant role being played around the land by the various junior golf foundations, including my Jack Newton Junior Golf Foundation in NSW. Our charter, when the foundation was formed in 1986, was to get more kids playing the game, through clinics and tournaments. It was based on the theory that the broader the base of a pyramid, the higher the peak. We're discovering and nurturing new talent and they are taking their place on the world stage.

There was no such nursery back in the early '80s, when it was single-minded determination that brought success. Craig Parry slept in the back of his van at tournaments and now earns $1 million plus a year. Brian Jones was broke in the mid-'80s and grew to multi-million-dollar status playing in Japan. Wayne Grady, the product of a working-class background and my successor as chairman of the Australasian PGA Tour, succeeded through sheer hard work and a dream. So, too, did David Graham and Bruce Devlin.

We've developed that pyramid now. It rises from the junior foundations through to the various institutes of sport and the excellent Australian Institute of Sport golf program established by Ross Herbert, who died in early 2001 at the age of forty-one after a short battle with cancer. His magnificent contribution to Australian golf should never be forgotten. We've been able to bring kids through from the grassroots start of the junior golf foundations. In the case of my own program, it is incredibly satisfying. Each year since 1986, we've had the Jack Newton Celebrity Classic on Queensland's Sunshine Coast to raise funds for the development of junior golf, with not a cent going to a middleman, and in 2000 we reached $1 million. It makes me proud and I guess part of the fruits of our endeavours is the fact that NSW won the last four junior (under 18) interstate amateur series of the twentieth century and the first one of the new millennium.

What a varied life I've had since the accident. Golf has remained my passion, but harness racing and rugby league have been pretty close tied at second.

When I was a youngster my father took me regularly to the Harold Park trots in Sydney. Originally he was stationed at Ryde when he joined the police force, but he was later transferred to Balmain, which meant that Harold Park was in his precinct. Dad always seemed to be on duty when there was a trotting meeting and I suspect this was more by good management than good luck.

Harness racing became an on-going interest for me, too, and in New Zealand in 1971 I met well-known Kiwi trainer–driver Tommy Knowles. The following year I stayed on his farm at Kumeu and each morning before heading to the golf I drove work for him. After winning the City of Auckland Classic in 1972 and doing well in other NZ tournaments, I was cashed up and asked Tommy to buy me a well-bred horse at the next yearling sales. I left $8000 with him – small change these days to the likes of Gai Waterhouse – and he bought one for $2200, giving me money back.

Blair Logie turned out a pretty useful horse, winning a couple of minor cup races in New Zealand. We sold him to America for $35 000, which wasn't a bad return on your money, especially in the '70s. Newt was the next horse, and he won a race on the final night of the Interdominion in Auckland. All up he probably won around $35 000 in prize money until he, too, was sold to the US.

When Jackie and I moved to Newcastle in 1976, I formed a syndicate with my mates Dick Maclean and Brian Hayes, and we used the letters of our surnames for the syndicate name of Hanema. Our horses all bore the name of royalty plus 'Hanema' – Duke of Hanema, Duchess of Hanema, Lady of Hanema, Prince of Hanema. We had a breakthrough buying one horse, already named Lots of Vic, who went on to win thirty-two races. Then Dick and I went out on our own, though I did own a few horses independently. The best of the batch was Catch the Action, who won around twelve races. I still hold high hopes of finding a true champion among the current horses in the paddock.

And rugby league! Nothing quite stirs the blood like this sport. Originally I was a Western Suburbs supporter (before Rupert Murdoch got his hands on the game – the club is now known as the Wests Tigers after the merger of Balmain and Western Suburbs) but swapped my allegiance to Parramatta when my parents moved into nearby Carling-ford. That was until the Newcastle Knights joined the competition in 1988.

Newcastle – the city, that is – has had quite a bashing through the years. There was the earthquake in 1989 and BHP closing down its operations in 1999, but the football team has always been a bonding factor. It's that little touch of life and sanity in a community pummelled by outside forces. (These include the fact that it is the safest of safe Labor seats because of its mining background, so it's basically ignored by federal politicians both Labor and Liberal. While I was brought up with very strong Labor roots, I think perhaps it is time for local councils and politicians to recognise we're losing many smart young kids from the area because of lack of opportunity.)

One of the most rewarding things we did as a family during the early post-accident years was join the Newcastle Knights rugby league club as foundation members. Rain, hail or shine, we turned up to watch the matches, and although Jackie, Kristie and Clint initially had limited knowledge of the game, we loved it from the start and still do. Perhaps those who have done their best to destroy the game of rugby league have overlooked its value as a tool for family bonding!

One day in 1997, 27 September to be exact, will always live in my memory. It was one of the proudest days of my life because the underdog got up. People were strung out along the road from Newcastle to the Central Coast to wish the Knights good luck as they travelled on their bus to the Sydney Sports Stadium and the grand final of the Australian Rugby League competition. They beat the silver-tailed Manly, with Darren Albert scoring the winning try with just seconds to go. Never before or since have I witnessed such scenes, not just at the ground but back in Newcastle. As the saying goes, you can take the boy out of Newcastle, but you can never, ever, take Newcastle out of the boy. The Knights that day epitomised everything I've ever stood for: never give in, no matter the adversity thrown your way.

On the team's way home, the highway was lined with people standing in drizzling rain to salute their heroes. Emotions ran high that night; they poured out in unison with the rain, and Jackie and I were fearful we would be crushed by the tide of joyous people who gathered at the Workers' Club to welcome the victorious team back. It was magic; it was Newcastle.

Clint recently played first-grade rugby league for the first time. To witness him playing in the distinctive red and blue of the mighty Knights alongside one of the greatest-ever players – Andrew Johns – not only filled me with pride and joy but made the events of eighteen years ago seem very distant and irrelevant.

Epilogue

From an early age sport shaped me, whether it was through participating, observing, socialising or, later, business activities. I am sure my life would have taken a vastly different course had it not been for sport – in particular, golf, and this is the main reason why I have always felt it important to put something back into the game. Among my activities in this area were my stint with the Australian PGA Tour as board member and chairman, and my initiatives in promoting junior golf.

Recently some educators have been talking about reducing sporting activities in schools. After discussions on this issue with many of my peers, the consensus of opinion seems to be that school sport was definitely worth having – at worst, it broke the monotony; at best, it was the only reason some of us went to school at all!

While some people might disagree with me, it is my

contention that if we can get our kids away from the computer and into a healthy, active environment playing some form of sport, the chances of avoiding many of the problems in our society today will be increased. Team sport provides camaraderie, while an 'individual' sport such as golf offers the opportunity to play from a young age until well into retirement, and a chance to smell the roses while getting some exercise. It can be a great character builder as well as teaching the importance of rules, honesty, integrity, etiquette, dress standards and discipline.

I urge the decision-makers to accept that sport is an integral part of the Australian life and psyche. Sportspeople have been possibly our most well-known export, particularly in the large markets of the USA, Europe and Japan. They are generally much better role models than our politicians and corporate leaders, and I suspect that most successful people wouldn't have made it to first base in pursuit of their dreams if they had followed the examples of business and government rather than those of their sporting heroes.

As an Aquarian, and with my background, it is little wonder that I am a fierce competitor who loves to win. I've always been prepared to give 110 per cent to achieve my goals. I would also classify myself as a 'front foot' player who has a distinct lack of patience and can be decidedly pig-headed, belligerent and outspoken, if I see the need. My disposition has often enabled me to break down barriers and get things done – but over the years it has also landed me in hot water, supplying fodder for my detractors and opponents.

In my view, you're a wimp if you don't truly believe in a cause, be it golf, football or any facet of life. There are those who sit back and criticise if they perceive something is wrong. They won't get off their backsides in a bid to rectify the situation. But you can't sit back and say, 'Let someone else do it.' Nothing will ever happen. At times, with the Junior Golf Foundation, I've come home to Jackie after running into brick walls and said to her, 'What the hell am I doing this for?' I know the answer: you have to suffer petty jealousy, hypocrisy and innuendo, but they only make you stronger. It has always been my passion to help junior golf, but sometimes what I want hasn't meshed with the AGU's or state association's thoughts. I won't back away even when they seem to have a different agenda from mine – which is a genuine desire to help kids in golf, and in life for that matter. No matter the number of times I get kicked up the backside, I'll keep trying.

My attitude has always been to tell it the way I see it, coming in the front door instead of the back door. Obviously over the years I've ruffled a few feathers. You do create enemies, but that's the legacy I've got – and I wouldn't have it any other way. I know people either like me or dislike me, but I make no excuses. I can't apologise for that. As a sportsperson, you have to be pretty self-centred – maybe even arrogant – if you're going to be successful. Tall-poppy syndrome still exists; it's a matter of how you deal with it.

When you're lying in a hospital bed, not knowing if you're going to live or die, you realise that life is far too short to elevate yourself to a pedestal above others. My philosophy has always been: 'Set your goals, achieve those goals and be proud to be Australian, but always do it with humility.'

Some people might suggest that I've already had nine lives. All I can say is that when judgement day finally arrives for me, I hope my epitaph will be: 'At least he had a go!'

Career record

AMATEUR
NSW schoolboys' championship 1965, 1966, 1967
NSW amateur championship 1968
NSW amateur mixed foursomes (with Jan Stephenson) 1968
Amateur foursomes championship of Australia (with Barry Burgess) 1969
Australian amateur championship semifinalist 1969

1970
2nd NSW PGA championship – Castle Hill CC, Sydney
4th South Pacific Open – Surfers Paradise GC, Qld
Top 10 Queensland Open – Keperra GC, Brisbane

1971
Top 2 NSW PGA – Mona Vale GC, Sydney
Top 5 New Zealand Open – Balmacewan GC, Dunedin, NZ
Top 6 Otago Classic – St Clair, Dunedin, NZ
Top 7 BP Open – Olgiata GC, Rome, Italy
Top 9 South Australian Open – Kooyonga GC, Adelaide

1972
Winner Benson & Hedges Golf Festival – Fulford GC, York, England
Winner Dutch Open – Haagsche G & CC, Wassenaar, The Netherlands
Winner Forbes Classic – Forbes GC, NSW
Winner City of Auckland Classic – The Grange GC, Auckland, NZ

2nd Caltex Tournament – Paraparaumu Beach, Wellington, NZ

2nd Martini International – Abridge GC, Essex, England

3rd Penfold Bournemouth Tournament – Queens Park GC,
      Bournemouth, England

3rd New Zealand Open – Paraparaumu Beach, Wellington, NZ

Top 3 Christchurch Garden City Classic – Russley GC,
      Christchurch, NZ

Top 5 John Player Trophy – Bognor Regis GC, West Sussex,
      England

Top 8 Carrolls International – Woodbrook GC, Dublin, Ireland

Top 8 Scottish Open – Downfield GC, Dundee, Scotland

1973

2nd Wills Open – Kings Norton GC, Birmingham, England

Top 2 Swiss Open – Crans-sur-Sierre GC, Switzerland

4th Benson & Hedges Festival – Fulford GC, York, England

Top 6 Sumrie Better Ball (with John O'Leary) – Blairgowrie
      GC, Scotland

9th Texaco pro-amateur – Southport and Ainsdale GC,
      Merseyside, England

Top 9 Martini International – Royal Burgess Golfing Society,
      Edinburgh, Scotland

Top 10 Dutch Open – Haagsche G & CC, Wassenaar, The
      Netherlands

1974

Winner Benson & Hedges matchplay championship – Downfield
      GC, Dundee, Scotland

Winner Nigerian Open – Ikoyi GC, Nigeria

2nd Carrolls International – Woodbrook GC, Dublin, Ireland

2nd Wills Tournament – Kings Norton GC, Birmingham, England

2nd Coca-Cola Young Professionals Championship – Long Ashton GC, Bristol, England

Top 2 New Zealand Open (lost sudden-death play-off to American Bob Gilder) – Shirley Course, Christchurch GC, NZ

Top 5 City of Auckland Classic – The Grange GC, Auckland, NZ

Top 10 Otago Classic – St Clair, Dunedin, NZ

1975

Winner Sumrie Better Ball (with John O'Leary) – Queens Park GC, Bournemouth, England

2nd British Open (lost 18-hole play-off to Tom Watson) – Carnoustie, Scotland

4th New Zealand Open – St Andrews Course, Hamilton GC, NZ

Top 8 Irish Open – Woodbrook GC, Dublin, Ireland

10th Chrysler Classic – Royal Melbourne GC

1976

Winner NSW Open – Royal Sydney GC

Winner Mufulira Open – Zambia

Winner Cock o' the North – Ndola, Zambia

2nd Zambian Open – Lusaka GC, Zambia

7th Australian Open – The Australian GC, Sydney

Top 10 South African Open – Houghton GC, Johannesburg, South Africa

Top 10 Chrysler Classic – Royal Melbourne GC

1977

Top 2 Colgate Champion of Champions – Victoria GC, Melbourne

Top 3 Australian PGA – Yarra Yarra GC, Melbourne

5th Australian Open – The Australian GC, Sydney

Top 10 Colgate Hall of Fame Classic – Pinehurst Resort & CC,
North Carolina, USA

1978

Winner Buick Open – Warwick Hills CC, Grand Blanc,
Michigan, USA

Top 2 Queensland Open – Brisbane GC

3rd Caltex Festival of Sydney Open – The Lakes GC, Sydney

Top 4 NSW Open – Manly GC, Sydney

Top 7 Victorian PGA – Woodlands GC, Melbourne

1979

Winner Australian Open – Metropolitan GC, Melbourne

Winner NSW Open – The Lakes GC, Sydney

2nd Queensland Open (lost sudden-death play-off to Jeff
Senior) – Indooroopilly GC, Brisbane

Top 4 Australian Masters – Huntingdale GC, Melbourne

Top 9 Tournament Players Championship – Sawgrass,
Jacksonville, Florida, USA

1980

Top 2 US Masters – Augusta National GC, Georgia, USA

Top 2 Greater Greensboro Open – Forest Oaks CC, North
Carolina, USA

Top 4 Kemper Open – Congressional CC, Bethesda, Maryland,
USA

Top 8 Australian Open – The Lakes GC, Sydney

Top 10 British Open – Muirfield, Scotland

Top 10 New Zealand Open – New Plymouth GC, NZ

1981

Top 3 Tooth Classic – Coolangatta & Tweed Heads GC, NSW

5th Westlakes Classic – Royal Adelaide GC

5th Australian Open – Victoria GC, Melbourne

1982

2nd New Zealand PGA – Mount Maunganui GC, Tauranga, NZ

Top 2 Tasmanian Open – Tasmania GC, Hobart

Top 3 Air New Zealand – Shell Open – Titirangi GC,
    Auckland, NZ

Top 5 Westpac Golf Classic – Royal Adelaide GC

Top 10 Byron Nelson Classic – Preston Trail GC, Dallas, Texas,
    USA

Top 10 New Zealand Open – Christchurch GC, NZ

1983

2nd Western Australian Open (lost sudden-death play-off to
    Terry Gale) – Lake Karrinyup GC, Perth

3rd Victorian Open – Metropolitan GC, Melbourne

3rd Tasmanian Open – Devonport GC, Tasmania

Top 5 Australian Masters – Huntingdale GC, Melbourne

Top 5 South Australian Open – Kooyonga GC, Adelaide

Index

NOTE: *Individual golf courses and clubs are listed under 'courses and clubs'. Individual tournaments are listed under 'tournaments and championships'.*

ABC (Australia) 193–5, 196, 202, 236
ABC (USA) 203
Aberdale Hotel, NSW 213
Adidas 211
African circuit 54–6, 116
Age [Melbourne] 197, 204
Agnew, Spiro 140
AGU *see* Australian Golf Union
Albert, Darren 243
Alexander, John 20
Allen, Mark 200
Allenby, Robert 142, 238
Alliss, Peter 193
amateur golf associations 235
American Express 35, 143
American tour *see* US circuit
amputee championships 226
ANZ Banking Group 237
appearance money 119, 133, 229–34, 238
Appleby, Stuart 142, 238
Archer, George 41–2, 140
Ashford, Murray 193–4
Asian circuit 35, 51–2, 53, 236
Athletics Australia 12
Australasian PGA Tour 235–7, 240, 245
Australasian PGA Tour Productions 236–7
Australian circuit 42, 53, 95, 143, 153
Australian Golf Union (AGU) 225, 232, 234, 235, 247
Australian golf writers' dinner 126
Australian Indoor Tennis Championships (1985) 189
Australian Institute of Sport 241
Australian PGA *see* Professional Golfers' Association

Australian Rules football
Melbourne 166
Sydney Swans 166–7, 190, 206
Victorian Football League (VFL) 166–7

Baba, Amadu 55
Baddeley, Aaron 239
Baker, Vinny 35, 37, 40, 49
Baker-Finch, Ian 200–1, 238
Baldwin, Michael 169–70, 185
Baleson, Gary 44
Ball, Alan 116
Ball, Teddy 51
Ballesteros, Seve 106, 107, 108–11, 119, 120, 173, 174, 240
Bannerman, Harry 40, 44–5, 158–9
Barber, Miller 106, 232
Barclay's Bank 55
Barker, Sue 131
Barnes, Brian 32, 39, 59, 70, 155
Bartlett, Kevin 183
basketball 236, 237
Bass-Walker, Patsy 37
BBC TV (UK) 200, 202
Beard, Frank 140, 147
Beaumaris Bay Motel 120–1
Beman, Deane 146, 151
Benaud, Richie 112, 195–6
Bennetts, Vic 29
Benson & Hedges 134
betting 24, 56–7, 71–2, 104–5, 156–60, 220, 222
BHP Recreational Club 221
Billings, Phil 10
Bland, John 200–1
Bolton, Bobby 47, 56–8
Bonallack, Michael 26
Briggs, Mac 112
British Airways 53, 63
British Caledonian Airways 54

British circuit 43, 51, 173
British Open *see* tournaments
'Bull' *see* Williams, Charles
Burgess, Barry 28, 30
Butterworth, Christopher (brother-in-law) 38, 79
Butterworth, John (brother-in-law) 79, 103
Butterworth, Jackie *see* Newton, Jackie
Byman, Bob 232

Caldwell, Rex 147
Calfee, Bill 161
Campbell, Michael 238
Cathay Pacific 53
Cawley, Evonne (née Goolagong) 20, 184
Cessnock, NSW 3-5
Chalmers, Greg 239
Channel Four TV (UK) 195
Chappell, Ian 174, 195
Charles, Bob 35, 41
Charlton, Tony 231, 233
cheating 52
Chifley Labor government 4
Claassens, Tertius 35-8, 39, 40
Clark, Clive 201
Coachman restaurant 183
coalminers' strike (1949) 4-5
Connery, Sean 70
conscription 116
Cole, Bobby 73, 74, 75, 77, 147
Coles, Neil 32, 49
Connor, Frank 158
Cooney, Bob 152
Cooney, Marlene 152
Corfu 145
Corrigan, Brian 116
Cotton, Henry 19
Couples, Fred 200-1
course design 89, 97, 202, 207-10
courses and clubs
　Arcadian Shores (USA) 112
　Atlanta Athletic Club (USA) 146
　Augusta National (USA) 53, 87-8, 92-112
　　Amen Corner 94, 109-10
　Australian (NSW) 28, 136, 170, 231, 232
　Bay Tree Plantation (USA) 104, 157, 183

Belmont (NSW) 217, 218, 226
Bournemouth (England) 71
Carnoustie (Scotland) 1, 69-78, 80-4, 88
Castle Hill (NSW) 31, 198, 207-8
Cessnock (NSW) 8
Commonwealth (Vic.) 207
Concord (NSW) 193-5
Crail (Scotland) 75
Crans-sur-Sierre (Switzerland) 34, 133
Dalmahoy (Scotland) 70
Downfield (Scotland) 116
Dundee (Scotland) 49
Elanora (NSW) 13-14
Frankfurt Main-Neiderrad (Germany) 26
Fulford (England) 40
Glen Abbey (Canada) 149-52, 154, 174
Gleneagles (Scotland) 134, 200
Gosford (NSW) 10, 11
Goulburn (NSW) 223
Grange, The (SA) 207
Greensboro (USA) 98, 100
Haagsche (The Netherlands) 40
Hillside (England) 37
Hoylake (England) 19, 25
Huntingdale (Vic.) 154, 207
Ikoyi (Nigeria) 54
Juo (Japan) 208-9
Kennemer (The Netherlands) 34
Kingston Heath (Vic.) 206-7
Kooyonga (SA) 207
Lakes, The (NSW) 119, 208
Long Reef (NSW) 10
Metropolitan (Vic.) 107, 119, 120, 121, 124-31
Moor Park (England) 145
Mufulira (Zambia) 56, 59, 63
Muirfield (NSW) 8-9, 10-11, 13, 15-16, 20, 21, 216
New South Wales 19, 20, 207
Ndola (Zambia) 56, 59
Newcastle *see* Stockton
Noosa (Qld) 218-20, 222
North Myrtle Beach (USA) 157
Northbridge (NSW) 10
Palm Meadows (USA) 203
Queens Park (England) 39
Rio Pinar (USA) 142
Riversdale (Vic.) 207

Roseville (NSW) 15–16
Royal Adelaide (SA) 28
Royal and Ancient Golf Club,
  St Andrews (Scotland) 26, 73,
  80, 133, 156, 200
  Valley of Sin 200–1
Royal Birkdale (England) 34, 117
Royal Canberra (ACT) 110
Royal Dublin (Ireland) 168
Royal Liverpool see Hoylake
Royal Lytham and St Annes
  (England) 48
Royal Melbourne (Vic.) 97, 120,
  141, 199, 222, 227, 233
Royal Porthcawl (Wales) 45
Royal Sydney (NSW) 98, 118
Ryde-Parramatta (NSW) 20
St Andrews see Royal and Ancient
St Nom La Breteche (France) 26
Sandwich (England) 144
Shortland Waters (previously
  Steelworks, NSW) 226
Steelworks (later Shortland
  Waters, NSW) 221
Stockton (NSW) 225–6
Sunningdale (England) 21–3, 25
Tory Pines (USA) 137
Troon (Scotland) 75
Turnberry (Scotland) 145, 158
Victoria (Vic.) 84
Warwick Hills (USA) 147
Wentworth (England) 40
Westchester (USA) 33, 152–3
Winged Foot (USA) 33
Woodlands (USA) 160
Yarra Yarra (Vic.) 20, 71, 206–7,
  231
Court, Margaret 20
Cowen, Peter 58
Crafter, Brian 194, 197
Crail Golfing Society (Scotland) 75
Crampton, Bruce 20, 21, 137–8, 161,
  222, 230
Crenshaw, Ben 149, 232
cricket 7, 8, 17, 95, 224
  Epping RSL cricket club 8, 17
  Northern Districts League,
  Sydney 8
Critchley, Bruce 200
Croker, Peter 156

Daly, Fred 19

Daly, John 213
Darcy, Eamonn 55, 205
D'Arcy, Frank 166–8, 190
Davidoff Asian PGA Tour 236
Davis, Rodger 97, 219, 221
de Vicenzo, Roberto 26
Dent, Phil 20
Devlin, Artie 223–4
Devlin, Bruce 20, 21, 33, 40, 87,
  152, 174, 223, 232, 240
Dobson, Keith 188
Dobson, Sandra 188
Donohoe, Kevin 10, 29
dress 67, 134
Dulwich College 48
Dumphy, John 212–13
Dunhill 119, 234
Dunk, Billy 31, 121–2
Durex 43
Dye, Pete 207, 208

East Bros 10
Edwards, Danny 149, 150, 151, 231
Eisenhower Medical Centre 139–40
Elkington, Steve 238
Epping Boys' High School 12–13,
  14–15, 17, 221
Epping Congregational Church 8
Epping Primary School 6
Epping RSL cricket club 8
Erskine, James 236
European circuit 32, 35, 39, 40, 43,
  51, 54, 106, 108, 126, 146, 173,
  205

Faichney, Sandy 20
Faldo, Nick 233, 240
Fats, Minnesota 160
Fermanis, Dulcie 120
Fermanis, Nick 120
Financial Times [UK] 193
Floyd, Raymond 152, 158, 209, 240
Footjoy shoes 92
Ford, Doug 94–5
Ford, Gerald 140
Fox Sports 237
Fraser, Neale 20
Fujita, Kazuo 208

Gale, Terry 162–3, 235
Garaialde, Jean 26, 27
Garcia, Sergio 239

Gardiner, Scott 239
Gardner, Buddy 161
Gaudion, Neil 166, 224
Gilbert, Gibby 111
Ginn, Sam 43
Ginn, Stewart 43, 44, 48, 126, 208, 231
Gleason, Jackie 160
Golf World (magazine) 35
golf-club industry 211–13
Good, David 44
Goolagong (later Cawley),
   Evonne 20, 184
Gordon Rugby Union Club 12
Gorton Liberal government 117
Grace Bros 211
Grady, Wayne 119, 123, 238, 241
Graham, David 32, 71, 107, 119,
   120, 207, 232, 233, 240
Graham, Jim 103–4
Graham, Lou 232, 233
Grant, Graeme 206–9, 209
Grant, Trevor 204, 206
Great White Shark Enterprises 234
Green, Hubert 119, 120
Gregson, Malcolm 40
gymnastics 8

Hagen, Walter 240
Hain, Jackie 185
Hall, Geoff 119
Hammond, George 49
harness racing *see* horse racing
Harold Park Paceway, NSW 241
Harrison Shield 13–14
Hart, Paul 120
Hawke, Bob 61, 174, 219, 220
Hay, Alex 200–1
Hayes, Brian 169, 187, 242
Hayes, Dale 26–7, 35
Hayes, Susan 33–4
Hayes, Toni 168
Hazell, Craig 176–7
Heard, Jerry 147, 231, 232
Henning, Harold 22
Henry, Bunkie 160
Henshaw, Dianne 218
Herald [Melbourne] 204
Herbert, Ross 241
Hetherington, Rachel 239
Hewes, Jeff 149
Hill, Michael 174

Hilton Hotel 102, 205
Hinkle, Lon 158, 232
Hoare, John 183
Hobday, Simon 35, 40, 46, 61
Hogan, Ben 70, 89, 109, 240
Holland *see* Netherlands, The
Hollows, Prof. Fred 169–70, 185
Hong Kong 52–3
Hope, Bob 139
Hope, Dolores 139
Hopman, Harry 22
horse racing 24–5, 103, 237, 242
   Sires Stakes horse races 188
   Spring Racing Carnival 237
Hoysted, Bob 183
Huish, David 73, 74
Hunt, Bernard 27
Hurlstone Agricultural College 17
hustling *see* betting

Ingham, Mike 37
International Management Group
   (IMG) 234–7
Irwin, Hale 119, 233, 240
ITV (UK) 193

Jack Newton Junior Golf
   Foundation 218, 240, 245, 247
Jacklin, Tony 32, 38, 71, 146, 158–9
Jaeckel, Barry 153
Japan 208–10
Japanese circuit 52, 136, 240
Jenkins, Dan 80, 84
Johnson, Tony 120
Johnston, Malcolm 218
Jones, Bobby 89, 90, 240
Jones, Brian 159, 209, 240
Jones, Robert Trent 207, 208
Jordan, Mickey 143

Katontoga, Bob ('The Cat') 56–8
Kaunda, Kenneth 60–1
Kennedy, Charlie 5
Kenya 54, 55, 61
Kite, Tom 143, 231, 232
Kmart 211
Knievel, Evel 136–7
Knowles, Tommy 242
Kumagai corporation 208

Lake, Ron 166
Langer, Bernhard 203

Laver, Rod 81
Lavin, David 223
Lawrence, Don 126, 204
Laws, John 230
Lees, Authur 19, 21–2, 23
Legrange, Cobie 27
Leonard, Tyson 157
Lietzke, Bruce 100, 102, 232
Lindsey, John 234
Littler, Gene 140
Locke, Bobby 67–73, 156
Lovett, Graham 174

Macbeth, Don 117–18
McCallum, Greg 166, 174, 217
McGregor, Annette 181, 183
McGregor, Col 51, 181, 183
Mackenzie, Alister 89, 97, 209
Mackie, Charlie 48, 77
Maclean, Denise 168–9, 171
Maclean, Dick 102–3, 169, 171, 187, 242
McLean, James 238
MacPherson, Rod 166
Mahaffey, John 147
Maltbie, Roger 153
Mangrum, Lloyd 68
Mario's restaurant 121
Marsh, Graham 29, 44, 53, 74, 121, 125, 127–30, 136, 195, 207, 235
Marsh, Rod 183, 227
Marshall, James 123–4
Marshall, John 123
Martin, Ed 104–5
Mason, Doug 154
Massengale, Rik 141
Matabele ants 59–60
May, Phil 95
media 123, 127
Melbourne courses 119–20, 209–11, 231
Melbourne syndrome 120
Melbourne VFL club 166
Mesnil, Bob 29
Miller, Allen 216, 222, 231
Miller, Brady 149, 150, 152
Miller, Johnny 74, 75, 76, 77, 78, 149, 151, 155, 209, 231, 233, 240
Milner, Aaron 60
Mitchell, Alfie 12
Mitchell, Jeff 107
Moffatt, Brian 12–13, 14–17

Moody, Orville 147
Moody, Peter 26, 158
Moore, David 64–5
Moore, Tommy 13
Morris, Noel 20
motor racing 237
Mt Wilga [Rehabilitation] Centre 185–7
Murdoch, Rupert 243
Murray, Alan 51
Murray, Ross 29

Nagle, Kel 44, 51
National Amputee Golf Association (USA) 226
Neilson, Peter 187
Nelford, Jim 122, 147
Netherlands, The 34–5, 39–40
New South Wales Golf Association 54, 244
New Zealand circuit 35, 137, 143
Newcastle Knights rugby league club 243–4
Newcastle Workers' Club 243
Newcombe, John 20, 81
Newton, Bill (grandfather) 3–4, 5–6, 42, 219
caddying for Jack 10–11
Newton, Clint (son) 132, 169, 175, 179–81, 212, 224, 243, 244
Newton Golf Company 211–12
Newton, Grant & Spencer company 207–10
Newton, Isobel (grandmother) 4, 42, 115, 173
Newton, Jack
accident 162, 165–90, 193, 195, 205, 211, 215, 220, 222, 241, 244
benefit tournament 183–4
colostomy reversal operation 215, 217
continuing difficulties 206, 215
first drink after 184
jokes about 187
media attention 171, 172, 173–4, 182–3
playing golf after 215–27
professional status 224–5
technique 223
rehabilitation 185–7, 217
support from players 174
trust appeal 174, 183–4, 189–90

Newton, Jack (cont.)
  Africa 54–65, 88
  amateur status 20–1, 27
  appearance money boycott 233–4
  Australasian PGA Tour, chairman
    of 235–6, 245
  biorhythms 125
  British Open loss to Watson 2, 84,
    88, 111–12, 131, 133, 146, 148,
    154, 173
  Cardiff, NSW (house) 190, 221
  children 152–3, 154, 161, 165,
    169, 171, 174–5, 179–81, 182,
    212–13, 224
  concentration 107–8
  course design 202, 207–10
  courtship 41
  disqualification 150–1
  drinking 30–1, 36, 47, 57, 68, 80,
    84, 90, 95, 121, 122, 131, 132,
    153, 166, 184, 189, 190, 193
  early years 3–17
    academic aptitude 8
    caddying for his father 9
    church 8
    Epping Boys' High School
      12–13, 14–15, 17
    Epping Primary School 6
    grandfather's influence 5–6, 10
    handicap (golf) 9
    Higher School Certificate 20
    I.K. Harrison Shield 13–14
    move to Sydney 5
    Muirfield Golf Club 9, 13
    NSW junior golf team 11
    NSW schoolboys'
      competition 10
    sports 7, 8, 9, 12, 13, 16
    telegram boy 8
    West Cessnock Primary
      School 5
  employment 30
  first win in Europe 40
  first win in USA 100, 148
  handicap (golf) 221–2
  holiday on Corfu 145
  horses 103, 241–2
  injuries 115–17, 161
    ankle 116–17
    foot 88, 92, 95–6, 107, 117–18,
      137, 161
    football 115

  golfer's elbow 112, 161
  knee 115–16
  thumb 144–5
  see also accident
  Ireland, honorary citizen of 205
  leaving the USA 161
  lessons, giving 61
  living in the USA 142–4, 149,
    154, 161
  Locke, Bobby, tips from 71
  management 33–4, 123–4
  marriage 48
  Myrtle Beach, South Carolina 144,
    184
  nervousness 119, 219
  nicknames 36, 39, 104, 112, 227
  opinion of
    appearance money 229–34
    Asian circuit 51–2, 53
    Australian Open 232
    Ballesteros, Seve 106, 109
    Dunk, Billy 122
    European circuit 51
    Gale, Terry 163
    his own play 119
    one-arm practice 222
    other golfers 155–6, 237–40
    school sport 245–6
    Sydney courses 210
    television commentating 203
    water features 210–11
    Webb, Karrie 239
    Woods, Tiger 237–8
  play-offs 148, 154
    see also British Open loss to
      Watson
  political leaning 243
  prequalifying (PQ) 98, 138, 141–3,
    144, 146, 149
  prize money 34, 35, 40, 96, 144,
    145, 146, 148, 153
  proposal to Jackie 47–8
  relations with
    Bannerman, Harry 44–5
    Katontoga, Bob 56–8
    Miller, Brady 149–52
    Norman, Greg 126
    officials 11, 53
    press 35–6, 108
    Thompson, Peter 196–200
    Trevino, Lee 155
  renewal of vows 181

reputation 34–6
speaking engagements 205–6
sponsorship 32, 54, 62, 98
sports writer 197, 204
standard shot 83
television commentator 63, 162,
    193–205, 218, 221
turning pro 29–30, 33–4
US card 136
Warners Bay, NSW (house) 154,
    187
wind, playing in 19–20, 76–7
Newton, Jack (father) 3–6, 8–9,
    10–11, 12–13, 34, 45–6, 80, 112,
    117, 121, 131–2, 152, 153, 173,
    174, 175, 217, 222, 241
advice on turning pro 34
back injury 117
British Amateur Championship
    (1973) 45
caddying for Jack 45, 120, 131
Cessnock Golf Club 8
dealing with Jack's accident 170,
    172, 173, 182
death 132
employment 3–5, 8
Muirfield Golf Club 8–9, 10–11
NSW police force 8, 45, 241
retrenchment 5
teachers, dealings with Jack's 12,
    14–15
Newton, Jackie (née Butterworth,
    wife) 37–43, 44, 46–8, 58, 60, 70,
    73, 75, 78, 79, 82, 88, 97, 108,
    120, 123–4, 131, 141–5, 147–8,
    161, 165, 183, 195, 242, 243,
    247
dealing with Jack's accident
    168–85
marriage 48
meeting Jack 37
meeting Jack's family 42
mother 62–3, 64
Piccadilly girl 37, 44
pregnancy 147, 152
proposal of marriage 47–8
religious belief 177
renewal of vows 181
speeding fine 99–100
Newton, Kristie (daughter) 132,
    152–3, 154, 169, 171, 175,
    179–81, 243

Newton, Meg (mother) 3, 6, 10, 36,
    45, 46, 120, 131, 152, 153, 170,
    173, 174, 180, 215–16, 217, 218
Nicholas, Geoff 226
Nicklaus, Jack ('The Golden
    Bear') 72–6, 78, 81, 91, 93, 106,
    109, 133, 136, 137, 140, 146, 154,
    156, 158, 174, 184, 232, 237, 238,
    240
Nida, Norman von see von Nida,
    Norman
Nield, Jim 169–71, 176, 185
Nigeria 54–5, 61
Nine TV network 195, 218
Norman, Greg ('The Great White
    Shark') 53, 112, 121, 123–4, 125,
    126–7, 130–1, 159, 174, 199–200,
    203, 208, 230, 234, 238, 240,
    245
Normanhurst High School 221
North, Andy 106

O'Brien, Seamus 236
Oceanic Sports Group 236
O'Connor, Christy, Jr 39, 205
O'Connor, Christy, Sr 45–6, 55, 205,
    223
Ogilvy, Geoff 239
Ogle, Brett 211
O'Leary, John 71–2, 205
O'Meara, Mark 142
Oosterhuis, Peter 32, 39, 40
Oosthuisen, Andries 76
Order of Merit 235
Ormsby, John 203
Ozaki, Jet 203
Ozaki, Jumbo 209

Packer, Kerry 28, 232
Palmer, Arnold 21, 109, 149, 158,
    160, 231, 240
Parry, Craig 240
Parslow, Geoff 231
Pate, Jerry 209, 232
Pavarotti, Luciano 230
pay TV 202
Pearce, Eddie 143, 231
Peete, Calvin 159–60, 184
PGA see Professional Golfers'
    Association
PGF see Precision Golf Forging
Phiri, David 61, 63

Player, Gary 20, 21, 22, 34, 100, 119, 120, 125–30, 174, 231, 240
pool 160
Precision Golf Forging (PGF) 10
Price, Dan 102–3
Prince, Dave 12, 13
Prince of Wales Hospital 169, 171, 185
Pritchard, Bill 193–4
prize money 94, 96, 119, 230–1, 237
Professional Golfers' Association (PGA)
  Asia 236
  Australia 31, 174, 233
  Britain 54, 58
  New South Wales 31
  United States 23, 100, 135, 146, 150, 151, 153, 184, 230, 237
psychology 71, 81, 138, 155–6

Qantas 126
Quintex 236

Rafferty, Bruce 29
Rafter, Pat 81
Raison, Mrs (landlady) 6
Ransom, Henry 22
Raymond, Salli 37–8, 49
Reasor, Mike 34
Rees, Dai 65
Rhodesia 61
Riddell, Sam 144
Riley, Wayne 211
Roberts, Clifford 87, 89–91, 95, 96, 97, 98
Robertson, Paul 217
Roche, Tony 20, 81
Rodriguez, Chi Chi 151
Rogers, Bill 209, 232
Roosenburg, Tony 235
Rosewall, Ken 81
Rothmans 37, 56
Royal and Ancient Golf Club see courses and clubs
rugby league 7, 8, 9, 16, 167, 237, 241, 243–5
  Balmain 243
  Manly 243
  NSW schoolboys' team 8
  Newcastle Knights 243–4
  Parramatta 243
  Western Suburbs 243
  Western Tigers 243

rugby union 12, 15
  Gordon 12
  Waratah Shield 15
rules of golf 51, 138, 151
Rumford, Brett 239
Russell, Art 118
Russell, Neil 213
Russucks hotel 70, 73, 79

sand greens 54
Sanders, Doug 133–7, 140, 160
Sanudo, Cesar 49
Sarazen, Gene 89, 240
SBS TV 202
Schroeder, John 143, 231
Scott, Adam 239
Scully, Vince 91
self-regulation 152
Senior, Jeff 118
Seniors circuit (US) 159, 197, 204
Seven TV network 202, 235, 236
Shade, Ronnie 55
Shaw, Liz 173
Shearer, Bob ('Shears') 20, 29, 44, 48, 74, 103, 122, 125, 126–7, 128, 130, 141, 143, 144, 149, 153, 156–8, 160, 174, 183, 195, 231, 232, 233
Shearer, Kathie (née Melvin) 44–5, 153, 195
Shimono 212
Sillett, Keith 174
Simon, Deray 120, 121
Simpson, Bob 194
Simpson, Scott 122
Singapore 52
Singleton, John 183
Sires Stakes horse races 188
Skase, Christopher 202, 236
Slazenger 20–1, 29, 30, 55, 104, 174
Sloan Morpeth Trophy (1969) 29
Smith, Gary 64–65
Smith, Stan 81
Smithies, Janet (née Newton, sister) 5, 16, 132
  children 132
Snead, J.C. 155, 233
Snead, Sam 69, 240
Sneed, Ed 102, 106, 232
snooker 47
soccer 7, 8, 9, 12, 13, 116, 236
South Africa 61–2, 69, 88

South Melbourne VFL club 167
Southern Cross hotel 183
Spain 43
Spencer, John 207, 209
sponsorship 32, 54, 62, 126, 143, 236
Spring Racing Carnival, Melbourne 237
Stadler, Craig 102, 107, 147
Stanley, Ian 43–4, 48, 126, 183, 189, 231
Steele, Tony 211
Sterling, Jack 150
Strange, Curtis 136
Sullivan, Frank 6–8
Sullivan, John 20
Sullivan, Mike 148
Sunday Tribune [South Africa] 61
Sun-Herald [Sydney] 204
Sutton, Hal 159
Swanton, E.W. 196
Sweden 117
swimming 16
Switzerland 34
Sydney Cricket Ground 166
Sydney Swans VFL club 166–7, 190, 206

Tallis, Patrick 24
Tarbuck, Jimmy 70
television coverage 79, 88, 90–1, 98, 186, 232, 235, 236–7
Ten TV network 236–7
tennis 7, 13, 81, 95, 158, 223
Thomas, Warwick 177, 181
Thompson, Leonard 155
Thomson, Peter 20, 35, 44, 48, 51, 194, 196–200, 204, 207
Thunderbird hotel 88
Timms, Sam 184
Tiriac, Ion 39
touch rugby 13
tournament organisation 51–3
tournaments and championships
  Andy Williams San Diego Open (1977) 137
  Asahi Glass Four Tours 159
  Atlanta Classic (1978) 146
  Augusta National Invitational (1934) 89
  Australian amateur (Royal Adelaide, 1969) 28–9

Australian Masters (Huntingdale) 202, 207, 234
  1979 154
Australian Match Play 235
Australian Open 17, 28, 122, 126, 127, 202, 232, 233, 234
  1976 (Australian) 136
  1979 (Metropolitan) 107, 119–31, 156, 173
  1980 (The Lakes) 234
  1983 (Kingston Heath) 207
  1985 (Royal Melbourne) 199–200
  1986 (Metropolitan) 97
  1991 211
  1999 238–9
  2000 238–9
Australian PGA 233, 234
  1978 (Royal Melbourne) 233
  1984 (Monash) 197
  1985 (Castle Hill) 198–9
Benson & Hedges tournaments
  1972 (Fulford) 40, 54
  1977 144
Bicentennial Classic (Royal Melbourne, 1988) 222
Bob Hope Classic (Palm Springs, 1977) 138–41
British amateur
  1969 (Hoylake) 21, 26, 87
  1973 (Royal Porthcawl) 45
British Columbia (BC) Open (1978) 153
British matchplay
  1973 (Dundee) 49
  1977 144
British Open 19, 26, 70, 78, 81, 84, 96, 117, 145, 159, 197, 202
  1947 (Hoylake) 19
  1948 (Muirfield) 19
  1957 (Carnoustie) 69
  1963 (Royal Lytham and St Annes) 41
  1970 (St Andrews) 133
  1971 (Royal Birkdale) 34
  1973 (Troon) 71, 75
  1974 (Royal Lytham and St Annes) 48
  1975 (Carnoustie) 1–2, 69–85, 93, 112, 116, 131, 173
  1977 (Turnberry) 145–6

tournaments and championships
(cont.)
    1979 (Royal Lytham and
      St Annes) 106
    1984 (St Andrews) 200–2, 204,
      205
  British PGA 233
    1972 (Wentworth) 40
    1977 (Sandwich) 144
  Buick Open (Warwick Hills, USA,
    1978) 100, 147–8
  Canadian Open (Glen Abbey)
    1978 149–52
    1979 154
    1983 174
  Carrolls International (Dublin,
    1972) 39
  Cathay Pacific (Hong Kong,
    1972) 52–3
  Christy O'Connor pro-am 223
  Chrysler Classic 233
    1973 (The Lakes, NSW) 231
  Citrus Open (USA, 1977) 142–3
  City of Auckland Classic (The
    Grange, NZ, 1972) 41, 242
  Coca-Cola Young Professionals
    (Bristol, 1973) 46
  Cock o' the North (Zambia,
    1976) 56, 59
  Colgate Champion of Champions
    (Vic.) 154–5
  Colgate Hall of Fame Classic
    (Pinehurst, USA)
    1977 146
    1978 153
  Colonial invitational (USA,
    1977) 144
  Double Diamond (England,
    1979) 124
  Dunlop Masters (South Africa,
    1972) 61
  Dutch Open
    1971 (Kennemer) 34, 35
    1972 (Haagsche) 39–40, 44, 54
  Dutch pro-am (1971) 35
  French Open
    1969 (St Nom La Breteche) 26
    1973 45
  German amateur (Frankfurt Main-
    Neiderrad, 1969) 26
  German Open (Frankfurt Main-
    Neiderrad, 1969) 26

Glen Campbell Los Angeles
  Open 141
Gosford annual (NSW, 1964) 10,
  11
Greater Greensboro Open (Forest
  Oaks, USA)
  1978 106, 146
  1979 100
  1980 107–8
Hawaiian Open (1977) 138
Heineken Classic (The Vines,
  WA) 235
Heritage Classic (Harbour Town,
  USA) 100
Houston Open (USA) 160
I.K. Harrison Shield (NSW, 1965)
  13–14
Indian Open (1971) 53
Irish Open 204, 223
  1983 (Royal Dublin) 168
Jack Newton Celebrity
  Classic 218–21, 241
Jackie Gleason Inverrary Classic
  (USA) 141
Jaguar–Rover competition
  (Australia) 224–5
John Player Classic (UK) 158, 193
  1972 41
John Player Trophy (Bognor Regis,
  UK, 1972) 39
Johnnie Walker Classic 234
Madrid Open (1973) 43
Martini International
  1973 (Royal Burgess,
    Scotland) 39
  1975 67, 70
Memorial invitational (USA,
  1977) 144
Mufulira Open (Zambia)
  1975 61
  1976 56, 64
New Orleans Open (1978) 146
NSW amateur (1968) 28
NSW Open 202, 235
  1976 (Royal Sydney) 98, 118
  1978 (Manly) 154
  1979 (The Lakes) 119, 123
  1983 (Concord) 193–5, 196
  1990 211
NSW PGA
  1970 (Castle Hill) 31
  1980 234

NSW schoolboys 10
New Zealand Open
  1971 (Balmacewan) 35
  1976 97
Nigerian Open (Ikoyi, 1974) 54
Otago Classic (St Clair, NZ,
  1971) 35
Palm Meadows Cup (USA,
  1988) 203
Penfold Bournemouth Tournament
  (Queens Park, 1972) 39
Piccadilly Medal tournament
  (England, 1972) 37
Piccadilly world matchplay
  (England) 49
Players' Championship (USA,
  1979) 100
Queensland Open 202, 235
  1976 118
Sammy Davis Hartford Open
  (USA) 141
Scottish Open
  1972 (Downfield) 39
  1989 200
Singapore Open (1972) 52
Skins (Port Douglas, Qld) 202
Sloan Morpeth Trophy (NSW,
  1969) 29
South African Open (Houghton,
  1976) 61
Southern Open (USA, 1982) 161
Spalding Masters (NZ, 1971) 53
Sumrie Better Ball (Queens Park,
  1975) 71
Swiss Open (Crans-sur-Sierre) 133
Tam o' Shanter (USA) 68
Test match (Australia v. UK) 202
Uniroyal International (Moor
  Park, England, 1977) 145
USI Classic (USA, 1972) 40
US Masters (Augusta
  National) 202
  1957 94
  1969 41–2
  1976 87–113, 116
  1977 97, 98
  1978 100, 119, 232
  1979 100–6, 119
  1980 106–13, 173
  1981 113
  1987 97
  1988 97

US Open 159, 202, 226
  1977 (S. Hills, Tulsa) 119
  1978 (Cherry Hill, Denver) 146
  1979 (Inverness, Toledo) 119
  1987 (Olympic, San
    Francisco) 122
  1988 (Brookline,
    Massachusetts) 136, 203
  1989 (Oak Hill, Rochester) 136
  1991 (Hazeltine, Minnesota) 203
US PGA 109, 202
  1979 (Oakland Hills,
    Michigan) 119
  1991 (Crooked Stick,
    Indianapolis) 203
  1995 (Riviera, California) 238
Victorian Open 231
  1977 (Yarra Yarra) 231
Victorian PGA (Woodlands,
  1978) 153
Westchester Classic (USA)
  1969 33
  1978 152–3
Western Australian Open (Lake
  Karrinyup, 1983) 162
Western Open (USA) 107
Westlakes Classic (Australia,
  1979) 124
Wills Masters 95
  1974 (Australian) 231
  1975 (Vic.) 84
World Series (USA, 1983) 184
Zambian Open (Lusaka,
  1976) 56–7
tradition 81, 90, 95
Trevino, Lee 32, 88, 106, 107, 151,
  154, 155, 158, 159, 174, 199, 231,
  239, 240
Trimble, Ken 211
Tuttle, Scott 125

US circuit 34, 96, 98, 122, 138, 141,
  144, 146, 152, 153, 158, 160, 173,
  216
US players' school, Brownsville,
  Texas 135
US PGA see Professional Golfers'
  Association

van Gulpen, Becky 27–8
Vanier, Gary 119
Vicenzo, Roberto de see de Vicenzo,
  Roberto

Victorian Football League
 (VFL) 166–7
Vines, Randall 31
von Nida, Norman ('The Von')
 19–21, 22–5, 26, 29, 31, 34, 51, 90

Wadey, Gordon 47, 56–7
Wadkins, Bobby 232
Wadkins, Lanny 154, 158
Walker, Bobby 37
Walker, Jimmy 58
Watson, Linda 79
Watson, Tom 1–2, 74–9, 81–4,
 145–6, 154, 158, 184, 240
 1975 British Open win over
  Newton 2, 84, 88, 111–12, 131,
  133, 146, 148, 154, 173
Webb, Karrie 239
Weibring, D.A. 147
Weiskopf, Jean 75
Weiskopf, Tom 71–3, 75, 158, 209
West Cessnock Primary School 5
Western Suburbs Rugby League
 Club 243

Western Tigers Rugby League
 Club 243
Whitaker, Jack 90, 193
Wickens, David 23, 25, 31–2
Williams, Andy 135
Williams, Charles ('Bull') 91–2, 95,
 100–2
Williams, Peter 183
Wimbledon 39, 47
Wolveridge, Mike 207
Wood, Jack 35–6
Woods, Earl 237
Woods, Tiger 112, 142, 229, 234,
 237–8, 240
Woy, Bucky 32
Wright, Ben 193

Young, Cliff 183

Zambia 54, 56–64, 88
Zambian Airways 62–3
Zoeller, Fuzzy 102, 106, 119, 120,
 199